BARON JOHN MALTRAVERS

1290–1364

BARON JOHN MALTRAVERS
1290–1364

'A Wise Knight in War and Peace'

AND HIS FOREBEARS AND DESCENDANTS 1066–1435

CAROLEEN McCLURE

Copyright © 2020 Caroleen McClure

The moral right of the author has been asserted.

Apart from any fair dealing for the purposes of research or private study, or criticism or review, as permitted under the Copyright, Designs and Patents Act 1988, this publication may only be reproduced, stored or transmitted, in any form or by any means, with the prior permission in writing of the publishers, or in the case of reprographic reproduction in accordance with the terms of licences issued by the Copyright Licensing Agency. Enquiries concerning reproduction outside those terms should be sent to the publishers.

Matador
9 Priory Business Park,
Wistow Road, Kibworth Beauchamp,
Leicestershire. LE8 0RX
Tel: 0116 279 2299
Email: books@troubador.co.uk
Web: www.troubador.co.uk/matador
Twitter: @matadorbooks

ISBN 978 183859 125 0

British Library Cataloguing in Publication Data.
A catalogue record for this book is available from the British Library.

Printed and bound in the UK by TJ International, Padstow, Cornwall
Typeset in 11pt Adobe Garamond Pro by Troubador Publishing Ltd, Leicester, UK

Matador is an imprint of Troubador Publishing Ltd

For Andrew

CONTENTS

Maps		ix
List of Illustrations		xii
Preface and Acknowledgements		xiii
The name 'Maltravers', 'Mautravers', 'Matravers'		xv
Introduction		xvii
1.	Hugh Maltravers: The Norman Conquest, 1066	1
2.	Maltravers Knights and Lords of the Manor, 1100–1290	9
3.	John Maltravers V and his son, Baron John Maltravers: War, Rebellion and Exile, 1290–1326:	26
4.	Baron John Maltravers: The Death of a King? 1326–1330	47
5.	Baron John Maltravers: Exile, Secret Mission, Crécy and Calais, 1330–1347	74
6.	Baron John Maltravers: Black Death, Channel Islands, Pilgrimage and Restoration, 1348–1354	88
7.	Baron John Maltravers: Last Years, 1355–1364	105
8.	Agnes de Bereford, later Argentein, then Nerford, then Maltravers	114
9.	Roger Maltravers I and II; Edward Maltravers I and II; William Maltravers IV	122
10.	Robert Maltravers and the Maltraverses of Crowell and Hooke; Browning and Strangways Descendants	126

11. Joan Maltravers, later de Keynes, then Rous	135
12. Eleanor Maltravers, later Arundel, then Cobham	141
Family Trees	154
Abbreviations for notes and references	157
Notes	159
Index of Maltravers Lands	189

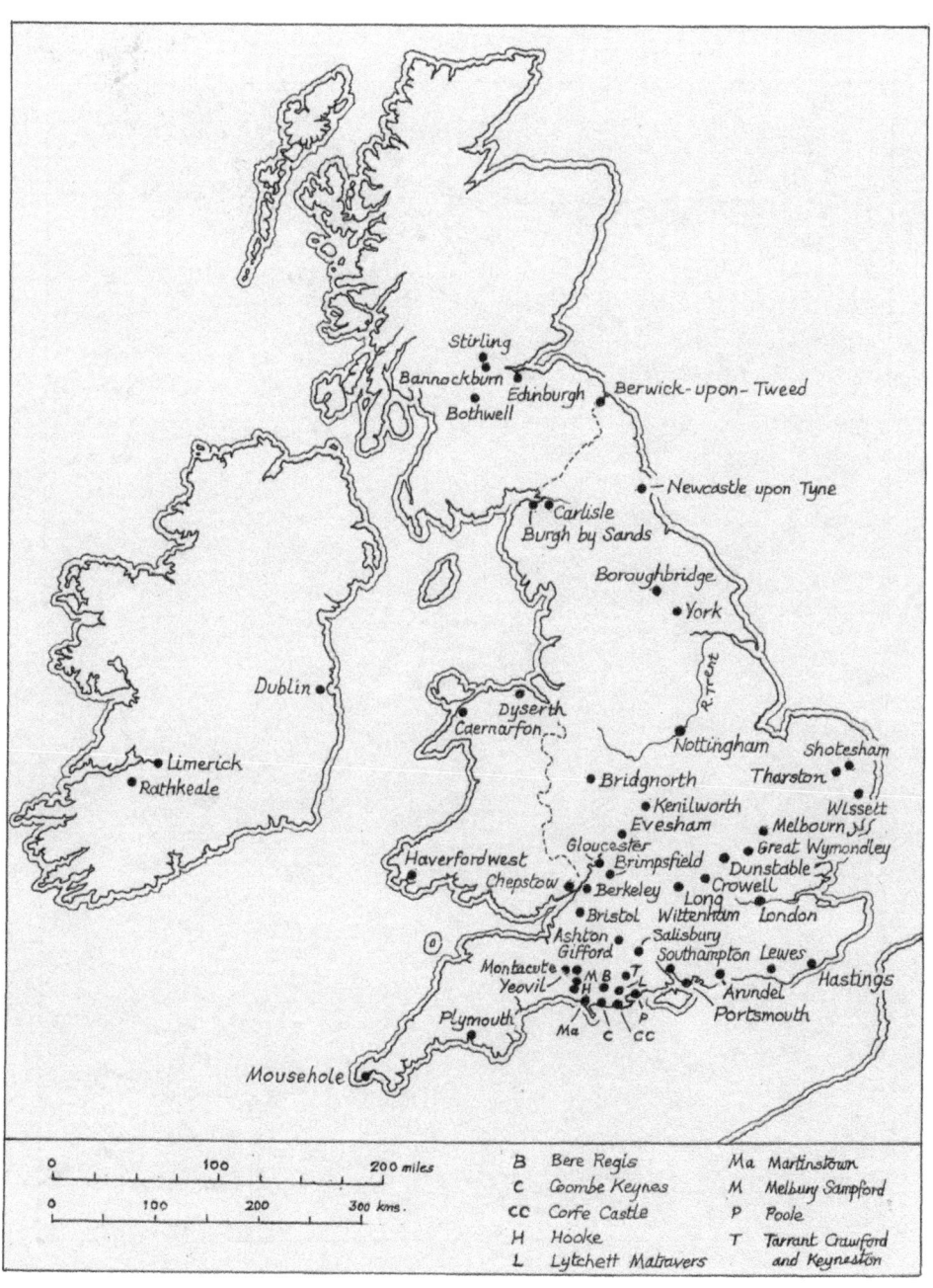

Map 1. British Isles

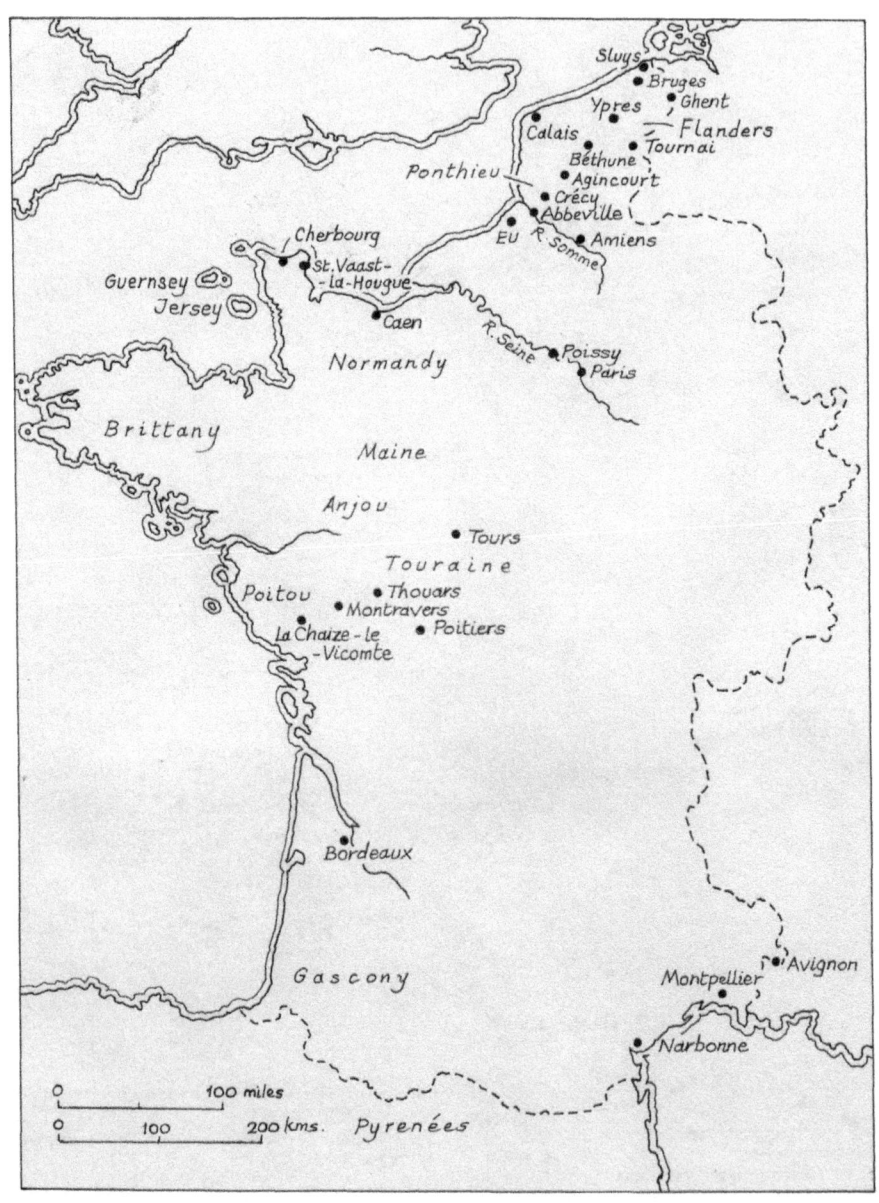

Map 2. France

Map 3. Manors and other lands in England held by Baron John Maltravers in 1364. He also held Rathkeale in Ireland.

LIST OF ILLUSTRATIONS

The Maltravers arms, illustration © Nick Griffiths FSA
The Norman knights landing in England, © iStock
Hugh Maltravers in Hinton Blewett, Exon Domesday, © The Dean and Chapter of Exeter Cathedral
The Church of St Nicholas, La Chaize-le-Vicomte, author's photo
Chepstow Castle, © iStock
Corfe Castle, author's photo
The Church of St Mary the Virgin, Lytchett Matravers, author's photo
Castle Cornet, Guernsey, author's photo
Mont Orgueil, or Gorey, Castle, Jersey, © iStock
The gravestone of John Maltravers in 2019, photo © John Evans
The gravestone of John Maltravers in 1810, © The British Library Board
Arundel Castle, © iStock

The copyright holders listed above have kindly given permission for the images to be reproduced in this book.

PREFACE AND ACKNOWLEDGEMENTS

The starting point for this study was the work of the late Peter Beebe Matravers, who spent many years researching the history of his family. It was this Peter Matravers who first suggested that the Hugh Maltravers in the *Domesday Book* may have come from Montravers in Poitou and who contacted the mayor of that village in the 1990s. Peter was well aware of the mystery surrounding the fate of Edward II and the possible part played by John Maltravers. While taking note of Peter's research, I have approached the story anew, and I am responsible for the contents of this book and the conclusions reached. I have also revised the family trees, as far as the evidence permits.

I am very grateful to Shirley Percival, historian of Lytchett Matravers and leader of Upton and Lytchett U3A Local History Group, for getting me involved with John Maltravers in the first place, for lending me her copy of Peter Matravers's notes, and for her advice and encouragement. Thanks are due to members of the Group for their continuing interest in the project. The late Antoine Fruchard of Montravers, who is much missed, contributed to the Maltravers quest with immense enthusiasm.

I thank both Dr Cindy Wood of Winchester University and Barbara Docherty for their useful advice. Many thanks also to the staff of the libraries, archives and other organisations contacted in the course of research: Dorset Libraries and LibrariesWest, Exeter Cathedral Library and Archives, Lambeth Palace Library Archives, The National Archives, The British Library, les Archives municipales de Thouars, the States of Jersey Library, la Société Guernsiaise, Boydell & Brewer, British History Online, the Parliament Rolls of Medieval England.

This book is greatly enhanced by the maps and Maltravers arms drawn by Nick Griffiths FSA and by the family trees drawn by Paul Futcher: thank you.

Thanks to the staff of Matador for guiding me through the publishing process.

And not least, thanks to my husband, Andrew, who has lived with my Maltravers obsession for nine years so far and who has accompanied me on the journey, both literally on our travels to France – including Normandy, Crécy, Poitiers and Montravers – and mentally sharing the stresses of research and writing.

THE NAME 'MALTRAVERS', 'MAUTRAVERS', 'MATRAVERS'

In the period covered in this book, from 1066 to 1435, the source documents are mainly written in the version of French known as Anglo-Norman and nearly always spell the family name 'Mautravers'. When a document is in Latin, the name is often Latinised as 'Maltravers', 'Malus Traversus', 'Malus Transitus' or similar.

Modern historians nearly always use the form 'Maltravers' for the medieval members of the family. I have used 'Maltravers' for personal names throughout the text, except in Chapter 1 where I am particularly discussing the different forms of the name. The barony of Maltravers descends from the first baron, who is the main subject of this book.

For place names, for example Lytchett Matravers, I have used the modern form 'Matravers'. As a present-day surname, the spelling is usually 'Matravers' or 'Mattravers'.

INTRODUCTION

Hugh Maltravers, a knight of obscure origin, fought for Duke William in the Norman Conquest and was rewarded with ten manors in South West England. His descendants were lords of many manors in Dorset, Somerset, Wiltshire and Gloucestershire for 300 years.

Like many knights, the Maltraverses could be found wherever fighting was to be done for the Norman and Plantagenet kings. A 'knight' in the early days was just a skilled warrior on horseback, but, as time went on, the term came to mean a man of a certain social status, and the Maltraverses became knights in this sense too.

Their story is one of social advancement. Military service brought them into contact with powerful families: the Berkeleys, the Giffards and the Mortimers. Land was the key to wealth, and manors were acquired by marriage, purchase or royal favour. When the king and his barons fell out, there might be civil war, and then it was essential to be on the winning side. If not, manors could be forfeited, and the lord might be imprisoned or even executed, unless he could slip away and evade capture. When things became calmer, lost lands could be regained and personal position restored.

Such conflicts were not frequent, but when they occurred the Maltraverses navigated the storms with considerable skill and luck. They were also fortunate in continuing the male line through nine or ten generations: one or two Hughs, a Walter, and then no fewer than seven Johns.

The sixth John Maltravers (c. 1290–1364) had an extraordinary life. Knighted at the age of sixteen, he was taken prisoner at Bannockburn a few years later. He and his brother-in-law Thomas Berkeley were appointed guardians of the deposed Edward II. Under the Mortimer regime, Maltravers was summoned to parliament as a baron, thus becoming the first Baron

Maltravers. At the fall of Mortimer, Maltravers was in deep trouble; he was tried for treason (in his absence as he had fled abroad) and sentenced to death. His enforced exile continued for twenty years. All that time, he hoped that a way would be found for him to clear his name and return home.

His son, the seventh John Maltravers, fought at Crécy, but both he and his only son, Henry, succumbed to the Black Death. The Maltravers heiress, Eleanor, married a younger son of the earl of Arundel. Through a quirk of fate, Eleanor's descendants inherited the earldom of Arundel in addition to the barony of Maltravers.

1

HUGH MALTRAVERS
THE NORMAN CONQUEST, 1066

Maltravers Origins

The Maltravers or Mautravers knights settled in South West England at the time of the Norman Conquest. They were the lords of several manors in Dorset, Somerset, Wiltshire and Gloucestershire for over 300 years. The first of them, Hugh Maltravers, is mentioned in the *Domesday Book* of 1086.

The present-day surname Matravers, Maltravers or Mattravers has been a puzzle to both historians and etymologists, who have thought it must be either a place name or a nickname. As there is no town or village with a name like that in Normandy, it has been concluded that it is a personal name derived from the French words '*mal*' and '*travers*' meaning bad passage or crossing; obstacle, trouble, mishap or misfortune; or a place with a difficult ford. Therefore, a Maltravers is perhaps 'a man difficult to pass', 'a stout soldier' or 'an unlucky man'.[1]

But it is a mistake to assume that Hugh Maltravers must have come from Normandy. Duke William's army in 1066 contained not only Normans but also soldiers from other areas – such as Flanders, the Paris region, Brittany, Maine and Aquitaine.[2] Aquitaine includes Poitou, and it is in Poitou that a possible homeland of the Maltravers knights can be found. In the *département* of Deux-Sèvres, there is a village which is today called Montravers, but which was called Mautravers in the Middle Ages and up to the time of the French Revolution. Documents dating from 1189 to 1199 mention people there called 'Hugues de

Mautravers' and 'Simon de Mautravers'. In Latin the name was given as Malus Traversus, and it was well named since, in the past, even as late as the nineteenth century, it was a notoriously difficult place to travel through.[3]

If this was indeed the birthplace of Hugh Maltravers, there was an obvious way for him to have become involved in the invasion of England. Among those who responded to Duke William's call to arms was Viscount Aimery of Thouars, who was one of the four viscounts of Poitou, and Maltravers's overlord. Aimery's own overlord was the count of Poitou, who was also duke of Aquitaine. The viscount of Thouars was an important magnate, governing a large territory stretching eighty miles westward to the coast from his inland stronghold of Thouars.[4] Viscount Aimery was not obliged to support Duke William, who was not his feudal overlord. Probably, he joined the expedition to enhance his own prestige, and reckoned that if the campaign were a success, and William became king of England as well as duke of Normandy, William would be a very powerful friend and ally. As the village of Mautravers was squarely in Aimery's territory, it could have been under his banner that Hugh Maltravers set out for adventure and fortune. Aimery took a large number of fighting men with him to Normandy, although the 4,000 that used to be claimed is probably an exaggeration.[5] It is now thought that the total number of men in William's army at Hastings was about 14,000[6] or 15,000,[7] and – as the majority would have been Normans – the contingent from Poitou was perhaps in the hundreds.

The Battle of Hastings, 14 October 1066

Aimery was one of the most prominent commanders on the Norman side at the Battle of Hastings. Duke William positioned his troops in three divisions. The Normans were in the centre, and soldiers from other regions were on either side. The Flemings and the French were on one wing. On the other wing were the Bretons, the Poitevins and the men from Maine, commanded jointly by Alan le Roux of Brittany and Aimery of Thouars;[8] their troops were on the left wing of the army.[9] After the stunning victory and the death of the English king, Harold, Aimery – a member of the duke's inner circle and 'a man whose eloquence equalled his prowess' – advised William to get himself crowned king of England without delay.[10] William was crowned at Westminster Abbey on 25 December 1066.

Viscount Aimery did not settle in England but returned to his own lands in Poitou: if he had acquired an estate in England, it would have been difficult for him to govern lands in two countries so far apart. By 1069 he was back home at Thouars, and at around the same time he built a castle and a church dedicated to St John the Baptist at La Chaize-le-Vicomte, where he already had a hunting lodge. Later, near the castle, he founded a priory with its own large church dedicated to St Nicholas. Work on this church started in about 1080, and it was consecrated in 1099, but he did not live to see it completed because he died in 1093.[11]

Some among those who came to England with Aimery may have decided to stay. Perhaps they were younger sons or others without prospects. Attempts have been made to identify the Poitevin settlers, but only a few have been found.[12] In fact, it is generally only possible to name for certain a few soldiers among the thousands in the Norman army. Sources produced soon after the event – such as the biography of Duke William by William of Poitiers, a history written by Orderic Vitalis,[13] and the Bayeux Tapestry – list only about twenty-one of the most important commanders. These are the only people who we can be sure were at the battle, and these named combatants include Aimery of Thouars but not Hugh Maltravers, who was a person of lesser status. The narrative poem *Roman de Rou*, composed by Wace *c.* 1160–1170, contains about 116 names, including Aimery de Thouars but, again, not Hugh Maltravers.

In later centuries, lists were compiled using sources of varying degrees of reliability. The best known are the Battle Abbey Roll, the Dives Roll and the Falaise Roll.

1. **The Battle Abbey Roll**, a parchment list of combatants, was kept at Battle Abbey in the Middle Ages. It later came into private hands and was finally lost in a fire in 1793. Before its loss, copies were made by several antiquaries, and these copies differ considerably from each other. Historians have been very dismissive of the roll, saying that it was an unreliable fourteenth-century list, and that the monks were willing to add names of supposed 'Companions of the Conqueror' on request. Some of the men on the list were definitely not at the battle; this does not mean that none of them fought at Hastings, merely that the roll does not constitute proof. Bearing that in mind, Mautravers – or its variants – is found in all the well-known versions:

    † 'Mantravers' in the Battle Abbey Roll as ascribed to John Brompton, 1436 (this spelling appears in no other list, and may be a misreading of the manuscript);

- † 'Mautrauers' in the Battle Abbey Roll as given by Guillaume le Tailleur, 1487;
- † 'Montravers' in the Battle Abbey Roll as copied by John Leland before 1550;
- † 'Montravers' in the Battle Abbey Roll as published by Raphael Holinshed, 1577; and
- † 'Mautrauers' in the Battle Abbey Roll as published by André Duchesne, 1619.

The surname Mautravers seems to have sometimes morphed into Montravers as early as the sixteenth century. The Battle Abbey Roll does not include forenames.[14]

2. **The Dives Roll**, a list of some 475 'Companions of William the Conqueror', was compiled for the 800th anniversary in 1866 and engraved on a stone plaque set up in the church at Dives-sur-Mer in 1862. The editor of the list is the French historian Léopold Delisle, who states that he used contemporary histories, English charters from the reign of William I, and 'above all' the *Domesday Book*. He says he did not use English lists of the fourteenth and fifteenth centuries (such as the Battle Abbey Roll, perhaps?), or the aforementioned *Roman de Rou*. The Dives Roll includes Aimery de Thouars, who is simply listed as 'Le Vicomte'; William d'Eu, who was later Maltravers's overlord; and 'Hugue Mautravers'. On the plaque, the letter 'V' is used for both 'U' and 'V', and so Hugh's name is engraved as 'HVGVE MAVTRAVERS'.[15]

3. **The Falaise Roll**, compiled by an international committee of historians in 1927–31, lists 315 'Companions' whose names were engraved on a bronze tablet placed in the Château of Falaise in 1931. It includes about 100 names from the *Roman de Rou*, and other names from chronicles and documents. The Falaise Roll includes Aimery of Thouars, but not William d'Eu or Hugh Maltravers.[16]

To sum up, it is not possible to be sure that Hugh Maltravers fought at the Battle of Hastings. The lists in which his name appears as one of the 'Companions of William the Conqueror' are of dubious authenticity or are using the *Domesday Book* as a major source. The *Domesday Book* shows who held lands in 1086, and it is likely that many of the *Domesday Book*'s listed tenants did indeed 'come with the Conqueror'. It is also possible that some of the people in the *Domesday Book* came to England after 1066. Whatever the origins of Hugh Maltravers, the first certain mention of him is in the *Domesday Book* as a sub-tenant of a Norman, William d'Eu.

Domesday Book, 1086

After the Norman Conquest, King William I allocated lands to his tenants-in-chief, and they in turn installed sub-tenants, known as 'mesne tenants', with each holding one or more manors. In the process, nearly all the Anglo-Saxon landowners were dispossessed.

When the king met with his nobles at Christmas 1085, he ordered a survey to be carried out – county by county, and manor by manor – of everyone's land and livestock. Within a few months, the returns came in. It was realised that the whole thing was too unwieldy and contained much unnecessary data. In the final version, some of the detail was omitted, such as the number of sheep, cattle, pigs and other livestock on each manor. Unfortunately for the family historian, another piece of information left out was the surname of many of the under-tenants, such as Hugh Maltravers, who – not being a tenant-in-chief – was simply listed as 'Hugh'. There were, of course, many tenants called 'Hugh', and to identify Hugh Maltravers among them requires some detective work and deduction.

The detailed returns were sent to Winchester, where they were collated, rendered into the agreed format and copied neatly into the *Great Domesday Book*. The actual writing is thought to have been done by a single scribe. The completed manuscript is in The National Archives (TNA) in London. After the passage of over 900 years, the parchment and the ink have survived remarkably well, and the writing is still clearly legible. The *Domesday Book* has been published several times in translation.[17] Particularly useful is the Phillimore edition, with a volume for each county which contains the Latin text, an English translation and notes.[18] The *Great Domesday Book* is also available online, is searchable by place names and personal names, and has the facility to display facsimiles of the original entries or whole pages.[19]

For the south-west counties, the earlier draft survey, which included surnames of under-tenants, has also survived. This document, known as the *Exon Domesday*, is kept in the archives at Exeter Cathedral Library. The *Exon Domesday* has not been published in facsimile, but the translation in the Phillimore edition includes, in small print, the extra details in the *Exon Domesday* that were omitted from the *Great Domesday Book*. The *Victoria County History of Somerset* also includes the *Exon Domesday* details, in inverted commas, within the translation of the *Domesday Book* text.

The *Exon Domesday* contains the only two instances in the *Domesday Book* of the full name Hugh Maltravers. The manor of Hinton Blewett, or 'Hantone', was held by Ralph Blewitt from the tenant-in-chief William d'Eu. It consisted of eight hides of land – a hide being about 120 acres – and was worked by seven villeins, three borderers and four serfs. There was arable land, a strip of woodland that was a league long, sixty acres of meadow and a mill. The livestock comprised one horse, five cows, seventeen pigs and twenty-five goats. 'Of the aforesaid eight hides HUGO MALTRAUERS [Maltravers] holds half a hide from William [d'Eu].'[20]

The *Exon Domesday* includes the geld (tax) return. The entry for the hundred of Chewton, which included Hinton Blewett, states that 'the king has had no geld from the one virgate [part of a hide, usually a quarter] which HUGO MALUS TRANSITUS holds.'[21]

Hugh Maltravers was the mesne tenant of several manors in 1086, all held from the same tenant-in-chief, William d'Eu. The core Maltravers lands were three manors that figure prominently and frequently in the later history of the family, and where there can be no doubt that the 'Hugh' in the *Domesday Book* is Hugh Maltravers. These are the two Dorset manors of Woolcombe and Lytchett Matravers, and a Somerset manor in Yeovil, which is later referred to as 'Hendford'. To these can be added Mappowder in Dorset, which the *Domesday Book* says is held by the same tenant as that of Lytchett Matravers.

Less securely identified are some manors held by 'Hugh' from William d'Eu in 1086, and for which there is later evidence of Maltravers interest: Stock Gaylard in Dorset, bracketed with Caundle (probably Stourton Caundle) and Charlton in Wiltshire, bracketed with Grafton.

More doubtful still are two other manors held by 'Hugh' from William d'Eu, for which later evidence is lacking: Sopworth, Wiltshire; and Shipton (probably Shipton Dovel), Gloucestershire.

The Lands of Hugh Maltravers in 1086

All Hugh Maltravers's lands were held from William d'Eu, as follows:

DORSET
† Hugh holds Mappowder[22] from William; the same Hugh holds Lytchett Matravers[23] from William;
† Hugh holds Woolcombe[24] from William;
† Hugh holds Stock Gaylard[25] from William; the same Hugh holds Caundle (Stourton Caundle)[26] from William.

SOMERSET
† Hugh holds Yeovil[27] from William;
† Ralph Blewitt holds Hinton Blewett from William; Hugh Maltravers holds half a hide of this land from William.[28]

WILTSHIRE
† Hugh holds Charlton (in Hungerford, now in Berkshire)[29] from William; the same Hugh holds Grafton[30] from William;
† Hugh holds Sopworth[31] from William.

GLOUCESTERSHIRE
† Hugh holds Shipton (Shipton Dovel) from William.[32]

The Downfall of William d'Eu

In 1087, King William I died, and his realm was divided between his two elder sons: William II (William Rufus), king of England from 1087–1100; and Robert 'Curthose', duke of Normandy from 1087–1106.

In 1096, William d'Eu – Hugh Maltravers's overlord – conspired with other barons to replace William II with Stephen of Aumale, the king's cousin. The rebellion failed, and William d'Eu was punished by being castrated and blinded; he died soon afterwards. The chronicler Orderic Vitalis tells us that the punishment was inflicted on him at the suggestion of the earl of Chester, whose sister William d'Eu had married, but William was unfaithful to her, fathering three children by another woman.[33] Hugh Maltravers continued to hold Lytchett Matravers and his other lands after the fall of his overlord.

Hugh Maltravers Donates Land to Montacute Priory

In 1100, William Rufus died in mysterious circumstances while hunting in the New Forest. Henry, the third son of King William I, became king as Henry I, and in 1106 defeated his brother Robert 'Curthose', duke of Normandy, in battle. From 1106, Henry I ruled both England and Normandy.

Around this time, Hugh Maltravers gave some land to the newly founded Priory of Montacute in Somerset. He granted to the church and brethren of Montacute his land near Preston 'which Alwi Croinge holds by Southbrook, free from all services except the royal service'. Preston is the manor that was later known as Preston Plucknett; it adjoined Hugh's manor of Hendford and was three miles from Montacute.[34]

The charter recording Hugh Maltravers's gift to Montacute is not dated, but is assumed to date from the same period as a charter of William, count of Mortain – that is, 1095–1104; a reasonable guess is about 1102.[35] It is possible that the donor was the first Hugh Maltravers, if he was born in about 1040, fought at Hastings in 1066, was a sub-tenant of William d'Eu by 1086 and was still living in 1102. On the other hand, perhaps it was a son of the original Hugh, who could have been born about 1070.

From obscure beginnings, Hugh Maltravers had become the lord of up to ten manors in the west of England and a benefactor of the Church.

2

MALTRAVERS KNIGHTS AND LORDS OF THE MANOR, 1100–1290

William Maltravers I, *c.* 1100–1136, Royal Administrator

In the reign of Henry I (1100–35), the Maltravers family was represented by William and Walter. They may have been sons of Hugh Maltravers (I or II, in Chapter 1), but there is no definite evidence of the relationship.

William was the first of the family to be directly involved with the royal household. He was in the king's entourage in England and Normandy, and witnessed several charters between 1121 and 1133.[1] He paid the king the enormous sum of 1,000 marks to obtain the honour (a collection of manors) of Pontefract in West Yorkshire. The Lacy family had held Pontefract from the Norman Conquest until about 1114, when Robert de Lacy was banished from England by the king. Hugh de Laval then held it until his death in about 1129. Pontefract was then awarded to William Maltravers. In addition to the 1,000 marks, which he probably paid in instalments, Maltravers paid the king £100 so that he could marry Dameta, Hugh de Laval's widow. The arrangement was that he would hold the territory, and have the benefit of Dameta's dower and marriage portion, for fifteen years from 1130.[2] William Maltravers has been criticised by historians for failing to make the customary grants to religious institutions, and has been called an 'asset-stripping apparatchik',[3] a harsh description of a young man on the make.

William Maltravers did not enjoy his new status for long. Henry I died in December 1135, and his daughter Matilda should have become queen in accordance with the late king's wishes, but she was unpopular, and some said a woman could not be a monarch. Her cousin, Stephen of Blois, son of Henry I's sister Adela, claimed the throne and was crowned. Fighting broke out between supporters of Matilda and those of Stephen: there were numerous acts of violence and lawlessness, and the settling of old scores. The monk, Richard of Hexham, gave a graphic account of events when the firm rule of Henry I was suddenly removed: 'Justice and peace perished in both Normandy and England. Violence and rapine, slaughter and devastation, unheard-of cruelties and endless calamities, tyrannized far and wide.'[4]

Among the victims of this anarchy was the unfortunate William Maltravers, who was attacked and fatally wounded by one of the de Lacy knights. Richard of Hexham says: 'At this period William, surnamed Transversus, who by a grant from king Henry held the lordship of Pontefract, having received at that place a mortal wound from a knight named Pain, died three days afterwards, having assumed the monastic habit.'[5] The manner of his demise, and its use by the chronicler as an example of the anarchy, has made William Maltravers the first (but not the last) of his family to be mentioned in general history books. Ilbert de Lacy, son of Robert, regained his family lands at Pontefract in 1136. Thus, we can date the murder of William Maltravers to the early part of that year.

The struggle between Stephen and Matilda continued for several years, but, in the end, Matilda retired to France, and Stephen agreed that her son Henry should become king after him. When Stephen died, Henry II (who reigned from 1154–89) became king of England. He was already count of Anjou by inheritance from his father, Geoffrey of Anjou, and he was duke of Normandy as a result of his father's conquest of the duchy. In 1152, he married Eleanor, duchess of Aquitaine in her own right, whose territory stretched from Poitou to the Pyrenees.

Walter Maltravers I, *c.* 1095– *c.* 1172, Holder of Lands in Dorset and Berkshire

Walter is thought to be William Maltravers I's elder brother since he was a landowner. In 1130–31, he held land in Dorset and Berkshire. In respect of his Dorset lands, he received 25 shillings by the king's writ, and in Berkshire he was charged 20 marks for a judgment in a land dispute with Payn Fitzjohn. His wife inherited land in Leicestershire, and Walter had to pay 50 marks for her inheritance. The precise location of his estates is not recorded.[6]

John Maltravers I, *c.* 1130– *c.* 1200,
Constable of Striguil; Ordeal by Water

In the generation after William I and Walter, we meet the first of several Johns in the Maltravers family. The scanty information available for this period, without dates of birth and with no firm evidence of relationships, causes problems in constructing the family tree. A 'John' is mentioned in various documents between 1157 and 1200: we know of his dealings with the king's treasury, of his two marriages, of him being accused of a crime and of his death in about 1200. But is this all about John Maltravers I or do the documents sometimes refer to his son, who would be John Maltravers II?

'John Maltravers' owed the royal treasury 2 marks in 1157,[7] and 100 marks as a penalty or amercement in 1164.[8] Both debts were paid in instalments. In 1172, he paid a fine of 10 marks to have possession of his lands. This may have been the point at which his father died, and the fine was the customary fee paid in these circumstances to the overlord or, in the case of a tenant-in-chief, to the king. Walter Maltravers I, if he was John's father, must have been over seventy by then, which is a venerable age but not impossible. Alternatively, the payments between 1157and 1172 may refer to two people named John Maltravers, John I in 1157 and John II in 1172.[9] In the present book, rather than introduce an extra John Maltravers whose existence is doubtful, all the references to John Maltravers from 1157 until his death in 1200 are ascribed to John Maltravers I.

John Maltravers I was in trouble with the law in 1185, but, fortunately for him, one of his sons (Walter II or John II) underwent the ordeal by water on his behalf. In an ordeal by water, the accused person was bound hand and foot and lowered into a pond. If he sank, he was innocent, but if he floated he was guilty. This is not much of a choice. It appears that the son floated and failed the test, as the father had to pay 100 marks 'to be quit of his plea regarding the King's peace'.[10] Trial by ordeal ceased after 1215, when the fourth Lateran Council withdrew the Church's support.

The Maltravers knights held the position of constable of Striguil (Chepstow) Castle, an obligation attached to their tenure of Hendford manor in Yeovil. It is not clear when this obligation began, although they had held Yeovil from the time of the *Domesday Book*. The first mention of this position is in 1190 when the famous William Marshal became earl of Pembroke and earl of Striguil, and 'a retainer, John Maltravers, [held] under him Henneford, co. Somerset, by the service of constable of Striguil Castle'. From then on, the Maltravers knights held the hereditary position of Constable of Striguil Castle,[11] associated with Hendford.

John Maltravers I married Alice Fitzgeoffrey firstly, and they had two sons: Walter Maltravers II and John Maltravers II.[12] In or before 1180, Alice Fitzgeoffrey died, and it looks as though John I married Alice de Bendeville almost immediately afterwards. The two sons of the second marriage, Thomas and William (William Maltravers II), were born in about 1180–81.[13] John Maltravers I died in 1199 or 1200. There were violent scenes as he lay on his deathbed, and a family feud erupted soon afterwards, as described under the subsequent section on John Maltravers II.

Walter Maltravers II, *c.* 1150– *c.* 1201, Crusader

Richard I, son of Henry II, became king in 1189 and devoted most of his energy to the third crusade in the Holy Land. Walter II, the elder son of John Maltravers I, went on crusade with the king, returning to England in 1192. The crusaders failed in their principal aim, which was to capture Jerusalem from the Saracens, but they succeeded in taking Acre and Jaffa, and negotiated the right of pilgrims to visit Jerusalem. On the way home, disastrously, the king was captured and handed over to the German emperor. A ransom of 150,000 marks was demanded and heavy taxes were levied to pay it, or most of it, before the king was released in 1194.[14]

It may have been Walter II who instigated the building of the church at Lytchett Matravers after he returned home. The oldest surviving part, the tower, dates from about 1200. The rest of the church has seen some rebuilding and enlargement.[15]

Walter II built up a holding of lands even in his father's lifetime. In 1183 and 1184, he was assigned some lands in Wiltshire, which had belonged to his late mother, Alice Fitzgeoffrey. These were the manors of Great Somerford (sometimes called Somerford Mautravers), Filands and Coate.[16] In 1193, Walter II took part in a rebellion by Prince John (later King John), and forfeited his lands in Wiltshire as a result. Walter Maltravers II died in or before 1201.[17]

John Maltravers II, *c.* 1155–1220;
Maltravers Versus Turberville: A Feud; and Magna Carta

In June 1199, John Maltravers I lay sick, approaching the end of his life. He was visited by his son John. Walter de Turberville arrived with five men and, in a seemingly motiveless act of aggression, captured two retainers of the younger John, took them to the byre and hanged one of them. The intruders also stole 10 marks' worth of chattels.

An explanation for the ill will between the two families soon became clear. Within the year, the elder John was dead and his widow, Alice de Bendeville, had married Walter de Turberville. A dispute arose about some land at Woolcombe, and some goods of the Maltravers family that were now in the possession of Walter de Turberville and his new wife. The younger John, feeling that he was being done out of his inheritance, went to law. Two preliminary hearings in May/June 1200 set the date for a full trial soon after Michaelmas (September 29) that year.

John II grew impatient at the law's delay, and decided to take back at least some of his rightful property. Accordingly, on 6 August 1200, he went to Walter de Turberville's house with three of his men. Things turned ugly, and, in the affray, the house was set on fire and six of Turberville's men were killed.

At Michaelmas 1200, the matter came before the court. First, with respect to the land of Alice de Bendeville, the court was asked to decide if John Maltravers I had held on the day he died three carucates of land at Woolcombe, which land was held at the time of the hearing by Walter de Turberville and Alice, his wife. Turberville said no inquiry was needed, since John I had given the land to Alice before he died, and Turberville produced a charter of John Maltravers senior, witnessed by John's elder son, Walter II. The case was adjourned until November.

Then John Maltravers II demanded from Walter de Turberville and Alice three charters – comprising two of King Henry I and one of the earl of Striguil, possibly regarding the constableship – and also five 'loricas' (breastplates or other items of body armour). Turberville admitted that he had possessed the charters, but said that they had been stolen or burned when his house was set on fire. As for the breastplates, the elder John had had only one, which he had given to his son Walter II, together with 10 'librates' of land, in the seventh year before he died. John Maltravers II refused to accept this explanation, and continued to demand the charters and the five suits of armour, which his father had been required to possess for use in a Welsh war. Turberville left the court without permission, and so Maltravers was adjudged to have won by default.

In the spring of 1201, the court considered the events when Walter de Turberville had intruded on the Maltravers household as John I lay dying, and the alleged murder and theft of chattels. Walter de Turberville denied everything and offered 40 shillings to have an inquiry into it. A hearing at the King's Bench was promised for mid-Lent.

Now it was the turn of John Maltravers II to be on the defensive, as Walter de Turberville accused him of burning his house and destroying charters and chattels to the value of £100 the previous August. John II's three accomplices, who were outlaws, had been seen by Turberville himself and another witness. John II said they were not outlaws and what he had taken belonged to him by right. A hearing was arranged, as in the previous case.

The case was adjourned twice more, to June 1201, but it is not known if a clear result was ever achieved.[18] They were still arguing about a carucate of land in Woolcombe as late as 1219, when it was claimed by Thomas Maltravers, son of Alice de Bendeville, who said that it had been his before his father, John Maltravers I, died. John Maltravers II declared that, on the contrary, it had belonged to John Maltravers I right up to the latter's death.[19]

The Maltravers lands in Wiltshire – Great Somerford and Coate – that were forfeited by Walter Maltravers II for taking part in Prince John's rebellion in 1193, were restored to John Maltravers II after the deaths of his brother Walter II and his father, John Maltravers I.

In the reign of King John (1199–1216), the Angevin empire of Henry II and Richard I was split up. In 1204, England lost Normandy to France, keeping only the Channel Islands. In the next two years, more territories were lost: Anjou, Touraine and parts of Poitou. With difficulty, the English retained Gascony in South West France; the sea route to Bordeaux would always be a concern for later medieval kings.

Barons who held land in both England and Normandy had to choose which lands to keep, as they could no longer hold land in both countries. Barons based in England were angered at the loss of their Norman lands. Because of this and other grievances, many barons rebelled against King John and forced him to agree to a charter setting out their rights: Magna Carta 1215. The king sought help from the pope, who annulled the charter. This led to civil war again between the barons and the king. John Maltravers II took the side of the barons and, as a result, his lands at Woodchester in Gloucestershire, and at Coate, Great Somerford, Easton and other places in Wiltshire were forfeited to the king.[20]

King John died of a sudden illness on 19 October 1216 and was succeeded by his son Henry, who was aged only nine (Henry III, 1216–72). The elderly and much respected earl of Pembroke, William Marshal, acted as protector of the king and regent of the realm. In 1217, John Maltravers II, being in the retinue of the earl of Pembroke, declared his allegiance to the new king, as did many other barons and knights. The sheriffs of Gloucestershire, Wiltshire, Berkshire, Somerset and Dorset were ordered to restore John Maltravers's lands to him in 1219.[21]

By May/June 1220, John Maltravers II had died, leaving a widow, Hawise. Their son, John Maltravers III, was born in about 1208. They also had a daughter, Alice. Margaret may have been another daughter, but the relationship is not certain.

John Maltravers III, *c.* 1208–1262?; His Sisters Alice and Margaret; Fighting in Gascony, Wales and Ireland; and His Arms, 'Sable Fretty Or'

Because John Maltravers III inherited as a minor, the family estates were once again escheated (taken into the king's hands). On 26 April 1221, the sheriff of Gloucestershire was ordered 'to take into the king's hand without delay all land formerly of John Maltravers in his bailiwick, with all chattels found therein, and to keep it safely with the same chattels so that nothing is removed therefrom until the king orders otherwise.'[22]

In 1222, Hawise claimed her dower land at Yeovil from William Maltravers II, her late husband's half-brother (son of John Maltravers I and Alice de Bendeville). True to form, the de Bendeville son protested that the land in question belonged to him and not to Hawise, because he had acquired it from his father. John Maltravers III, being underage, was unable to pursue the claim at this time, and it is not known whether the matter was resolved.[23]

Acting as head of the family since their father had died, he arranged a prestigious marriage for his sister Alice to Elias Giffard (lord of Brimpsfield, Gloucestershire) and gave her the manor of Ashton in the Wylye Valley, Wiltshire, as her dowry. Ashton, later called Ashton Gifford, was to be held by Elias and Alice, and then by their heirs, from John Maltravers III and his heirs. Elias Giffard and Alice Maltravers had a son, John, who was born in 1232. This

Giffard marriage was the start of a connection between the Giffards and the Maltraverses that was to last for several generations.[24]

Margaret Maltravers was probably another sister of John Maltravers III. She was a lady of the royal household. In 1235, the marriage was arranged between the king's sister Isabella and Frederick the German emperor. The royal bride, magnificently attired and bejewelled, accompanied by her 'damsel' (a lady in waiting) Margaret Maltravers and by a huge retinue, set off for Cologne. After the wedding, Frederick sent almost all of his bride's retinue, including Margaret Maltravers, back to England. From this point onwards, Isabella seldom saw outsiders and she died in 1241.

Meanwhile, in England, the royal accounts show occasional gifts of money and robes to Margaret, until she herself married Sir Richard Ashburnham in about 1241: '26 January 1241. 46s. 8d. paid for a robe for Margaret Maltravers of the king's gift, being a tunic and supertunic, and a cloak with trimming of linen and an edging of rabbitskin (furrura de cuniculis).'[25]

John Maltravers III was summoned to the king's service in 1230, and thereafter took part in several military campaigns in Gascony, Wales and Ireland.[26]

South and South East Wales had long been held by Norman Marcher lords, but the north of Wales was ruled by Welsh princes. King Henry III tried to extend his rule to North Wales and built several castles, including Dyserth, which was put under John Maltravers III as its constable. Although in a strong defensive position on a hilltop, Dyserth was difficult to reprovision in the event of a siege, as happened in 1245. It is recorded that John Maltravers re-provisioned the castle at his own expense. He claimed £70 14s. 10½d. from the royal treasury; this sum was repaid to him in 1246. Eventually, after a further siege in 1263, Llywelyn ap Gruffydd took and destroyed the castle.[27]

John Maltravers III was given respite from taking up knighthood in July 1256 until the following summer, implying that he was knighted in 1257.[28] At the Norman Conquest, a knight was simply a mounted warrior. Later, the rank carried a privileged status. As time went on, it became considered an expensive and not altogether welcome burden.

The arms of John Maltravers were 'sable fretty or' (on a black background, interlaced bands in gold). The design is an example of 'canting' arms, which is a play on the user's name. The criss-cross pattern looks like a barrier – something difficult to cross – referring to the literal meaning of Maltravers, as discussed in Chapter 1. These arms are found in Glover's Roll, dating from 1258 or earlier.

Heraldry, as an organised system, only became popular in the twelfth century, and it is very unlikely that the fretty design was used by the original Hugh Maltravers. It is not clear which John Maltravers was the first to bear these arms, but we can be fairly sure that John Maltravers III did so.

The name of John Maltravers III's wife is not known. He had two or three sons: John IV, William III and possibly Walter III. John Maltravers III may have died in 1262, as in that year a 'John Maltravers' renewed Hugh Maltravers's charter granting land at Preston Plucknett to Montacute Priory: 'John Maltravers of Yeovil, quit-claims to the church and monks of Montacute, all right, claim and service which he holds in the land of Prestone which is called Bysuthebroke, which Hugh Maltravers gave to the said church.'[29] This may have been the point where John Maltravers III died and John Maltravers IV inherited his estates.

William Maltravers III, *c.* 1242–after 1280; Fighting at Lewes and Evesham; and the Death of Simon de Montfort

William Maltravers III was a younger son of John Maltravers III, but his story will be told before his brother's, as the notable events of his life occurred first.

In the early years of the reign of Henry III, relations between the king and his barons were fairly harmonious, in contrast to the reign of King John when conflict led to Magna Carta (1215) and a civil war. By the 1250s, however, the barons had several complaints: they felt sidelined by the king's tendency to consult only his foreign relatives, especially his half-brothers (the sons of his mother, Isabella of Angouleme, with her second husband, Hugh X of Lusignan). Also, the king had incurred huge debts in his ill-advised attempt to make his second son, Edmund, king of Sicily. At the parliament of 1258, the barons proposed, in the Provisions of Oxford, a council of fifteen magnates who would appoint people to official positions and who would, in effect, have power over the king. Sometime afterwards, the king regained power, but the leader of the barons, Simon de Montfort, insisted on the Provisions of Oxford, and, in 1264, the country again came to civil war.

At the time, full-scale battles were rare, and warfare was more a matter of skirmishes and sieges. Now, for the first time in over forty years, there was a battle on English soil. Knights were mounted on their great war horses, clad in coats of mail, and armed with shields, swords and lances. Their heraldic devices were depicted on their shields and on the surcoats they wore over their armour. They were accompanied by a large number of foot soldiers carrying various weapons: swords, daggers, pikes, or bows and arrows.

The Battle of Lewes took place on 14 May 1264. King Henry III and his son Prince Edward (the future king Edward I) were opposed by Simon de Montfort. Among the hundreds of knights and thousands of other soldiers in Simon's army were William Maltravers III and his cousin John Giffard, son of Elias Giffard and Alice Maltravers.

William III bore the Maltravers arms of 'sable fretty or' with the Giffard arms of 'gules three lions passant guardant argent' on a canton. William's arms are depicted in the Dering Roll of about 1275, which is now kept in the British Library.

At an early stage in the battle, John Giffard, William Maltravers III and others were captured by the king's side and imprisoned in Lewes Castle. The fighting continued all day. The battle turned against the king, who had to take refuge in Lewes Priory, where Prince Edward joined him. The town and even the priory church were set alight, but the royalist defenders held out. Eventually, a truce was reached, and details of a settlement were negotiated the next day, with friars from the priory acting as intermediaries, and going back and forth between the parties. Some of the prisoners in the castle were released, including John Giffard and William Maltravers III, but it was agreed that King Henry III and Prince Edward should be in de Montfort's custody.

It appeared that de Montfort had won the battle, and, for the next few months, he more or less ruled the country. Traditionally, the king's Great Council consisted of nobles and leading clergy. Earlier in the reign of Henry III, for the first time, two knights from each shire were also summoned to the council. The parliament that Montfort summoned in January 1265 was a significant development in that it also included two burgesses from each town.

Simon de Montfort's arrogance made him many enemies. Some of his supporters felt they had never intended to replace King Henry III with King Simon. Gilbert de Clare, earl of Gloucester, who was previously a foremost ally, deserted Simon. John Giffard left de Montfort's retinue and joined that of de Clare. As well as dissatisfaction with his erstwhile leader, Giffard was motivated by the fact that de Clare was the dominant magnate in Gloucestershire where the main Giffard estates were located. William Maltravers III followed his cousin into the anti-Simon, or pro-royalist, camp.

As de Montfort moved around the country, he dragged his prisoners – King Henry and Prince Edward – with him. In May 1265, Edward – supposedly exercising his horses near Hereford with the permission of his gaolers – suddenly escaped and galloped away to Roger Mortimer at Wigmore. (Mortimer was the grandfather of the famous Roger Mortimer of the reign of Edward II.) Together with de Clare, they assembled an army, and the stage was set for the second battle.

Prince Edward and Simon de Montfort finally confronted each other at the Battle of Evesham. De Montfort had only a part of his army, as his son – another Simon – was making his way from Kenilworth with the rest of the force. On the morning of the battle, 4 August 1265, de Montfort thought he saw his son's contingent arriving, but one of his men – who was an expert in heraldry – climbed the bell tower at Evesham Abbey and reported that it was, in fact, the royal army. De Montfort was hopelessly outnumbered, and the battle was particularly bloody. A small group of royal knights were given the task of seeking out and killing Simon de Montfort. Roger Mortimer killed de Montfort by striking him through the neck with his lance. The knights then fell upon de Montfort's body, and William Maltravers III cut off his feet and hands. They then cut off de Montfort's head and his testicles, which were 'hung on either side of his nose', and the head was sent to Roger Mortimer's wife in this state. 'Such was the murder of Evesham for battle was it none.' The killing continued in the fields and town of Evesham, and even in the church. When it was over, some of Simon de Montfort's friends carried the remains of his body to Evesham Abbey's church for burial before the high altar.[30]

There were many cases of forcible entry, robbery and usurpation of lands during the troubles between King Henry III and Simon de Montfort. John Maltravers IV, William III's brother, was the victim of such an armed robbery, when William Padel and many others broke into his house at Woolcombe and carried off his goods and chattels. John IV made a complaint in the court of King's Bench in 1267 regarding the wrong done to him.[31] If this case is an example of the politically motivated lawlessness, it may indicate that John Maltravers IV was a combatant in that war, presumably with his brother William III at the Battle of Evesham in 1265. This is the extremely flimsy and circumstantial evidence that has been used to place 'John de Maltravers of Dorset' with 'William de Maltravers of Dorset and Berkshire' among the royalist gentry. No information about William Padel has been found.[32]

As far as is known, William Maltravers III did not marry and had no direct descendants. At Christmas 1271, he was at the home of the Ferrers family in Groby, Leicestershire – perhaps invited as a bachelor friend, not having his own household. Anne Ferrers was pregnant at the time and gave birth to a son, William, in the following month. The Christmas festivities, and the presence at them of William Maltravers III, were recalled 21 years later, in 1293, when it was necessary to prove the date of birth of William Ferrers. Various witnesses recounted what they were doing at the time, and why they could be sure that William Ferrers was now of age and could take possession of his estates.[33]

On 26 June 1280, William Maltravers III and his brother John Maltravers IV witnessed a charter of Prince Edmund (the younger brother of Prince Edward), by which he gave his manor of Bere, Dorset, to the convent at Tarrant.[34]

There is no evidence of any lands being held by William Maltravers III, and a supposed connection with Ashton, near Codford, Wiltshire, is the result of an error in the sources. Ashton was the dowry of Alice Maltravers when she married Elias Giffard. When their grandson John Giffard died in 1322, it was initially said that the deceased had held Ashton from the heirs of *William* Maltravers, but further inquiry showed that it was held from the heirs of *John* Maltravers.[35]

John Maltravers IV, c. 1240–1297, Steward of the King's Household and Wrongly Said to be Keeper of the Forest; Land in Ireland; the Visit of Edward I and Military Service in Wales

The eldest son of John Maltravers III, John IV, was born in about 1240. It is possible that he fought alongside his younger brother at Lewes and Evesham as previously mentioned. In the reign of Edward I (1272–1307), he had connections with the royal household and took part in military campaigns.

John Maltravers IV was steward of the king's household in 1274. The steward was in charge of the domestic arrangements, overseeing the supply of food and drink for the court, and everything else needed for day-to-day life. Each evening, he met with the treasurer, known as the 'keeper of the wardrobe', to check the accounts. His was no small task, as Edward I's domestic establishment contained about 600 people and was often on the move. The steward was part of the king's inner circle.

It is not possible to say how long John Maltravers IV held this position. Unlike other government officials, who had letters of appointment that can be seen in the Patent Rolls, the stewards received no such letters. Instead, the main source for the names of the stewards is the Charter Rolls. These rolls contain details of charters issued by the king, together with the names of the courtiers and household servants who witnessed them. Unfortunately for our purpose, very few charters were issued in the first two or three years of the reign, and John Maltravers IV is not mentioned as a witness. The steward in these years, who witnessed some charters (but is only rarely listed as the steward) was Hugh fitz Otto.[36]

The one charter witnessed by John Maltravers IV as steward is not in the Charter Rolls since it is an ecclesiastical charter. This charter, granted by the king to the Collegiate Church in Wolverhampton, confirms the earlier charters issued by Edward the Confessor, William I and Henry II to the same church. It was witnessed by the archbishop of York, the bishops of Ely and Winchester, the earl of Lancaster, John de Warenne (the earl of Surrey), Roger Mortimer, John Maltravers ('steward of our household'), and others. The king granted this charter 'by his own hand' at Northampton on 8 May 1274. The witness Roger Mortimer is the same Roger Mortimer who was at Evesham.[37] The date is strange and may be an error. Edward I was out of England on crusade when he became king in 1272, and he did not return to his realm until August 1274. So how could he personally have authorised this charter in May 1274? Records of his travels show that he was indeed at Northampton that year, but not until 3–18 November. This may be the correct date for the Wolverhampton charter.[38] It is possible that John Maltravers was the steward only during the king's sojourn in Northampton.

John Maltravers IV is said to have been 'keeper of the king's forests this side of the Trent [south of the Trent]', and to have claimed 'from every forester, both within the forest of Savernake and elsewhere in the county of Wiltshire, when he should die, his horse, saddle and bridle, horn and sword, bow and barbed arrows. Inquis. Temp. Edw. I.'[39] This comes from a 1679 book by Thomas Blount, originally in Latin and later translated into English. It has been repeated by later historians, including Hutchins, and can be found on many genealogical websites.

'North of the Trent' and 'south of the Trent' are terms used by modern historians for clarity, but in the Middle Ages the expression was 'this side of the Trent (*citra Trentam*)' or 'the other side of the Trent (*ultra Trentam*)' depending on where the king was at the time: if he was at Westminster, the south of England was '*citra Trentam*', but if the king was at York, the north was '*citra Trentam*'. This may seem confusing to us, but appears not to have caused problems at the time.

In fact, John Maltravers IV did not hold the position of keeper of the king's forests on either side of the Trent. Blount had the wrong reign and the wrong John Maltravers. The names of all the justices of the forest under Edward I are known. The appointment of each person is noted in the Patent Rolls or in the Fine Rolls, and his predecessor is simultaneously ordered to surrender the memoranda and rolls concerning the office. There are no gaps in the sequence for John Maltravers IV to be inserted.[40]

JUSTICES OF THE FOREST SOUTH OF THE TRENT
- † Roger de Clifford the elder, 1265–70.[41]
- † Roger de Clifford junior, 1270–74[42] – Roger senior was on crusade with the king.
- † Roger de Clifford the elder again, 1274–81[43] – after having returned from crusade.
- † Luke de Tany, 1281–83.[44]
- † Roger le Strange, 1283–97.[45]
- † Hugh le Despenser, 1297–1307.[46]
- † Payn Tybotot, appointed August 1307.[47]

JUSTICES OF THE FOREST NORTH OF THE TRENT
- † Geoffrey de Neville, 1270–85.[48]
- † William de Vescy, 1285–90.
- † John de Vescy, son of William de Vescy, 1290–95.
- † William de Vescy (again), 1295–97.[49]
- † Robert de Clifford from 1298 to 1308.[50]

However, a later John Maltravers (VI), the grandson of John Maltravers IV, did indeed hold the position of keeper of the forest south of the Trent from 5 April 1329 until 1330.

Under the justices, each forest was governed by a warden (a 'custos'). The wardens of Savernake were all members of the Sturmy family from the time of the *Domesday Book* until the fifteenth century. No Maltravers ever held this position.[51]

John Maltravers IV and his wife, Joan, had at least four children: three sons (John Maltravers V, Roger Maltravers I and Robert Maltravers of Crowell) and a daughter (Anastasia). Walter Maltravers IV may have been another of their sons.

In 1281, John IV added to his lands by purchasing from Roger Waspail the Dorset manors of Langton (later known as Langton Matravers and part of the modern parish of the same name) and Witchampton. John IV paid Roger 100 marks for these transactions.[52]

In the same year, John IV gave Roger Waspail a life interest in the manor of Woolcombe, Dorset, in exchange for the manor of Rathkeale, plus some land in Loughill and Kilcolman, all in County Limerick, Ireland. John IV and his heirs were to hold these Irish lands in perpetuity, not just for a life interest. It is not known what prompted this sudden interest in acquiring property in Ireland, which was a long way from their existing lands in the south-west of England. It has been suggested that John Maltravers IV's wife, Joan, may have been an Irish heiress, but there is no real evidence for this, and it is uncertain how the marriage came about. Nothing is known about Joan's family. For several generations into the future from that point, the Maltraverses were to take a strong interest in their Irish estates.[53]

John Maltravers IV himself went to Ireland in 1280–81, and appointed attorneys to look after his interests in England while he was away.[54] In 1285, John IV and his wife were in England, but appointed agents to act elsewhere, probably in Ireland.[55] By 1289, the responsibility for the Irish estates had been passed to John IV's son, John Maltravers V. The younger John and his wife Eleanor stayed in England, but nominated agents in Ireland.[56]

John IV's daughter Anastasia married Herbert St Quintin. John IV gave his son-in-law some land in Woolcombe in 1285, presumably as Anastasia's dowry. The land was to be held by Herbert St Quintin and his heirs from John Maltravers IV and his heirs. Evidently, the manor given to Roger Waspail did not comprise the whole of Woolcombe. A son, also named Herbert, was born to Anastasia and Herbert St Quintin in 1285 or 1286.[57] Hutchins and other older histories are wrong in saying that Anastasia was previously married to John de Haddon: that was a different Anastasia.

John Maltravers IV must have felt greatly honoured when King Edward I paid his first visit to Lytchett Matravers on 28 November 1285. On the two previous days, the king was at Canford Magna, then on the 28th he was at both Blandford and Lytchett Matravers.[58] If he spent the night at the Lytchett Matravers manor, it must have been a massive task to entertain, accommodate and feed the royal household, including the household knights, officials and servants, with their horses and baggage train. The king was on his way to Corfe Castle, where he spent the next five days. He had conceived the idea of establishing a new town, to be called Newtown, near Ower on the shores of Poole Harbour. The project was discussed in the following year, but it came to nothing.

The 1290s was a decade full of wars in Gascony, Wales, Scotland and Flanders. In 1294, as forces were being mustered at London and Portsmouth to go to Gascony, news came of widespread revolt in Wales. Edward I's castles at Harlech, Conwy and Criccieth were under siege, and the castle at Caernarfon was being destroyed. The king learned of these events in early October and immediately ordered the troops that were still at Portsmouth to turn around and go to Wales. Other forces were mobilised, including an unprecedented 35,000 foot soldiers. On 15 October, a writ was sent to John Maltravers IV, summoning him to be at Worcester on 21 November to perform military service against the Welsh. The king himself reached Chester on 5 December. Conwy was back in the king's hands in time for him to celebrate Christmas there. His strategy of building fortresses where they could be reprovisioned from the sea was a great success, as compared with inland castles such as Dyserth, which was besieged in 1245. John Giffard, cousin of John Maltravers IV, commanded the force that relieved the castle of Builth in November 1294.[59]

John Maltravers IV died in early 1297. When a tenant-in-chief – or a person who was possibly a tenant-in-chief – died, an inquiry was held to find out what lands had been held at the date of death, from whom they had been held and who the heir was. In the case of John IV, a writ ordering an Inquisition Post Mortem of his lands was issued on 28 February 1297. He was found to have held the following:

BERKSHIRE
† Childrey (now in Oxfordshire): a court and land held from Hugh de Say.

SOMERSET
† Hendford: the manor held from the earl Marshal, by service of being constable of Chepstow (Striguil).

GLOUCESTERSHIRE
† Woodchester: the manor held from the king in chief.

DORSET
- † Langton Matravers: land held from the king in chief, and other parcels of land held from John de Clavile, Robert Fitzpayn and Ingram le Waleys.
- † Lytchett Matravers: the manor with advowson of the church held from Joan, Countess of Gloucester and Hertford.[60]
- † Witchampton: the manor and advowson of the church held from the same countess.

John IV's heir was found to be his son John V, who was aged 30 in the previous September (on the feast of St Michael), and therefore born in 1266.[61]

Walter Maltravers III

Master Walter Maltravers III was the parson of Yeovil. The title 'Master' (Magister) indicates that he had received a university education. In 1280, he was required to respond to a writ of Quo Warranto, and to say by what right he held a market in Yeovil. He successfully claimed that he and his predecessors as parsons had held the market since time immemorial.[62] He may have been a son of John Maltravers III, but the relationship is not proved.

3

JOHN MALTRAVERS V AND HIS SON, BARON JOHN MALTRAVERS WAR, REBELLION AND EXILE, 1290–1326

John Maltravers V in Flanders and Ireland, 1290–1299

John Maltravers V and his wife, Eleanor de Gorges, had three sons and a daughter. Their first son, John Maltravers VI, was born in about 1290. The other two sons were William, who became rector of Lytchett Matravers in 1314, and Edward. Their daughter was Matilda.

In 1297, John V, as a knight holding lands or rents valued at £20 or more, was summoned to perform military service in person, with horses and arms, beyond the seas and to attend the muster in London on 7 July.[1] Unusually, the country where he was to fight was not stated, perhaps because the whole enterprise was a matter of dispute between the king on the one hand, and his magnates and the Church, angered by heavy taxes, on the other. Earlier in 1297, the king had wanted to send a force to Gascony to assist the earl of Lincoln, but he was met with a refusal by many nobles, who argued that their feudal duty did not require service outside the realm. Roger Bigod, earl of Norfolk and the hereditary marshal of England, said he would only go on a campaign overseas in the company of the king.

'By God, Earl,' said the king, 'you shall either go or hang.'

'By the same oath, O King,' replied Bigod, 'I will neither go nor hang'; he then left the court.[2]

The hereditary constable, Humphrey de Bohun, earl of Hereford, took the same line. When they were later asked to go to Flanders, this time with the king also to go in person, they again refused. The stand-off continued during the summer, and the king eventually departed for Flanders on 23 August with fewer soldiers than he had wished for, and with Geoffrey de Geneville as marshal and Thomas de Berkeley, first Baron Berkeley of the powerful Gloucestershire family, as constable. The king finally returned to England on 14 March 1298, having agreed a two-year truce with France.[3]

In 1299, John Maltravers V went to Ireland in person, presumably to visit Rathkeale and his other estates. He was accompanied by four men: his brother Roger, Thomas de Newbury, Thomas de Dumore and Melior le Brun.[4]

John Maltravers V in Scotland, 1286–1305

John V was caught up in Edward I's protracted efforts to bring Scotland into his domains. At first, this was attempted by diplomatic means. King Alexander III of Scotland died in 1286, leaving his granddaughter Margaret, the 'Maid of Norway', as his sole direct heir. The plan was for her to marry Edward I's son, Edward of Caernarfon, later King Edward II. If they had a child, this would unite the kingdoms of England and Scotland in the next generation, which was a union that, in the event, did not occur until 1603. Unfortunately, Margaret died in 1290, aged seven, possibly having contracted food poisoning on her voyage from Norway to Scotland for the wedding. Since there was then no generally agreed successor to the throne of Scotland, the Scots asked Edward I to assist in choosing between the rival claimants. John Balliol was chosen to be king in preference to the other main claimant, Robert Bruce.

Edward regarded himself as overlord of Scotland, which was a status that the Scots only accepted under duress. Between 1296 and the end of his reign in 1307, Edward I led his army into Scotland on six occasions: in 1296, 1298, 1300, 1301, 1303 and 1306. Some expeditions were more successful than others in terms of battles won or castles captured, but there was always the difficulty of supplying and paying the troops over a campaign that might last several months.

In 1300, John Maltravers V – as a knight with lands worth £40 per year – was ordered to present himself at Carlisle on 24 June; he was one of 1,700 knights in all. In addition, there were 9,000 foot soldiers, who were to be paid wages from a tax levied in Wales. They fought an inconclusive campaign in South West Scotland, and many of the foot soldiers deserted when their wages were not paid.

In 1301, two armies were levied: one in the east, led by the king; and one in the west, led by Prince Edward, then aged seventeen. From Ireland came cavalry and foot soldiers: the magnates of Ireland were told that their debts to the Crown would be cancelled if they participated. John Maltravers V was summoned from Wiltshire to perform military service in person against the Scots, and to attend the muster at Berwick-upon-Tweed on 24 June.

It is also recorded that a 'John Maltravers of Ireland' was summoned to the war in Scotland in 1300, 1301 and 1302, receiving a 'letter of credence'. This may be John Maltravers V, or 'John Maltravers of Ireland' may be a different person altogether.

A further campaign from 1303–1304 had a successful outcome from the English point of view. John Balliol had been forced to abdicate in 1296, and the Scottish leader was now Balliol's nephew, John Comyn; in March 1304, Comyn and 130 other Scottish landowners swore allegiance to Edward I. After the king had left Scotland, William Wallace, the popular Scottish military leader, was captured by his compatriots and handed over to the English to be tried; he was executed for high treason in August 1305, and Edward I probably regarded his troubles in Scotland as being at an end.

Edward I's Second Visit to Lytchett Matravers, 1306

By the end of 1305, King Edward I's territories in England, Wales, Ireland, Scotland and Gascony were all at peace. He was sixty-six years old, and still fit and active. His second wife, Margaret of France, had given him two sons to join Prince Edward, who was the sole surviving son of his first marriage to his late and beloved Queen Eleanor. The king spent Christmas 1305 at Kingston Lacy, Dorset, which was a manor house of his old friend Henry de Lacy, earl of Lincoln. This was Edward I's fifth visit, and he stayed for three weeks.[5] In January 1306, he spent a week at Bindon Abbey near Wool, and then travelled around Dorset and Hampshire, no doubt indulging in his favourite sports of hunting and falconry.

On 9 February 1306, he visited the manor house at Lytchett Matravers, and presumably spent the night there. He was at Frampton the night before and the night after, so perhaps he only took a small number of household knights and servants with him to Lytchett Matravers. What excitement for John V and Eleanor Maltravers, the lord and lady of the manor, and for their sons! The eldest, John VI, was about sixteen years old, so on the brink of manhood. No doubt they recalled the king's visit twenty years previously, which was in the time of John V's father, and the recent campaigns in Scotland, which were now happily resolved.[6] Maybe the family's minstrel entertained the royal guest. There was a Maltravers harpist called Melior who had played for the king at Plympton, Devon, in 1297 'while the king was bled', and who had been rewarded with a gift of 20 shillings. If Melior was still in John Maltravers V's employ in 1306, he would no doubt have been called upon to delight the king with his music again.[7]

During the visit, the king made a grant 'to John Maltravers and his heirs of free warren in all their demesne lands in Lytchett Matravers, Dorset'. This conferred the exclusive right to hunt the beasts and fowl of the warren on their lands; that is to say, hares, foxes, rabbits, pheasant and partridge, but not the beasts of the forest, deer and wild boar.[8]

Crisis in Scotland: The Knighting of John Maltravers V and His Son, John VI; and the Feast of the Swans, 1306

After his visit to Lytchett Matravers, the king went to Frampton, West Parley, Ringwood and Lyndhurst (on 15 February), from where he set out for Winchester, arriving on 18 February. Sometime in that week, the appalling news reached him of the murder of John Comyn by Robert Bruce on 10 February, and of the latter's intention to be crowned king of Scotland, the ceremony for which took place at Scone on 25 March. This Robert Bruce was the grandson of the Robert Bruce who had been one of the claimants to the throne of Scotland in 1290. The news coincided with, and perhaps caused, a sudden decline in Edward I's health, and when he left Winchester in May, he was carried in a litter. However, he was not too ill to make plans for renewed intervention in Scotland.

The king decided that an army would be assembled at Carlisle, and that it would be led by his son Prince Edward. He announced that the prince would be knighted on Whit Sunday, 22 May, and that others who wished to be knighted with him should present themselves at Westminster on that day. Among the 267 or so men who responded to the call were the Maltravers father and son who had received the king so recently. On the appointed day, the king knighted his eldest son, and Prince Edward then knighted all the others. The ceremony concluded with a magnificent 'Feast of the Swans', with a centrepiece of two swans decorated with gold nets. The event recalled the legend of King Arthur and his knights renewing their oaths at Pentecost.

In the following days, the clerks were busy issuing letters of protection (against legal actions in their absence) for those intending to set out for Scotland. Among them were 'John Maltravers senior' (John V), Roger Maltravers I and Walter Maltravers IV, all in the retinue of Maurice de Berkeley. John Maltravers junior (John VI) is not mentioned, possibly not needing letters of protection because of his youth, but it is difficult to believe that, having just been knighted, he was sent home again and not allowed to ride northwards. Roger Maltravers I was a younger brother of John V. Walter Maltravers IV was probably also a brother of John V: he cannot have been a younger brother of John VI or he would have been under sixteen and too young to fight. Maurice de Berkeley (1271–1326, later the second Baron Berkeley), had just been knighted with his father, Thomas de Berkeley (1245–1321), the first Baron Berkeley. In the future, there were to be close ties between the Berkeleys and the Maltraverses.[9]

Another of the new knights was Roger Mortimer of Wigmore, the grandson of the Roger Mortimer who had fought at the Battle of Evesham in 1265. At the age of nineteen, Roger Mortimer of Wigmore was already head of his family and with his own retinue, since his father, Edmund, had died young. Roger had been knighted with his uncle Roger Mortimer of Chirk.[10]

The advance force had already left for the north, to be followed by Prince Edward and the main army, and then, slowly and laboriously, by King Edward I. Initially, in 1306, the English defeated Bruce, who fled to Ireland, while his captured supporters and family were executed or imprisoned. In February 1307, Bruce returned to Scotland, now more popular than ever. The king at last arrived at Carlisle in March, and continued to direct military operations from the rear, but was frustrated by the lack of success. Finally, in late June 1307, he made a heroic attempt to ride out at the head of his troops; after a few days, he was forced to stop at Burgh by Sands on the Solway Firth, where he died on 7 July 1307. On the death of Edward I, the campaign in Scotland against Robert Bruce was abandoned.

The Early Years of King Edward II, 1307–1313

At the beginning of the new reign, John Maltravers V was a person of some standing in his community. In December 1307 and again in March 1308, he was appointed a conservator of the peace in Dorset.[11]

Soon afterwards, he was himself a victim of crime. He complained that thieves and poachers had broken into his park at his manor of Woodchester, Gloucestershire, and had hunted his game and carried away his goods. On three occasions between 1308 and 1310, justices were appointed, '*oyer et terminer*', to hear and determine the case against the malefactors. One of the thieves, a certain Luke le Warner, was convicted of taking a buck and four does from the park, and was kept in prison for over a year until his brother paid a fine of 40 shillings to obtain his release.[12]

From time to time, John V took an interest in his Irish lands at Rathkeale. In 1307 and 1308, John V and Eleanor Maltravers appointed attorneys in Ireland. In 1310, they actually went there: 'John Maltravers the elder and Eleanor his wife, going to Ireland, have letters nominating John de Middleton and Henry de Glanville their attorneys for two years.'[13]

John Maltravers V appears in a roll of arms, known as the Parliamentary Roll, in which he is given the status of 'banneret'. That is, a person who displays his arms on a square banner in battle; an ordinary knight has a triangular pennon. The document starts with the bannerets: '*Ces sunt les nons e les Armes a Banerez de Engletere* [These are the names and the arms of the bannerets of England].' There follow 169 names: the king, thirteen earls, the bishop of Durham and 154 bannerets. This includes, at number 148 in the list, 'Sir John Maltravers, "sable fretty or"' (on a black background, a criss-cross pattern in gold). Then come the ordinary knights arranged by county. In all, there are about 1,100 names. The Parliamentary Roll can be dated to 1307–11, since the third name on the list (after the king and the earl of Gloucester) is the king's friend, Piers Gaveston, earl of Cornwall, one of Edward II's first acts as king having been to ennoble his favourite in August 1307. The roll cannot be later than 1311, as it includes Antony Bek, bishop of Durham, who died in that year. The roll gives an idea of the status of the Maltravers family at this time. Having started in 1086 as the holders of manors from William d'Eu, they had advanced significantly up the social scale as a result of service to kings and nobles, military enthusiasm, and the good luck of having continued the male line thus far.[14]

But what of John the younger, John Maltravers VI? For him, the highlight of the years after the Scottish expedition was undoubtedly the Dunstable tournament of 1309. Armed and mounted nobles and knights assembled in teams to fight a mock battle, aptly described as a 'mêlée', which could easily become as dangerous as it sounds. We have the names of some 235 warriors who took part, among them 'Sir John de Maltravers', bearing the arms 'sable fretty or, a label of three points argent'. The label indicates a son of the principal bearer of the arms and is therefore the younger John. He is named under the heading 'de la commune' towards the end of the list. This probably means he was not contracted to one of the great lords but was allocated to a team on the day.[15]

Having recalled Piers Gaveston from exile in 1307, Edward II endowed him with lands and money, and gave him a prominent position at the court. The magnates felt excluded from affairs of state and were insulted by Gaveston's nicknames for them: the earl of Warwick was 'the Black Dog of Arden' and the earl of Lincoln was 'Burst Belly'. Twice they forced Gaveston into exile and twice he returned. Eventually, he was captured by the earl of Warwick and, after a sham trial, was beheaded on 19 June 1312 on the orders of the earl of Lancaster. The king was both devastated and enraged. He was unable to take action immediately, but never forgave Lancaster and looked out for an opportunity for revenge.

On 23 May 1313, King Edward II and Queen Isabella travelled to France, at the invitation of the king of France, for the knighting of Isabella's three brothers. In the large party from England was John Maltravers (probably John the elder [V]), in the retinue of Robert Fitzpayn, who had been steward of the king's household in 1308–10; Maltravers and Fitzpayn both held land in Dorset. John, like all the others in the party, was given protection during his absence 'beyond seas'. The festivities continued for nearly two months, and they all returned home in July 1313.[16]

Maltravers Family Matters, 1313–1314

There were two marriages in the Maltravers family in 1313. John V's daughter Matilda married John Lenham the younger. It was the custom for the bride's father to give her a dowry in the form of land or money, but that is not recorded in this case. It was also the custom for the bridegroom's father to endow the couple with land, and so John Lenham senior gave his son some lands in Farndon and in Bokland, both in Berkshire, which were to be inherited by the children of John Lenham the younger and Matilda.[17]

In the same year John V saw his son John (John Maltravers VI) married to Milicent (also called Ela) de Berkeley, a daughter of Maurice de Berkeley. This was a prestigious marriage for the Maltravers family; perhaps the contacts established at the Feast of the Swans in 1306 and on campaign in Scotland had inclined Maurice de Berkeley to favour the alliance. On the other hand, from the de Berkeley point of view, the Maltraverses were of a somewhat lower social status, and Maurice de Berkeley was not particularly generous in Milicent's dowry of only 500 marks. Oddly, the Close Rolls in October 1313 show that the 500 marks that Maurice de Berkeley owed to John Maltravers V (senior) is immediately cancelled out by 500 marks owed by 'John Maltravers the younger [VI]' to Maurice de Berkeley. It is hard to understand what is going on here.[18]

More conventional is the gift on 28 April 1314 to John Maltravers the younger and Milicent his wife, by William Maltravers, a clerk, no doubt acting for John Maltravers senior, of the manor of Loders Bingham, Dorset, and some more land in Berkshire. The land is to be held by John Maltravers junior and Milicent in their lifetimes and then by the heirs of John.[19] John Maltravers VI and Milicent had one son, another John Maltravers (VII), whose exact date of birth is unknown.

A royal charter permitted a market to be held at the Maltravers manor of Rathkeale: '1 May 1314. Grant to John Maltravers and his heirs of a weekly market on Tuesday at their manor of Rathkeale, County Limerick, and of a yearly fair there on the vigil, the feast and the morrow of Holy Trinity [the Sunday after Pentecost / Whit Sunday].'[20]

The Battle of Bannockburn, 1314

In the summer of 1314, the king at last turned his attention to Scotland. Since the beginning of his reign, he had only led one expedition north, in 1310–11. Robert Bruce had been attacking English-held castles one by one, and destroying their fortifications to prevent reoccupation, until only three remained in 1314: Stirling, Bothwell and Dunbar. Edward II assembled a huge force of over 20,000 men, not only from England but also from Wales, Ireland and even from Gascony. John Maltravers VI certainly fought at Bannockburn, as did his uncle Robert Maltravers; both are listed in the retinue of Maurice de Berkeley.[21]

In April, when about to set out for Scotland, the king appointed conservators of the peace in various counties, including, for Dorset, Robert Fitzpayn the elder and John Maltravers V. By June, reports were reaching the king, who was then on his way north, that great outrages were being committed, including unlawful assemblies by day and night, assaults, murders, and unauthorised hunting of deer in the parks of the king and his subjects. New instructions were sent to the conservators of the peace, in strong terms, that transgressors were to be pursued and taken into custody to await justice. Robert Fitzpayn the elder and John Maltravers V were reappointed for Dorset. It might be supposed that John Maltravers V did not join the royal army, because of his local duties, but the conservators of the peace for Gloucestershire included Thomas de Berkeley the elder in April and Maurice de Berkeley in June, both of whom certainly took part in the campaign.[22]

In Scotland, the two armies clashed near Stirling. The Battle of Bannockburn on 23–24 June 1314 was a celebrated victory for the Scots against a larger English army. In preparation for the battle, during the night of 23 June, the English crossed the Bannock Burn and positioned themselves in a narrow V-shaped piece of land bounded by the Bannock Burn and the Pelstream Burn; their idea was to avoid any obstacles placed on the main road and to advance towards Stirling Castle in the morning. At daybreak on 24 June, they found that the Scottish army had also moved in the night and were now arrayed against them, at the mouth of the V. The English knights on their heavy warhorses charged forwards, but they were met with stout resistance from the formations of Scottish pikemen. The battle became a mêlée in which men and horses were killed in hand-to-hand combat; because of the restrictions of the site, any outflanking manoeuvres were impossible. The English archers were too far behind to make an impact, and the thousands of foot soldiers were unable to reach the centre of the action. When all was lost, Edward II was led away to Dunbar on the east coast, where he took ship to safety. Seeing the royal banner depart utterly demoralised the English army and the defeat became a rout.

Humphrey de Bohun (earl of Hereford and the hereditary constable of the army), together with a group of lords, knights, men-at-arms and foot soldiers, fled the scene in the other direction, making for the western route to Carlisle. At Bothwell, south of Glasgow and twenty miles from Bannockburn, they paused, and their leaders were admitted to Bothwell Castle, which was in English hands. The constable of the castle, Sir Walter Fitzgilbert, then defected to Bruce, and the refugees from the battle, including Hereford, found themselves prisoners.

Maurice de Berkeley also fled, with a large force of Welsh foot soldiers, but many of the Welsh were either captured or killed before they could leave Scotland,[23] and Maurice de Berkeley was himself captured and imprisoned. It is not clear if he was held at Bothwell or elsewhere. Probably in this group of fugitives, and certainly imprisoned somewhere, were Maurice's father Lord Thomas de Berkeley; John Maltravers VI, 'the son'; and the latter's relation, John Giffard, grandson of Elias Giffard and Alice Maltravers.[24] An alternative version of the flight of the Welsh is that they were with Aymer de Valence, earl of Pembroke, who evaded capture.[25]

The local Scots plundered the English baggage train and captured for ransom as many of the nobles as they could, and while the Scots were thus occupied many soldiers managed to escape to England. The earl of Hereford was later released in exchange for several Scots held in England, and the others were ransomed. John Maltravers VI must have paid a ransom, but there is no record of the amount paid.

A particular humiliation for the English was the loss of the king's privy seal. It was found on the battlefield, and Bruce chivalrously returned it to Edward II in the care of a released captive, Ralph de Monthermer. The keeper of the privy seal, Roger de Northburgh, was also captured and released,[26] and Edward II was forced to use Queen Isabella's seal until his own was restored to him.

The shock of the defeat was keenly felt in England. The author of *Vita Edwardi Secundi* lamented: 'Oh! day of vengeance and misfortune, day of ruin and dishonour, evil and accursed day... So many fine noblemen [and] strong young men, so many noble horses, so much military equipment, costly garments and gold plate — all lost in one harsh day, one fleeting hour.'[27]

Berwick, 1315–1316

After the Battle of Bannockburn, Robert Bruce's status as king of Scotland was unquestioned within his realm, but the English were no more ready than before to concede the fact; perhaps even less so in view of their humiliating defeat. And so the war continued, with attacks by the Scots in northern

England. There was a raid in the Tyne Valley in December 1314, and Carlisle was besieged in July 1315. To add to the misery, 1315 and 1316 were years of heavy and incessant rainfall. Over all of Europe, crops could not ripen, cattle drowned in the waterlogged fields, and many people died of starvation. In the fourteenth century in general, the climate was significantly worse in comparison with the benign previous century, when agriculture had prospered and the population had increased.

Maurice de Berkeley was released from captivity, presumably having paid his ransom, and was appointed the warden of the town and castle of Berwick on 17 April 1315.[28] In his retinue were his second son, also called Maurice de Berkeley and born in 1298; John Maltravers, 'his knight' (probably John Maltravers VI); and Robert Maltravers. Thomas de Gurney, de Berkeley's yeoman, is probably the Thomas Gurney who, as we shall see, was notoriously associated with de Berkeley and Maltravers twelve years later. It was no easy task to defend the town and to ensure supplies: by October, de Berkeley was complaining to the king that the promised money and victuals had not arrived, and that if these did not come by All Saints' Day, the garrison would desert.[29] On 15 January 1316, the defenders fought off a surprise night attack by the Scots. In mid-February, things were so desperate that some of the garrison went on a foray, even though the warden told them not to go; they replied that it was better to die fighting than to starve. They seized some cattle and took many prisoners, but were intercepted on their way back by the Scots, losing twenty men-at-arms and sixty foot soldiers (who were killed or taken prisoner), most of their horses, and all the provisions they had gathered.[30]

By March, de Berkeley was so desperate that he wrote a letter of resignation to the king; the burghers were in debt, his men were dying of hunger, and only fifty of the 300 men-at-arms enrolled could be mustered, mounted and armed. He requested that another warden be appointed as his term ended at Easter and he was not prepared to remain any longer. Accordingly, a new warden was appointed in May 1316.[31]

De Berkeley was later paid £465 6s. 8d. for nineteen horses lost by himself and his retinue while he was warden. In each case, the horse was described and its loss attested by a member of his staff. The most expensive horse in the list was the black destrier (a heavy warhorse) with two white hind feet and a star, which was lost on 5 December 1315 and appraised for Sir John Maltravers (probably VI), his knight, at 66 marks (£44). Maurice de Berkeley's own horse, another black destrier with a star, was worth 60 marks (£40), and the values of the rest ranged down to £10. Five of the horses were lost on 16 January 1316, no doubt in repelling the night attack by the Scots. The payment to de Berkeley was authorised on 22 July 1316.[32]

Ireland and Scotland, 1315–1318

In May 1315, soon after Sir Maurice de Berkeley had taken up his post as warden of Berwick, the Scots opened a second front through the invasion of Ireland by Edward Bruce, brother of Robert. The aim was to make common cause with another Gaelic-speaking country in order to drive the English out of Ireland and to establish a base for an attack on England from the west. Edward Bruce was crowned king of Ireland, but – in spite of fine words about the friendly relationship, and ties of language and customs between the Irish and the Scots – the campaign soon became the usual trail of killing, looting and destruction.

The English government, still reeling from the defeat at Bannockburn, was slow to counter the threats by the Scots in Ireland and the north of England. In February 1316, while Maurice de Berkeley and his hard-pressed garrison were suffering in Berwick, parliament met at Lincoln and made plans to assemble an army at Newcastle upon Tyne in July. Shortly before the agreed date, the muster was postponed, and on 30 June fresh orders summoned John Maltravers (probably V) and others to attend a muster on 15 August.[33] In August the muster was postponed again and a general order of 30 August 1316 summoned all men holding land valued at £50 or more to muster under the king at Newcastle upon Tyne on the Octaves of St Michael, 6 October.[34] Those summoned included John Maltravers (probably V), who was ordered to come with horse and arms to Newcastle upon Tyne on 6 October for the Scottish war.[35] In the end, the whole intended campaign in the north of England was cancelled. This must have caused enormous confusion, as well as a lot of wasted journeys riding or marching northwards and back again.

John Maltravers V had no intention of going to Scotland, and decided instead to see for himself what was happening at Rathkeale. In June 1316, 'John Maltravers [V], going to Ireland' appointed attorneys to look after his interests in England for two years, and in July he was given protection (against legal action in his absence), which was also for two years.[36]

In November 1316, Roger Mortimer, who was enjoying the favour of King Edward II at that time, was appointed as the king's lieutenant in Ireland and charged with raising an army to expel Edward Bruce. On 4 January 1317, all lords with lands in Ireland were required to defend them against the king's enemies, either by going there themselves or by sending men for the purpose.[37] On the same date, certain individuals, including a 'John Maltravers', – not specified as 'the elder' or 'the younger' – were ordered to be at Haverford on 2 February, prepared either to join Mortimer's expedition in person or else to provide a sufficient force for the defence of the country. It is likely that John Maltravers the elder, (V), who was probably already in Ireland and was the landowner, was the intended recipient of the summons.[38]

While preparations for Mortimer's expedition were being made, Robert Bruce sailed to Ireland to aid his brother, landing in January 1317. The Bruces rode across the country, killing inhabitants and burning property as they went. By April, they had reached Castleconnell, near Limerick and only twenty-five miles from Rathkeale. After some delay, Mortimer's forces arrived in Ireland on 7 April 1317. When the news reached Edward and Robert Bruce, they realised their position was hopeless: added to the understandable hostility of the local inhabitants, who signally failed to join their cause, and the difficulty of sourcing supplies in famine conditions, was the knowledge that they were being pursued by an English army. They sped away towards Ulster, and Robert Bruce returned to Scotland in May 1317.

John Maltravers the elder (V) was still in Ireland on the king's service at the end of 1317, and, on 10 December, his protection was renewed until Easter 1318.[39] Roger Mortimer continued as royal lieutenant in Ireland until April 1318, when he was recalled to England. Edward Bruce was finally defeated and killed at the Battle of Faughart on 14 October 1318.

Land Transactions and Property Disputes, 1318–1320

In September 1317, John Maltravers VI purchased the manor of Philipston, Dorset, from Walter and Margery de Thornhill. For this, John VI gave the Thornhills 100 marks.[40] He was also involved in an attack on the earl of Pembroke's manor of Painswick, Gloucestershire, on 31 July 1318, in which the earl's property was damaged and 200 deer were killed. The other perpetrators were Thomas de Berkeley junior, his brother Maurice de Berkeley junior, and fifty-four associates, including Thomas Gurney. The affair was the result of a property dispute between the Berkeleys and Pembroke, the exact cause of which is not clear. At all events, John Maltravers VI was led into an act of violence in support of his wife's family and against the earl of Pembroke, who was a loyal supporter of the king. To make matters worse, the offenders then kidnapped the royal coroners who were appointed to inquire into the affair. The issue was not resolved until March 1320, when compensation was paid to the earl, and the offenders, including John Maltravers VI, were pardoned.[41]

The king was still well-disposed towards John Maltravers the elder (V), and, on 28 September 1318, granted to him and his heirs free warren in all their demesne lands in Witchampton, Woolcombe, Philipston, Loders and Chilfrome (all in Dorset); Yeovil (Somerset); Great Somerford, Coate, Hill Deverill, Sherrington and Sopworth (all in Wiltshire); Woodchester (Gloucestershire); and Childrey (Oxfordshire, formerly in Berkshire). Lytchett Matravers (Dorset) was not included, as it already had the charter of free warren granted by Edward I in 1306.[42]

Despite his lawless behaviour at Painswick, John Maltravers VI, now aged about twenty-eight, was a person of standing in Dorset, and he attended the parliament at York on 20 October 1318 as one of the two knights of the shire representing his county. In December, he was paid his expenses for attendance, and for the journey to and from York, at the rate of 5 shillings a day.[43]

The Scots captured Berwick-upon-Tweed in April 1318, and a campaign was mounted in 1319 to recover it. John Maltravers, probably the elder (V), received two summonses – the first on 20 March to be at Newcastle upon Tyne on 3 June, and the second on 22 May to be at Newcastle on 24 June, as the start date had been changed. Typically, the operation was shambolic and ill-prepared. The siege of Berwick took place in September 1319, but it had to be broken off when a Scottish force invaded Yorkshire. In December, a two-year truce with the Scots was agreed, bringing a temporary peace.[44]

In 1320, Edward Maltravers I, another son of John Maltravers V, indulged in a spot of park breaking, which seems to have been the usual method of pursuing a quarrel. On 3 February, a commission of oyer and terminer was set up to enquire into a complaint by Roger Damory, who was a friend of the king at this time, that Edward Maltravers I and others had broken his park at Tarrant Gunville.[45]

Maurice de Berkeley was appointed seneschal of Gascony on 28 February 1320, shortly before the pardon for the Painswick affair. Although it sounds like a prestigious appointment, the king may have intended to get Maurice and the other troublemakers out of the way for a while. Accompanying Maurice de Berkeley to Gascony were his two sons (Thomas and Maurice junior), and also John Maltravers VI with five others. De Berkeley was ordered to depart on his mission without delay, and therefore had to borrow 100 marks from Italian bankers for travelling expenses, a sum that was repaid to the bankers by the king. In fact, de Berkeley's tenure as seneschal only lasted six months, with his successor being appointed on 22 July 1320.[46]

In November 1320, John Maltravers VI gained the tenancy of land in Up Wimborne, Dorset, comprising a messuage, mill, land and rent to be paid to him of 18s. 4d. John VI and his heirs were to hold the tenancy in perpetuity, rendering to the chief lords of that fee the appropriate services.[47]

The Despenser Wars, 1321–1322

In 1321, there was trouble in the lands of the Marcher lords, the border land of England and Wales. After the young and childless earl of Gloucester had been killed at the Battle of Bannockburn, his lands were divided among his three sisters – Eleanor, Margaret and Elizabeth – who were married to the king's new favourites – Hugh Despenser the younger, Hugh Audley and Roger Damory, respectively. Hugh Despenser, Eleanor's husband, was a grasping man who was not content with the substantial lands that were his wife's inheritance, and he set about increasing his domains by any means. This aroused the ire of other Marcher lords: the earl of Hereford, Roger Mortimer, Maurice de Berkeley, John Maltravers VI, John Giffard, and even Hugh Audley and Roger Damory. They assembled what amounted to an army and rampaged over the Despenser lands, attacking farms and castles (including Newport and Cardiff), and destroying Despenser property. In all, their forces comprised 800 men-at-arms, 500 'hobelers' (light horsemen) and 10,000 foot soldiers. They stole thousands of farm animals — sheep, cattle, pigs and goats — as well as armour, kitchen vessels, locks, bars, windows and lead, and small but valuable items, including chessboards, and ivory and ebony chessmen.[48]

The king eventually conceded that the Despensers must be banished. Hugh Despenser the elder went to Bordeaux, and his son became a pirate, and in August–September 1321 the Marcher lords were all pardoned for anything done against the Despensers. Among those pardoned were John Maltravers VI,

Edward Maltravers I (John's brother) and Maurice de Berkeley, who was now Lord Berkeley following the death of his father, Thomas, on 23 July 1321.[49] The Maltraverses and Lord Berkeley were back in favour only for a few months, however.

Roger Mortimer of Wigmore and the earl of Hereford formed an alliance with the earl of Lancaster, and made further demands on the king. The king was determined to reassert his authority, and in December 1321 recalled the Despensers from exile and summoned a royal army to muster at Cirencester. The earls of Arundel, Surrey and Pembroke supported the king. Oliver Ingham and Robert Lewer were appointed to arrest and imprison some of the rebels, including Roger Damory, Hugh Audley, John Giffard and John Maltravers VI, and also to seize all their lands and goods, and place them in the king's hands.[50]

The Marchers retreated westwards, pursued by the royal army. In early January 1322, the two sides confronted each other across the River Severn at Bridgnorth, Shropshire. The earl of Hereford and Roger Mortimer set fire to the town and killed some of the king's servants. Later they attacked the castles of Elmley and Hanley. At the same time, further writs were sent out to arrest John (VI) and Edward (I) Maltravers, among others, and to seize their lands, goods and chattels.[51]

The king increased the pressure on 15 January 1322 by ordering the sheriff of Shropshire to call on all men in the county between the ages of sixteen and sixty to be equipped and arrayed to proceed against those who had committed the outrages at Bridgnorth: 'Furthermore, the Sheriff is commanded to raise the hue and cry against the earl of Hereford and his associates… and if the offenders are apprehended, they are to be committed to prison until the King shall otherwise direct.' The same order went out to all the other sheriffs throughout England.[52]

The rebels' success was short-lived. The earl of Lancaster did not come to help them as he had promised. Roger Mortimer and his uncle, realising that their situation was hopeless, surrendered to the king on 22 January on the understanding that they would be pardoned. Instead, they were imprisoned in the Tower of London, and all the castles, manors and other property of Roger Mortimer were forfeited to the king. Lord Berkeley also surrendered and was imprisoned in Wallingford Castle. Most of the other Marcher lords decided to fight on, and when the earl of Hereford went north to join the earl of Lancaster, John Maltravers VI went with him.

On 23 February, John Maltravers VI and the others were still on the move. By a writ issued at Wootton-under-Edge, the sheriff of Northampton, who had disregarded the king's previous orders and permitted the 'contrariants' to pass through his bailiwick in great numbers, was told to pursue and arrest them, and to report back to the king. The sheriff was warned that the king had appointed spies to make sure the sheriff carried out his orders, otherwise he would be punished with the same pain as the contrariants. John Maltravers VI was named among the rebels. Similar orders were sent to twelve other counties in the Midlands and the North.[53]

Although she was the wife of a rebel, on 9 March 1322, Milicent (the wife of John Maltravers VI) was awarded 100 shillings annually for her maintenance, to be paid out of the issues of John's lands in Gloucestershire, which were in the king's hands 'for certain reasons'.[54]

The Battle of Boroughbridge, 1322

The Battle of Boroughbridge, in Yorkshire on 16 March 1322, was the last stand of the rebels against the king, and it was a decisive royal victory. The earl of Hereford was killed, and the earl of Lancaster was captured and executed shortly afterwards. The usual punishment for treason was hanging, drawing and quartering, but Lancaster was beheaded in the presence of the king, so that he died in the same manner as Piers Gaveston. The king got his revenge at last. The king exacted severe punishment: twenty-seven other northern and Marcher lords, including John Giffard, were executed. Many contrariants were imprisoned, although some were released on payment of a fine; these included Thomas Gurney who had to pay £100. Roger Mortimer and his uncle, still imprisoned in the Tower of London, were sentenced to death, but the sentence was commuted to life imprisonment. The Despensers returned to power.[55]

Although John Maltravers VI took part in the rebellion, firm evidence that he was at the final battle of 16 March is lacking. He is listed on the so-called 'Boroughbridge Roll of Arms', with his arms of 'sable, frettée or, and a label of three pendants argent', but the roll cannot have been intended to record the participants in that battle, as many of the men named were in prison at the time or already dead. It may have been compiled a few years earlier for a different purpose.[56]

John VI was certainly neither killed nor captured. With the talent for disappearing, which often served him well, he had escaped and could not be found. Some say he fled 'beyond the sea' with five other 'rebels': John Botetourt, John de Kingston, Nicholas Percy, John de Twyford and William Trussell.[57] The authorities thought that he and some of the others were still at large in the west of England in the summer of 1322. On 2 August, the sheriff of Somerset and Dorset was ordered to pursue, arrest and imprison William Trussell, John Maltravers VI, John de Kingston, Matthew de Cliveden and Nicholas de Percy, who were wandering about in his bailiwick 'committing intolerable damage in contempt of the king and in breach of his peace'. Similar orders were sent to the sheriff of Warwick and Leicester, and to the sheriff of Wiltshire.[58] The whereabouts of John Maltravers VI at this time is a mystery. He may have been in Somerset in 1325, as in July that year a John Maltravers, specifically identified as 'John the younger', with some accomplices, broke into the king's manor at Kingsbury, and stole horses, oxen, cows and crops.[59]

John Maltravers V took no part in the rebellion of 1321–1322, and the officials were careful to distinguish between the forfeited lands of John VI and the retained lands of John V. For example, Woodchester, Gloucestershire – a manor of the elder John Maltravers, which had been seized by the king in the mistaken impression it was a possession of John Maltravers VI – was returned to John Maltravers V in July 1322.[60]

The Battle of Old Byland, 1322

Encouraged by his success at the Battle of Boroughbridge, the king decided to launch a campaign against the Scots. John Maltravers V was summoned to perform military service in person and was required to present himself at Newcastle upon Tyne on 24 July 1322,[61] but the campaign was a failure. Edward II's army invaded Scotland in August, but Robert Bruce, instead of giving battle, withdrew northwards, destroying food supplies as he went. Defeated by sickness and starvation, the English returned south of the border. Bruce pursued them, and they hastily retreated to Yorkshire, leaving Queen Isabella stranded at Tynemouth Priory, from where she managed to escape by boat. Bruce caught up with Edward II's depleted army near Old Byland, Yorkshire, and defeated them in a surprise attack. Fortunately for King Edward personally, he was staying nearby and avoided capture, but otherwise the campaign had been a disaster. Edward II was forced to admit that it was impossible to win victory in Scotland and concluded a thirteen-year truce with Robert the Bruce in May 1323.

This was, however, by no means the end of Edward II's troubles, and in some ways it was just the beginning. On 1 August 1323, Roger Mortimer escaped from the Tower of London in a daring and well-planned operation, and fled to France. There he met up with the other fugitives, possibly including John Maltravers VI.

The Threat from Gascony, 1322–1324

It was not long before the king had to confront a new threat. Aquitaine had been under the English Crown since the reign of Henry II (1154–1189), whose wife was the heiress Eleanor of Aquitaine. Parts of the territory had been lost to France piecemeal until by the fourteenth century all that remained was the area around Bordeaux known as Gascony. The English kings, who were still described as dukes of Aquitaine, held Gascony as vassals of the kings of France, and therefore had to perform an act of homage whenever there was a new French king. This happened several times in the reign of Edward II, as first the father and then the three brothers of his wife Isabella inherited the French throne in turn. In 1322, Isabella's youngest brother became King Charles IV of France, who proposed in 1323 that Edward II should come to do homage in the following year.

Before that could happen, however, a crisis arose in the form of an attempt by the French government to establish a bastide, or fortified town, at the village of Saint-Sardos in Gascony. A sergeant arrived in the village to claim it for France and erected a stake on which the arms of the king of France were displayed. Local nobles objected, hanged the sergeant at his own stake and burned the village. King Charles IV declared Gascony confiscate and sent in troops, who besieged the town of La Réole. The English did not have a large army in Gascony, as the duchy had been peaceful for many years, and so were only able to hold out for a few weeks before surrendering. This brief War of Saint-Sardos came to an end with a truce agreed in 1324, through which the Agenais – an area in the east of Gascony – became part of France.

Edward II was mistrustful of Queen Isabella and her French connections. In September 1324, all her land and property were confiscated, and in October her allowance for living expenses was drastically cut.⁶² It is somewhat surprising, therefore, that Edward II should have entrusted her with a diplomatic mission to France in March 1325, where she was to discuss with her brother Charles IV the question of the homage for Gascony and a final peace settlement.

At the same time, Edward II decided to send reinforcements to the duchy. John Maltravers V was among those summoned to be at Portsmouth on 24 March to join John de Warenne, earl of Surrey, who was about to sail for Gascony with a great force of men-at-arms and foot soldiers.⁶³ Even before the fleet set sail, there was mutiny among the foot soldiers. Roger Maltravers I, the brother of John Maltravers V, appears on a list of over 100 men of Gloucestershire who had been selected as foot soldiers but who refused to go. On 2 April, the sheriff of that county was ordered to arrest and imprison the reluctant soldiers, or face (unspecified) consequences.⁶⁴ On 28 April, the sheriff was notified of a further contingent of 100 men of Gloucestershire and the Forest of Dean, who had been taken to Portsmouth and been paid their wages, but who had returned home without the king's licence. They, too, were ordered to be arrested and imprisoned.⁶⁵ The fleet finally sailed on 22 May. De Warenne's tour of duty was supposed to last six months, but it was extended by the king in October, rather apologetically, with warm words about the earl's exemplary service.⁶⁶ De Warenne returned to England in 1326.

In September 1325, Edward II appointed his son, Prince Edward, to be duke of Aquitaine, and sent him to join Isabella in Paris. Prince Edward then performed the homage for Gascony on behalf of his father. In a shocking development, Isabella refused to return to England, and Roger Mortimer openly joined her court. Prince Edward and the king's half-brother – Edmund, earl of Kent – also refused to return to England and remained in France with Isabella.

By 1326, John Maltravers VI had joined her entourage. When exactly he did this is debatable; as we have seen, he was being sought in England in August 1322 and he was accused of lawless behaviour in Somerset in July 1325. However, he did join Isabella's court at some point, since 'John Maltravers the younger' was given lands in 1327 for 'service to Queen Isabella abroad and at home'.⁶⁷

The king was enraged by his wife's actions, but there was little he could do, apart from making preparations against a possible invasion. Castles were put in a state of readiness, and sheriffs were ordered to raise a force to defend the country, but many people hated the Despenser regime and were loath to help the king.

John Maltravers V, 1324–1325

John Maltravers V remained in England and, unlike his absent son, was still loyal to the king at first. On 9 May 1324, he was summoned by the sheriff of Gloucester to attend the Great Council to be held at Westminster on the 30 May.[68] By the next year, however, John V's support had waned: there is evidence that John Maltravers V did not join de Warenne's expedition to which he had been summoned, as we hear of him again as being in England in the autumn. In September, he caused a disturbance at the annual fair at Woodbury Hill near Bere Regis, Dorset, when he and a band of men assaulted the organisers and prevented the dues of the fair from being collected. As the victims included Richard and John Turberville, it is probable that the enmity between the Maltraverses and the Turbervilles, dating back over 100 years, had something to do with it. A commission of oyer and terminer was set up the following month to investigate the disturbance.[69]

John Maltravers V's first wife, Eleanor de Gorges, died in about 1325, and he then married Joan de Percy, the widow of the rebel Nicholas de Percy who had fought against the king at Boroughbridge, fled with John Maltravers VI after the battle and died in 1324. Joan was a Dorset heiress in her own right, born Joan de Foliot, and had inherited Melbury Osmond from her father Sir Walter Foliot. From her mother, Ada Sampford, she had inherited Melbury Sampford.[70]

The elder John Maltravers (V) played little part in national affairs thereafter, and, with his new wife, soon had a second family of three daughters. His son, John VI, however, was to become deeply involved in the turbulent politics of the following decade.

4

BARON JOHN MALTRAVERS
THE DEATH OF A KING?
1326–1330

Invasion and Abdication

Across the Channel, Queen Isabella and Roger Mortimer were preparing to invade England. They were greatly helped by William, count of Hainault, who – in return for the betrothal of his daughter Philippa to Prince Edward – provided troops, and also ships to convey them across the sea. They set sail in September and landed in Suffolk on 24 September 1326. Their numbers, initially small, grew quickly, whereas the king's frantic orders to officials all over southern England to send thousands of men-at-arms to him were not obeyed.[1]

Before long, King Edward II was fleeing westwards, with the invaders in pursuit, hoping in vain that the Welsh would come to his aid. At Bristol in October, the elder Hugh Despenser was captured, tried and executed. Prince Edward was declared to be the guardian of the realm which the king had abandoned. Edmund, earl of Arundel, a long-term enemy of Roger Mortimer, was captured and beheaded with little ceremony in November. The king himself was captured near Llantrisant in November 1326, together with Hugh Despenser the younger, the latter being tried and executed. The king was taken as a captive to Kenilworth Castle. John Maltravers VI had almost certainly returned to England with Roger Mortimer to take part in these events.

After this swift settling of old scores, the question of what to do with the king was considered more carefully. Some doubted that it was possible to depose an anointed king, and there was no precedent for such an action. A parliament was convened for January 1327. A John Maltravers (presumably John Maltravers VI) was in London at the time, although he had not been summoned either as a baron or as a knight of the shire for Dorset. He is listed among the 'barons' who took an oath of loyalty to Queen Isabella and her son Prince Edward on 13 January. A large number of men took this oath, including four earls and twenty-four barons, among the latter being Roger Mortimer and this John Maltravers.[2]

The king refused to attend the parliament. After several days of debate, it was decided that he was incompetent to govern and should be deposed. A delegation was sent to Kenilworth, where Edward II, deeply distressed at the people's rejection of him, abdicated the throne in favour of his son. Thus Edward III, at fourteen years of age, became king on 25 January 1327 and was crowned on 1 February 1327. A council was appointed to advise the young king, consisting of four prelates, four earls and six barons, but in effect the country was ruled by Queen Isabella and Roger Mortimer. The ex-king remained imprisoned in Kenilworth Castle.

Lands

John Maltravers VI was soon rewarded for his loyalty to the new regime. On 17 February 1327, the sheriffs of Oxfordshire, Berkshire, Somerset, Dorset and Wiltshire were ordered to restore his lands and manors to him.[3]

In March, he was granted for life, 'for service to Queen Isabella and the king [Edward III] abroad and at home', some lands that had been held by Hugh Despenser the elder: Winterborne Houghton in Dorset [4] and Sutton Mandeville in Wiltshire.[5] It is significant that Maltravers VI's service to Isabella 'abroad' is mentioned, showing that he was one of the rebels who joined her court in France. In April, also 'for service to Queen Isabella', he was granted for life the manor of Overstone, Northamptonshire,[6] which had been forfeited by Donald, earl of Mar. The rights to the advowsons and knights' fees for Winterborne Houghton and Overstone, for life, were confirmed in a grant in January 1329.[7]

In June 1327, John Maltravers (whether V or VI is not specified) – having acquired half of the manor of Stapleford, Wiltshire, from John Sturmy – was pardoned for entering the manor without licence and was permitted to retain possession.[8]

In September 1327, John Maltravers VI had occasion to complain of the theft of thirty-two oxen, eight cows and 300 sheep worth £100 from his manors of Loders and Philipston, Dorset, and a commission of oyer and terminer was appointed.⁹

In October 1327, Robert Fitzpayn and Ela, his wife – having entered into an arrangement by which they, or the survivor of them, would hold the manor and advowson of Marshwood, Dorset, in fee tail – granted the remainder (the ownership after their deaths) to John Maltravers the younger.¹⁰

First Rescue Attempt and Transfer to Berkeley Castle

In March 1327, there was a plot to free ex-king Edward II from Kenilworth Castle. The plotters may have been the Dunheved brothers: Thomas, who was a Dominican friar, and Stephen, a layman. The plot was discovered, and Roger Mortimer decided that Kenilworth Castle was not a secure enough prison. Possibly he did not trust its lord, Henry of Lancaster, who had succeeded his brother Thomas as earl of Lancaster.

Mortimer decided that the captive could be guarded more securely in the castle of his friend and ally Lord Berkeley. Here, too, there was a new generation in charge. Maurice de Berkeley had died a prisoner in Wallingford Castle in 1326, and his son, Thomas, was the new Lord Berkeley. Thomas, Lord Berkeley, was the husband of Mortimer's daughter Margaret and was also the brother-in-law of John Maltravers VI. Thomas de Berkeley and John Maltravers VI were given joint responsibility for guarding 'Lord Edward'.

Lord Berkeley and John Maltravers left Kenilworth Castle with Edward II on April 3, accompanied by Thomas Gurney and William Bishop. Gurney had been associated with the Berkeleys previously,¹¹ and William Bishop had served under Mortimer as a soldier in 1321.¹² The journey to Berkeley Castle, about 68 miles, took about three days, which was a normal duration for such a journey at that time. They made an overnight stop along the way at Llanthony Secunda Priory, Gloucester, a daughter house of Llanthony Priory, Wales. The Berkeley accounts show that provisions were sent to the castle for Edward II and his attendants, from his arrival on 5 April until 21 September.¹³

The chronicler Adam Murimuth says that to forestall attempts to free him from Berkeley Castle, the captive was taken by night to Corfe and other places, and then led back to Berkeley Castle, so that his whereabouts would be unknown.[14]

Another chronicler, Geoffrey le Baker, gives a different account of the transfer. From Kenilworth Castle, Edward II was taken to Corfe Castle and thence to Bristol Castle, where he stayed for some time, suffering ill-treatment, including being deprived of sleep, warm clothing and nourishing food. As the townspeople were becoming aware of the identity of the prisoner and were making plans to free him, he was taken to Berkeley Castle. Along the way, the guards subjected him to various forms of humiliation. They jeered at him, and Gurney made him a crown of hay. They forced him to shave off his beard with the aid of cold ditch water, to which Edward II added the warm water of his copious tears.[15]

Whether or not that is true, once installed in Berkeley Castle, his treatment may have improved a little. John Maltravers VI and Thomas de Berkeley were allowed the generous sum of £5 a day for his expenses. The first payment was authorised on 24 April and was backdated to April 4. The payments continued to the end of Edward II's life. Even if some of it went into their own pockets, there must have been enough left for food and other items for the prisoner. Records at Berkeley Castle show the purchase of capons, beef, cheese, eggs and wine for Edward and his attendants. Queen Isabella sent him gifts of fine clothes, linen and edible delicacies. Baker and Murimuth say that Edward II was treated humanely by Lord Berkeley, but Murimuth says that Maltravers treated him 'otherwise'. Murimuth also says that Berkeley and Maltravers took it in turns to guard their prisoner, a month at a time each.[16]

The Weardale Campaign

Meanwhile, Robert Bruce, who had held off from military action during the invasion by Mortimer and Isabella, was still seeking recognition as the king of an independent realm. Mortimer was willing to agree to this, but the earl of Lancaster and other northern lords were firmly against it. It was reported in March that the Scots were building up their forces, and so, in April 1327, the English government ordered a general muster. On April 5, John Maltravers V was summoned to be at Newcastle upon Tyne with horse and arms, to perform his service in the king's army, which was then on its way to Scotland. According to Hutchins, John Maltravers VI received exactly the same summons on the same day, although it was only two days after he had been appointed keeper of the dethroned king.[17] A John Maltravers was involved in the military preparations, for at the end of April 1327 Thomas de Berkeley, his brother (called, inevitably, Maurice) and John Maltravers (probably VI) were sent to Bristol Castle to collect 'armour etc. to be used in the northern parts'.[18]

The campaign, known as the Weardale Campaign, was not a success. It kept the English army in the north of England from late May until early August 1327, but it had no chance to fight a pitched battle. At one point, when the two armies were facing each other, the English camped for the night, but the Scots crept up on them while they slept, cut the ropes of their tents and slaughtered many of them. A few days later the Scottish army decamped at night and went home, leaving 300 leather cauldrons full of meat to cook as an insulting parting gift. This was the young king Edward III's first experience of warfare, and he no doubt learned lessons for the future.

Second Rescue Attempt

In early July 1327, news came to York that there had been another conspiracy, led by the Dominican friar Thomas Dunheved and his brother Stephen, in which Berkeley Castle had been ransacked, and the ex-king had actually been freed and was at liberty. There was consternation and a flurry of activity. On July 3, Lord Berkeley was charged with unspecified 'special business of the king' and relieved of his military duties against the Scots.[19] On July 11, both he and John Maltravers were appointed commissioners of the peace for Somerset, Dorset, Wiltshire, Hampshire, Gloucestershire, Herefordshire, Oxfordshire and Berkshire, to enable them to track down the conspirators. Despite the security breach, it appears that Mortimer still trusted de Berkeley and Maltravers to put matters right, or perhaps he did not want to publicise the disaster more widely.[20] We assume that the ex-king was back in custody quite soon, since a letter dated July 27 from Thomas de Berkeley to the chancellor, John Hotham, names the people who abducted Edward II, but it does not mention the need to recapture him. This letter is the only explicit statement we have that Edward II had been 'seized from the custody' of Lord Berkeley.[21] On August 1, de Berkeley was given the task of arresting the Dunheved brothers and eighteen other named malefactors.[22]

Third Rescue Attempt

Yet another plot to free Edward II came to light in September 1327. William de Shalford, Roger Mortimer's lieutenant in North Wales, wrote a letter to Mortimer on 14 September alleging that one Rhys ap Gruffydd and certain great men of England were planning to free the ex-king, and warning that if they succeeded, Mortimer and his associates would die a terrible death. Mortimer, who was in Abergavenny at the time, received the letter and sent it to Berkeley Castle by the hand of William Ockley. Ockley was to deliver it to the guardians at Berkeley Castle and to ask them to remedy the situation quickly (in a manner unspecified) in order to avoid great peril. Whereupon Ockley carried out his mission as he understood it (surely Mortimer would have given more precise instructions orally?), and it is said that Ockley and those who were guarding the ex-king traitorously murdered him, spilling royal blood.

The letter does not survive, and its content and the response to it by Mortimer and Ockley are only known because of a court case in 1331, in which – on the petition of an individual – Shalford was accused of bringing about the death of Edward II indirectly by writing the letter. The story only names Mortimer and Ockley, not those at Berkeley Castle who allegedly carried out the foul deed.[23]

Death of Edward II: The Official Version

On 21 September 1327, Edward II died at Berkeley Castle of natural causes, or at least that was the official story at the time. In any case, something happened on that day as Edward II was never seen alive again, as far as was known. Thomas Gurney immediately set out for Lincoln, to give the king (Edward III) a letter from Lord Berkeley telling him of his father's sudden death, which was announced at the Lincoln parliament a few days later.

Back at Berkeley Castle, the body of the former king was embalmed by a local woman. The heart was removed and placed in a silver casket, so that it could be kept by Queen Isabella for eventual burial with her when the time came. According to Murimuth, many abbots, priors, knights and burgesses of Bristol and Gloucester were invited to see the body, and they viewed it *'superficialiter'* (superficially). Perhaps he means that it was covered in cerecloth as was the custom, thus preventing close inspection. He says that there was a rumour among the populace that Edward II had been murdered *'per cautelam'* (cunningly, or by a trick), on the orders of John Maltravers VI and Thomas Gurney. He does not mention the red-hot poker story, which appeared later.[24]

Thomas de Berkeley and John Maltravers continued to be paid their £5 a day for custody of Edward II up to 21 October, when his body was transferred into the keeping of the abbot of Gloucester. The funeral and burial in the abbey (now Gloucester Cathedral) took place on 20 December 1327, and it was a splendid occasion.[25]

The closed coffin lay on a magnificent hearse decorated with gilded images of lions, angels and the four evangelists. On top of the coffin was a wooden effigy of the late king, dressed in his coronation robes and wearing a gilt crown. Many people came to see this amazing sight. In later years, the grave became a place of pilgrimage, and a shrine-like tomb was erected. Royal patronage and gifts from pilgrims enabled the abbey to remodel the east end of the church in the perpendicular style.[26]

After the funeral, the woman who had carried out the embalming was taken to Worcester, where the court had gone to spend Christmas. This was by order of the young king, in order that Queen Isabella could meet her. We can only speculate about this incident, and we do not know if she had any extra information to impart about Edward II's death.[27] In fact, the whole story of these three months is a mixture of ostentatious pageantry and suspicious circumstances, to which we will return later. For a year or two, no one openly questioned the official story, and John Maltravers VI achieved an even greater position.

Peace Treaty with Scotland

Negotiations for a peace with Scotland were concluded by a treaty in May 1328, in which – to the disgust of the earl of Lancaster – the kingdom of Scotland was recognised as fully independent, and Robert Bruce and his heirs as the rightful rulers. The agreement was cemented in July by the marriage of Edward III's young sister Joan, aged 7, to David, the 5-year-old son of Robert Bruce, king of Scotland.

Relations between Roger Mortimer and the earl of Lancaster grew ever more hostile. Apart from the shameful peace with Scotland, the earl complained of the rapacity of Queen Isabella, and of the way the young king was under the control of Isabella and Mortimer, excluding the council of nobles that was set up at the start of his reign. According to one chronicle, he accused unnamed persons, acting on the authority of Isabella and Roger Mortimer, of having murdered Edward II.[28] If so, this was the first open accusation of Edward II's murder. No doubt Lancaster's temper was not improved on learning of Mortimer's impressive new title of 'earl of March', which was granted at the Salisbury parliament in October 1328.

Both sides were building up armies, and it looked as if there would be civil war again. On Mortimer's side was the ever-dependable John Maltravers VI. Exchequer rolls record, in October 1328, a payment of £135 'to John Maltravers for bringing a force of men-at-arms and infantry to the king at Salisbury, there to remain in his pay until the crisis ends'. The crisis ended in January 1329, when first the earls of Kent and Norfolk, and then the earl of Lancaster capitulated.[29]

In the aftermath of the rebellion, a commission of oyer and terminer was set up in February 1329 to try those Londoners who had been rebels. John Maltravers VI was a prominent member of the commission, along with Oliver Ingham, John de Grantham (the mayor of London) and others.[30]

John Maltravers VI served on other commissions of oyer and terminer at around this time, dealing with cases of assault and theft. A particularly prevalent crime that he investigated was breaking into the parks and chases (private forests) of nobles, hunting therein without licence, and carrying away deer and trees. Queen Isabella complained of this in her chases in Gloucestershire, Somerset, Surrey and Berkshire, and on the Isle of Wight, in 1329–30.[31]

He was custodian of the king's stannary (tin mines) in Devon from October 1328 to November 1329. As he paid rent of £114 6s 8d per year for the privilege, it must have yielded a useful income for him.[32]

Steward of the King's Household

John Maltravers VI was appointed steward of the royal household for a few weeks in 1328 (3 March to 12 April), ousting John de Ros, a Lancastrian supporter.[33] He was reappointed on 1 March 1329, this time holding office for well over a year until 29 July 1330. In his capacity as steward, he witnessed fifty-six charters between January and July 1330.[34]

The steward was responsible for the day-to-day running of the household. In normal times, the king might have had cordial, even friendly, relations with his steward, whom he saw almost daily. These were not normal times, and the teenage king had reason to be wary of Maltravers VI. As a close associate of Roger Mortimer, Maltravers would report back on any words or actions of the king. If Edward III had suspicions about his father's captivity and death, he would have been well advised to keep them to himself.

Isabella's three brothers became kings of France, in turn. In 1328, the last of them, Charles IV, died. The atmosphere in England was too unsettled for any claim to the French throne to be made at this time on behalf of Edward III as Isabella's son, and so Charles IV's cousin Philip de Valois became King Philip VI of France. The question of the homage for Gascony arose again, and Edward III went to France to perform the ceremony in Amiens Cathedral on 6 June 1329. John Maltravers VI was in the royal party in his official capacity, and witnessed the deed of homage as 'seneschal de roy d'Angletere'.[35]

Keeper of the Forest South of the Trent

As if John Maltravers VI did not have enough on his plate, on 5 April 1329, shortly before the trip to France, he was made keeper (or warden) of the forest south of the Trent, responsible for enforcing the law of the royal forest in the south of England.[36] The sheriffs, bailiffs and others were to be answerable to him and were to 'summon before him knights and others as often as he shall require'.[37] The previous keeper, William la Zouche de Mortimer, was ordered to deliver to Maltravers the rolls, memoranda and other things relating to the forest, and Maltravers was to bring his rolls to the Exchequer at the end of each year. John Maltravers held this office until December 1330.

In John Maltravers's half of the country, there were several individual forests, each with its own warden. Within the forests, various officials had responsibilities for the 'vert and venison', that is, the vegetation, including trees (a valuable source of timber), and the beasts of the forest, especially the deer. The regarders inspected the forest from time to time, and the agisters gave permission for pigs and cattle to be pastured in the forest when this would not disadvantage the deer. People might be given a licence known as an arrentation, which allowed them to enclose land in the forest, but only with a small ditch and a low hedge, so that the deer could still come and go.

Periodically, the keeper had held an eyre, or a meeting of the forest court. In theory, this took place every seven years, but sometimes decades passed without the court being convened. An eyre was a major undertaking for the justices appointed, usually four of them, including the keeper of the forest for the appropriate half of England. John Maltravers VI held three, or possibly four, eyres between October 1329 and February 1330:

† at Windsor, Berkshire, starting on 16 October 1329;[38]
† at Guildford, Surrey, due to start on 4 December 1329;[39]
† at Salisbury, Wiltshire, scheduled for 15 January 1330, but postponed to 26 February 1330;[40] and
† at Southampton, Hampshire, for the New Forest, starting on 9 July 1330.[41]

The procedure for setting up the Berkshire eyre is described in the Close Rolls for 25 August 1329:

> To the sheriff of Berks. Order to summon archbishops, bishops, abbots, priors, earls, barons, knights, and all free tenants of lands within the bounds of the forest, and four men and the reeve from each town within the forest, and the foresters of the towns... to be at New Windsor on Monday [16 October], before John Maltravers and three others, whom the king had appointed his justices to make eyre upon this occasion, and to cause all foresters and verderers... to come, with all their attachments of vert and of venison... and to cause the regarders in his bailiwick to come [with] all their regards sealed with their seals, and to cause all the king's agisters of his bailiwick to come with all their agistments.[42]

Prior to the eyre, the officials of the king's treasury were ordered to 'send transcripts of all the arrentations made in the times of Edward I and Edward II in the forest of Windsor to John Maltravers and his fellows, justices in eyre for pleas of that forest'. The administration of the forest had been lax for some time, and it was necessary to look into the records of the previous sixty years.[43] In preparation for the eyre, a perambulation of the forest was held so that local officials could report to John Maltravers as to the state of the forest. For Savernake, records have survived that give the names of the thirty-three officials who rode round the 'metes and bounds of the Forest'.[44]

One of the aims of the eyre was to establish the correct boundaries of the forest in accordance with the Charter of the Forest 1217. Land taken into the forest wrongly between the accession of Henry II (1154) and the death of King John (1216) should have been disafforested, so that people holding land in what had been the forest were not subject to the onerous forest laws. After more than a century the charter had still not been fully implemented. Although some tenants would have liked to see the charter enforced, there were others – such as the Sturmy family, the hereditary wardens of Savernake – who would lose both status and income.

Malefactors had to appear before the justices to have their cases determined. For instance, in May 1329, John Maltravers had been ordered to release on bail three men imprisoned at Windsor for 'trespass of venison in Windsor Forest'. Those who stood bail for the three undertook to produce them before the next eyre of the forest.[45] Presumably, they appeared at the eyre in October 1329. This would have been swift justice. Due to the infrequency of the eyres, it was common to find that most of the accused persons had died before the coming of the justices; for example, a man in the New Forest who shot a deer with a bow and arrow in 1289 had died before the eyre of 1330. There was a similar situation in Wiltshire, where 104 people due to appear in 1330 were 'essoined' (excused for absence) by death.[46]

As well as holding eyres, Maltravers had to see to the repair of forest boundaries. In April 1329, he was ordered to repair the enclosures of Clarendon Park, near Salisbury, 'as the king understands that the enclosures are broken down so that his deer can go out of the park'.[47] A year later (April 1330), the wood for renewing the paling at Clarendon Park had not been delivered, and the sheriff of Hampshire was told to send it without delay, with payment for carriage to be made by John Maltravers on behalf of the king.[48]

On 10 December 1329 came a general order to John de Sitelyng and John de Farlegh to survey the underwood in all the forests south of the Trent under the supervision of John Maltravers VI, keeper of the forest, or his deputy, to cut down and sell the underwood where appropriate, and to use the money for the repair of the king's parks within the forests. Dead wood from hedges was to be spread on cut areas to protect regrowth from 'the biting of animals'. This sounds like a massive task, and one wonders how much interest John personally took in it.[49]

Edward II: Did He Survive?

If Roger Mortimer and Queen Isabella thought they had got away with any deceit over the death and burial of Edward II, they were about to be disabused. Their plot began to unravel, not with an accusation of murder, but with the claim that Edward II was still alive. Edmund, earl of Kent, Edward II's half-brother, learned of the ex-king's survival. Kent claimed that a Dominican friar had come to him and said he had 'raised up the devil, which declared unto him for certain that Edward his brother, sometime king of England, was alive.' This may have been in 1328 or early 1329.[50]

Kent put in motion a plan to rescue his half-brother. In July 1329, he visited the pope in Avignon and told him what was going on. The pope promised moral and financial support, although he later denied having had any involvement. Kent made contact with two exiles in Paris, Henry de Beaumont and Thomas Roscelyn, and then returned home to gather supporters. A good number of clerical and lay magnates rallied to his cause.

William Melton – the archbishop of York – went so far as to write a letter, which has survived, to Simon Swanland – mayor of London and a draper by profession – saying he had knowledge that 'our liege lord Edward of Caernarfon is alive and in good health, and in a safe place by his own wish'. He asked Swanland to purchase some items for Edward, including clothing, boots, belts, bags, coverlets and hangings, and to advise on how to obtain a large sum of money for the said lord.[51] The letter is dated 14 January, but lacks a year, which is probably 1329 or 1330.

King Edward III was beginning to assert himself, and, in September 1329, he appointed several of his own men to positions close to him; for example, Robert Wodehouse became treasurer and Richard Bury became keeper of the privy seal. John Maltravers VI, however, although an associate of Mortimer, remained as steward. William Montagu went to see the pope on the king's behalf. Edward III was anxious to find a way of authenticating his letters to the pope, and it was arranged that if a letter was endorsed '*pater sancte*' (holy father), in Edward III's own handwriting, it could be taken as coming from the king himself and not from Isabella or Mortimer. An example of such a letter was found in the Vatican archives.

Corfe Castle comes into the story once more. The keeper from 16 December 1325 was John Pecche. On 24 September 1329, John Maltravers VI was appointed as his successor. Around the same time, on 26 August 1329, the sheriff of Somerset was ordered to spend up to £20 on repairing the houses, walls and other buildings of Corfe Castle, to the approval of John Maltravers, keeper of the castle.[52] Over the winter of 1329–30, John Maltravers VI held three positions simultaneously: steward of the royal household, keeper of the forest south of the Trent, and constable of Corfe Castle. In addition, he sat as a judge on a case before the King's Bench in November, where he is called 'John Maltravers, baron'.[53] In Roger Mortimer's small close circle, this was a man who could be called upon for any important mission, and apparently, keeper of Corfe came into that category.

John Maltravers VI was still riding high, and, in January 1330, received in his own name a summons to the parliament that was due to meet in March, thus becoming known as Lord Maltravers.[54] He had been described as a baron twice before, first when he took the oath of loyalty to Queen Isabella and Edward III in January 1327, and again when he sat as a judge of the King's Bench in November 1329. The summons to the parliament made it official.

Although pleased with his new status, John Maltravers may have worried that hidden matters were about to come to light, with unpredictable consequences. Indeed, this was the case, as the earl of Kent was getting closer to his objective of rescuing his brother. In about January 1330, Edmund, earl of Kent heard that Edward II, who was supposed to have died in 1327, was at Corfe Castle. Many people in the village were aware of lights at the castle and a great commotion, as if an important person were staying there. The earl of Kent sent a Dominican friar to check. In the hall, the friar saw a man who appeared to be Edward II, the father of the current king, sitting at a table having his supper. The friar was not allowed to approach him or speak to him.[55]

On hearing this, the earl of Kent hastened to Corfe Castle, but John Deveril – a member of the garrison – forbade him access, acting – so he said – on the king's orders. The earl then wrote a letter to Edward (II) of Caernarfon, telling him that he would soon be freed from prison 'so that you will be king again as you were before' (fatal words). John Deveril agreed to pass the letter to the prisoner, but instead gave it to Roger Mortimer.[56]

At the Winchester parliament in March, Roger Mortimer brought matters to a head by accusing the earl of Kent of treason, and produced the earl's own letter to Edward II in Corfe Castle as proof. A court was assembled, and after a brief trial the earl was condemned to death. He made a full confession, implicating many co-conspirators, and threw himself on the king's mercy, but to no avail. He was executed on 19 March 1330 to the shock of those present.

Whatever was going on, it is hard to believe that John Maltravers VI had nothing to do with it, as the castle in his keeping was central to the story. Either Mortimer and his assistants lured the earl of Kent into revealing his treasonable intentions, or else Edmund had discovered the truth, and Maltravers really was concealing the ex-king in Corfe Castle.

Just two days after the execution of the earl of Kent, John Maltravers VI and five others were given a commission 'to make inquisition in the county of Southampton [Hampshire] to discover the adherents of Edmund of Woodstock, late earl of Kent, who has been condemned to death by his peers in the present Parliament for high treason'.[57] In spite of the obvious risk in being involved, many people believed that Edward II lived on. Some of them were still at large in August, when John Maltravers (VI, 'the son') and two others were given a commission 'to discover the adherents in the county of Dorset of Edmund, late earl of Kent'.[58] To counter any possible rebellion, in July, Mortimer ordered knights and other men-at-arms to be arrayed under the supervision of Roger Mortimer himself in Gloucestershire, Herefordshire, Shropshire and Worcestershire; under Simon de Bereford in Nottinghamshire and Leicestershire; under John Maltravers VI in Wiltshire, Hampshire and Dorset; and under five others in various counties.[59] With the earl of Kent dead and Edward II supposedly dead, one wonders why the government was so fearful.

The earl of Kent's property was distributed. The bulk of it went to Geoffrey Mortimer, Roger's son, and the rest was divided between Mortimer's and Isabella's supporters: the earl of Surrey, Hugh de Turplington, Oliver Ingham, Simon de Bereford, Bartholomew Burghersh, Thomas de Berkeley and John Maltravers VI.

John Maltravers VI was steward of the king's household until 29 July 1330, and he was replaced by Hugh Turplington on 1 August.[60]

Second Marriage for John Maltravers VI

John Maltravers VI's first wife (Ela de Berkeley) died, and he somehow found time in 1329 or 1330 to woo and wed a rich widow, Agnes de Bereford. She was the daughter of Sir William de Bereford, Chief Justice of the Common Pleas (died 1326), and her previous husbands were Sir John de Argentein (died *c*. October 1318) and Sir John de Nerford (died 5 February 1329).[61] She had one son from her first marriage: John de Argentein, who was born in about April 1318. She was probably related to Sir Simon de Bereford, a close associate of Roger Mortimer, who was granted the income from the Argentein estates in January 1327, due to the heir being a minor.⁶² Historians have speculated that Agnes was Simon's sister, but there is no definite proof. She was a strong-minded woman and was to be a staunch support to John Maltravers in the troubles that would shortly befall him.

Lands: The Giffard Inheritance

When John Giffard was executed in 1322 for his part in the rebellion against Edward II, his lands were forfeited to the Crown. Under the Mortimer regime, his estates were to be restored to the Giffard family, and inquisitions post mortem were held in February and March 1327 to determine who should be the heir or heirs. John Giffard left no children, but had an extended family of half-sisters and cousins, and their descendants. There was also a John Kellaway who claimed to be the rightful heir by descent from John Giffard's grandfather's sister.

The jurors in Gloucestershire said that the chief Giffard manor of Brimpsfield, and other manors in the county, should belong to descendants of John Giffard's half-sisters – Katherine and Eleanor – and so the heirs were James Audley (grandson of Katherine), and John Lestrange (son of Eleanor).⁶³ The jurors in Wiltshire confessed themselves baffled and unable to say who was the 'next heir according to the law and custom of the realm'. The jurors in South Wales also returned 'heir not known'.⁶⁴

Further enquiries clarified the position of Ashton, Wiltshire. The manor of Ashton was originally given to Alice Maltravers by her brother John Maltravers III as her dowry when she married Elias Giffard in about 1230. Ashton was to be held by Elias, Alice and their descendants, from John Maltravers III and his descendants. In 1327, it was decided that the heirs were James Audley and John Lestrange, as for Gloucestershire.⁶⁵

Although John Giffard had been executed, his widow Avelina was given the manor of King's Stanley, Gloucestershire, as dower. Avelina died in about September 1327, and King's Stanley was then allocated to descendants of John Giffard's three aunts: Maud, Isabel and Mabel. The heirs were Roger Bavant, great-grandson of Maud; Thomas de Grimstead, great-grandson of Isabel; and Richard Dauntsey, grandson of Mabel.⁶⁶

John Maltravers VI had an eye on the Giffard lands for himself, although he only had a claim for Ashton. Sometime in 1327, he was given the wardship of those lands of John Giffard that were still in the king's hands,[67] and, in November 1328, he became keeper of Carreg Cennen Castle in Carmarthenshire, which had been held by John Giffard.[68]

This was not the end of the matter. In 1329, the king (or Mortimer and Isabella acting in his name) declared that the Giffard lands should remain in the king's hands 'by reason of failure of heirs of John Giffard',[69] none of the claimants having been able to prove their entitlement. In a sweeping gesture, the king then granted all the Giffard lands to John Maltravers VI and his heirs, in consideration of 'the good services rendered to the king's mother and the king by him as steward of her household and the dangers and expenses incurred by him'. This probably refers to the period in 1326 when Queen Isabella and her son Prince Edward were in France. Accordingly, in May 1330, nearly all the Giffard lands (but not Ashton) were transferred to John Maltravers VI:

GLOUCESTERSHIRE

† Brimpsfield, King's Stanley, Rockhampton, Stonehouse, Stoke Gifford, Syde and Walls.

WILTSHIRE

† Boyton, Broughton Gifford, Codford, Elston, Orcheston, Sherrington and Stapleford.

WALES

† Carreg Cennen Castle and the surrounding area of Iskennen.[70]

John Maltravers V, Father of John VI

John Maltravers V, who was about 64 years of age in 1330, took no part in the events at Berkeley Castle or Corfe Castle, instead occupying himself with managing his estates, and personal and community matters. In May 1329, John Maltravers V, Robert Fitzpayn and John Peverel were appointed commissioners of the peace for Dorset.[71]

He continued to take an interest in his Irish lands. In February 1327[72] and again in July 1329,[73] he appointed two attorneys to deal with his estates in Ireland for three years while he stayed in England. On the second occasion, one of the attorneys was his younger son Edward Maltravers I.

John Maltravers V, like his eldest son, remarried sometime between 1325 and 1330, as previously mentioned. His new wife was Joan Foliot, the widow of Nicholas de Percy and an heiress in her own right. She inherited Melbury Osmond from her father (Walter Foliot), and Melbury Sampford from her mother (Ada, or Alda, Sampford). In 1330, Joan also inherited from her mother part of the town of Nantwich, Cheshire, and other lands in that county.[74] The marriage seems to have caused annoyance in the Percy family as, in 1337, William de Percy – parson of Folke, Dorset – was ordered to be arrested and imprisoned for having, with others, abducted Joan and stolen goods belonging to her husband John Maltravers V.[75]

Nemesis for Roger Mortimer

The autumn of 1330 was the eleventh hour for the rule of Isabella and Mortimer. By October, fear and suspicion was growing on both sides. Mortimer and Queen Isabella realised that the time was approaching when the young king would expect to take charge, with who knew what consequences for themselves. Edward III was frustrated by Mortimer's overbearing ways. When the court was at Nottingham Castle, Mortimer accused William Montagu and some of Edward III's young knights of plotting against him. They denied this, but with Edward III's agreement they decided to take action. On October 19, after dark, they entered the castle quietly by a secret tunnel cut into the rock. When they burst into the royal apartments, the alarm was raised by the steward, Hugh Turplington. He was promptly struck down and killed. Others rushed to the scene, and two more men were killed in the ensuing mêlée. Mortimer, Simon de Bereford and Oliver Ingham were overpowered and taken prisoner. Isabella called out to Edward III, 'Fair son! Fair son! Have pity on gentle Mortimer.'[76] But it was too late for that. She herself was placed under guard, and Mortimer and Simon de Bereford were sent to the Tower of London to await trial.

Promptly, on the following day, Edward issued a proclamation to be read by sheriffs in public places throughout the realm, stating that:

> The king's affairs and the affairs of his realm have been directed until now to the damage and dishonour of him and his realm and to the impoverishment of his people… wherefore he has, of his own knowledge and will, caused

certain persons to be arrested, to wit the earl of March [Mortimer], Sir Oliver Ingham and Sir Simon de Bereford, and he wills that all men shall know that he will henceforth govern his people according to right and reason, as befits his royal dignity, and that the affairs that concern him and the estate of his realm shall be directed by the common counsel of the magnates of his realm and in no other wise.[77]

Thus Edward III commenced his personal rule at the age of seventeen. His eighteenth birthday was three weeks later, on November 13, 1330.

The king made it clear to his mother, Queen Isabella, that – while she would live in honourable retirement – he was now in charge, and her participation in affairs of state was not required. She lost much of the wealth and land she had accumulated, but was given an annual allowance of £3,000, which was very generous in the circumstances.

On October 23, writs were issued summoning a parliament to meet at Westminster on November 26. John Maltravers VI received his personal summons confirming his status as Baron Maltravers, but by then he had heard what was afoot and did not attend. Instead, he made plans to flee the country. We can imagine that he just had time to take leave of his family in Lytchett Matravers: his father, John V; his son, another John (VII); and his wife Agnes de Bereford.[78]

At the parliament in November 1330, the main business was the trial of Roger Mortimer. He was accused of treason under fourteen headings, including ignoring the requirement for a council of bishops, earls and barons to advise the king, thereby usurping royal power for himself; having ex-king Edward II murdered at Berkeley Castle by himself and his followers; and, knowing full well that the former king was dead and buried, tricking Edmund, earl of Kent, into believing that he was alive and thereby procuring the earl's death. The peers considered the charges and found him guilty on all of them. He was sentenced to be drawn and hanged. A day or two later, on November 29, he was executed.[79]

Simon de Bereford was accused of being a helper and supporter of Roger Mortimer in all his treasons, felonies and evil acts, including the murder of a liege lord, the destruction of royal blood, and various other felonies and robberies. He, too, was sentenced to be drawn and hanged as a traitor. He was executed on December 24.[80]

John Maltravers VI was not accused of Edward II's murder. He was, however, found guilty in his absence of causing the death of Edmund, earl of Kent, 'inasmuch as he, knowing that King Edward [II] was really dead, by ingenious means and by false and evil subtleties led the earl of Kent to believe that he was alive'[81] and so caused the earl's death. The sentence on John Maltravers VI was to be drawn, hanged and beheaded as a traitor. As he had fled, a reward of 1000 marks (about £666) was offered for capturing him alive and bringing him to the king, 'and if he could not be taken alive, whoever should bring his head would be given £500'.

Bogo de Bayouse and John Deveril of the Corfe Castle garrison were also sentenced to death for entrapment of the earl of Kent. They, too, had fled. The reward offered for bringing Bayouse to the king alive was £100 or was 100 marks (about £66) for his head. For John Deveril, the reward was £66 alive or £40 for his head.[82]

Thomas Gurney and William Ockley were sentenced to death for 'falsely and traitorously' murdering Edward II. They had also fled. The reward for capturing Gurney alive was £100 or was £66 for his head. For Ockley, it was £66 alive or £40 for his head.[83]

These are the seven death sentences passed in the parliament. Apart from Roger Mortimer, the only person who was actually executed as a result of these parliamentary proceedings was Mortimer's associate, Simon de Bereford. If he was indeed the brother of Agnes Maltravers, this must have caused her great distress, in addition to that caused by the hasty departure of her husband in fear of his life.

Oliver Ingham was pardoned on 8 December and was later reappointed as seneschal of Gascony, which was a post he had held under Edward II.

Thomas de Berkeley made no attempt to flee, but appeared before the king in the parliament to deny any involvement in the death of Edward II. He claimed that he had not heard of the ex-king's death before the present parliament. Considering that it was he who had first written to Edward III informing him of Edward II's death, which occurred in Berkeley Castle, this was an extraordinary claim. He was asked how he could deny all knowledge and responsibility since 'he was lord of the aforesaid castle, and the ex-king was delivered into the keeping of Thomas [de Berkeley] and John [Maltravers] to be kept safely, and they received and accepted the keeping of the king'.[84] Then de Berkeley said that, at the time when 'it is said, the murder took place', he was at his castle of Bradley, suffering from such a severe illness that he remembered nothing about it. Further challenged that illness was not a sufficient excuse, he said that he had placed under him, to guard the ex-king, men whom he considered equivalent to himself and John Maltravers. The parliament met again in January 1331, and acquitted de Berkeley of murdering Edward II or of assisting the murder. As to the charge of appointing Gurney and Ockley, the murderers, the matter was postponed until the next parliament, when judgment would be given. Meanwhile, de Berkeley was released, and the charge of appointing Gurney and Ockley was eventually dropped altogether in 1336. Historians have examined the Berkeley Castle accounts, which show that he did not go to Bradley until a week after Edward II's death. There is no suggestion in the parliamentary record that Maltravers VI was, or should have been, there at the crucial time.

Somewhat belatedly, on 3 December 1330, an attempt was made to stop those of the accused who had fled – that is, John Maltravers VI, Thomas Gurney, John Deveril and William Ockley – from leaving the country. The seaports of Faversham, Dover, Hastings, Rye, Winchelsea, Romney, Hythe and Ipswich were to be watched, and if the wanted men were found, they were to be apprehended and brought to the king. Bogo de Bayouse is not in the list; perhaps he was of lesser importance or perhaps he was already known to have fled abroad.[85]

Maltravers and Gurney evaded capture by keeping clear of the obvious ports and instead taking ship at Mousehole in Cornwall. Two men from Mousehole were later accused of helping them to 'pass beyond seas from Cornwall in spite of the king's mandate to the keepers of all ports not to suffer them to leave the realm'. Afterwards, the Cornishmen had supplied Maltravers and Gurney with corn, armour and victuals, 'and they still render them continual assistance'. This was in July 1331.[86]

Maltravers and Gurney were still together in the spring of 1331 when they were seen in Burgos, northern Spain, by Isolda de Belhouse, an English pilgrim who was on her way to Compostella. This sighting of Maltravers VI is mentioned only in the French version of *The Brut* chronicle. Maltravers VI disappeared, but Gurney was arrested.[87] When news of Gurney's capture reached England, an agent – Giles of Spain – was sent out to take charge of him. Negotiations took place for the handover in summer 1331, but by then Gurney had vanished. He is next heard of in Naples in 1333. Again, an agent – this time William Thweng – was sent to bring him back. Thweng got as far as Bayonne with his prisoner, but there Gurney fell ill and died. In July 1333, William Thweng returned to England with Gurney's embalmed body and spent several days at Tynemouth with King Edward III. No doubt the king was anxious to learn if Gurney had given any more information about what really happened at Berkeley Castle.

William Ockley, accused in parliament with Gurney, had already disappeared without trace.

Of the two guards at Corfe Castle, Bogo de Bayouse fled to France and then to Italy, where his wife joined him. He died in Rome on 26 July 1334.[88] The fate of John Deveril is unknown, but in August 1331 he was thought to be still at large in the West Country. John Maltravers V and two others were given the task of arresting him wherever he was to be found and bringing him to the king, and also of imprisoning until further orders any persons in Somerset and Dorset who had sheltered him.[89]

John Maltravers VI forfeited all his manors, lands, goods and chattels on 15 December 1330. Sheriffs were ordered to take his possessions into the king's hands. The same applied to the other fugitives.[90]

The earl of Kent's son, Edmund, and the earl's widow, Margaret, presented petitions to the parliament on 7 December, saying that if there had been an error in the process by which the earl was put to death, it should be remedied, considering – among other things – that Sir Roger Mortimer, late earl of March, had admitted before the people at his death that the earl of Kent had been wrongfully killed. If true, this was a significant admission by Mortimer that the earl of Kent had been tricked. The petitions were carefully considered, and in view of the malicious deception that had been practised on the earl, leading him to try to release Edward II – which was clearly impossible because the late king had been dead for a long time – it was decided that the title of earl and the late earl of Kent's lands should be restored to his son Edmund, and that Margaret should regain her dower lands.[91] In March 1331, the restoration was put into effect.[92]

The Chroniclers' Version of Events

Now that it had been said officially that Edward II had been murdered, it was safe for monastic chroniclers to write up what they knew of the circumstances. Some simply said that he had died on a certain date, and some that he had died of an illness. Others stated that he had been murdered, and blamed John Maltravers VI and Gurney for the deed, in spite of the fact that Maltravers was never accused of the murder, either in the parliament of November 1330 or later.

Adam Murimuth was based in Exeter in 1327, and was the closest to Berkeley Castle. He made notes at the time and wrote, in about 1337, that Edward II had been suffocated by Maltravers and Gurney, acting on the orders of Roger Mortimer.

The northern version of *The Brut* chronicle, probably written after 1333, is the first to give the well-known story that the murder weapon was a red-hot copper rod inserted into the victim's anus to burn out his bowels, leaving no external mark on his body. Maltravers and Gurney are said to be the murderers, again on Mortimer's orders. One version of *The Brut* chronicle is unique in giving Corfe Castle as the site of the murder, but this error is corrected to Berkeley Castle later in the same chronicle, when describing the trials of Roger Mortimer and the others in 1330.[93]

Ranulph Higden, a monk of Chester, writing in around 1340, also mentions a red-hot iron, but does not name the murderer.[94]

Geoffrey le Baker, writing somewhat later (around 1350), gives full rein to his imagination in his graphic account of how Maltravers VI and Gurney carried out the murder. Their first idea was to keep Edward II for many days in a cell near a pit filled with rotting carcases, hoping he would be overcome by the stench. When that did not work, they resorted to more direct methods, first suffocation under heavy cushions and then a red-hot iron in his bowels. His screams of agony were heard within and without the castle, at which many were moved to compassion and to pray for his soul as it departed this world.[95] Baker's account is ludicrously improbable. There would hardly have been time to try and kill him by the miasma from rotten flesh. The aim would surely have been to kill him effectively but discreetly, and not to alert the whole neighbourhood.

All the chroniclers who name the murderers accuse Maltravers and Gurney of the deed, apart from one much later chronicler – Thomas Burton in the 1390s – who names Gurney only. They all say that Edward II died on about 21 September 1327; none say that he did not die at that time.

However, there is evidence that John Maltravers VI was not at Berkeley Castle at the time of the alleged murder, but instead he was in Dorset. In late September 1327, Thomas de Berkeley wrote two letters to John Maltravers, one addressed to him 'in Dorset' and the other addressed to him 'at Corfe'. It is intriguing if Maltravers was at Corfe as early as 1327, as he did not become constable of Corfe Castle until 1329. Payments to the messengers carrying these letters are recorded in the Berkeley Castle accounts, after a payment to Roger

Mortimer in Wales.⁹⁶ Roger Mortimer, having left the court at Nottingham, arrived in Abergavenny on about 14 September, so the two letters to John Maltravers VI were probably sent in mid-to-late September.

Also from the Berkeley Castle accounts, we see that a payment of £258 8s. 2d. was sent to John Maltravers VI at about the same time as the letters. The entry in the Berkeley Castle records is the second to last in an account that ends on 30 September 1327; therefore, dating it on or shortly before that date.⁹⁷ The payment is 'for service on behalf of the king's father in Dorset'. This ambiguous description may mean that Maltravers was in Dorset, but that the service was carried out elsewhere – for instance, at Berkeley Castle – or that the service was carried out in Dorset, perhaps at Corfe. If it was the latter, it shows that the ex-king was moved around the country as stated by Murimuth. Could it even mean that both Maltravers and 'the king's father' were in Dorset in September 1327? It is unlikely that anyone would put this in writing, even in the private castle accounts.

If there was a murder, the culprits were probably Thomas Gurney and William Ockley, and not John Maltravers VI, who was never accused of it and who was, in any case, elsewhere.

The Fieschi Letter, the Italian Connection and Further Pointers to the Survival of Edward II

The story of Edward II's death, whether natural or violent, in Berkeley Castle; his funeral at Gloucester; the erroneous belief of the earl of Kent that Edward had survived, leading to the earl's execution for treason; and the trial in the parliament of the guilty were generally accepted for centuries. John Maltravers VI was bracketed with the murderers because of the statement in Murimuth's chronicle, which others repeated, although Maltravers was, in fact, only convicted of the entrapment of the earl of Kent.

Then, after 500 years of this familiar narrative, came a sensational discovery that raised the possibility that Edward II did not die in 1327 after all, but escaped from Berkeley Castle and, after various travels, ended up in a monastery in Italy. This was the 'Fieschi letter', which was found by chance by a French historian, Alexandre Germain, in 1877 and published in 1878. It purports to be a copy of a letter sent to Edward III by Manuel Fieschi, a papal notary. Fieschi says he has spoken to Edward III's father in person and recounts

Edward II's story as the ex-king told it to him. The original letter, as received by Edward III in the 1330s, has not been found.

Fieschi's version of the story begins with Edward II's flight during the invasion of Isabella and Mortimer in 1326, followed by his capture, deposition and imprisonment in Kenilworth Castle and Berkeley Castle. Then Edward II describes his escape from Berkeley Castle in 1327. The servant who was keeping him came and said to him, 'Thomas de Gornay and Symon Desberfort, knights, have arrived with the purpose of killing you.' The servant offered to give his own clothes to Edward II, so that Edward II could avoid recognition and escape. Thus attired, at twilight, Edward II went out of the prison. At the last door, he found the gatekeeper sleeping, whom he quickly killed; and, having got the keys of the door, he opened the door and went out with the servant. The knights who had come to kill him, seeing that Edward II had fled, decided to put the body of the gatekeeper in a box, his heart having been extracted, and then they maliciously presented to the Queen the heart and body of the gatekeeper as the heart and body of her husband. Therefore, it was the body of the gatekeeper that was interred ceremoniously at Gloucester. After leaving Berkeley Castle, Edward II and his companion were received in Corfe Castle by Lord Thomas, castellan of Corfe, without the knowledge of Lord 'John Maltravers [VI], lord of the said Thomas'. He remained secretly in Corfe Castle for a year and a half. Afterwards, having heard that the earl of Kent had been beheaded for saying that Edward II was still alive, he took a ship and crossed to Ireland, where he remained for nine months. Then he returned to England, dressed as a hermit; crossed the sea to Normandy; visited Avignon, where he was received by the pope; went on pilgrimage to the shrine of the three kings at Cologne; and finished up in a monastery near Cecima in Italy. The letter ends with: 'In testimony of which I caused my seal to be affixed for the consideration of Your Highness. Manuel de Fieschi, notary of the lord pope, your devoted servant.'[98]

The letter had been copied into a bound manuscript volume of bishop's charters kept in the archives in Montpellier, southern France. The subject matter of the letter, therefore, has no connection with the other documents in the book. Nevertheless, as far as its handwriting and language are concerned, which are typical of an Italian writing medieval Latin, it appears to be genuine, and no one has been able to prove it to be a forgery.[99]

Fieschi must have spoken to someone extraordinarily well informed, if not to Edward II himself, as the details of his flight from Isabella and Mortimer, his capture, deposition, and imprisonment would not have been known to everybody. It is the only source giving a role at Berkeley Castle to Simon de Bereford. In parliament, he was convicted of helping Roger Mortimer in all his treasons, felonies and evil acts, including the murder of a liege lord and the destruction of royal blood. This could refer to either the murder of Edward II, or to the entrapment and death of the earl of Kent, who was a half-brother of Edward II. Simon de Bereford was the escheator south of the Trent under the Mortimer regime, but it has never been clear what exactly he did to merit a traitor's death. John Maltravers VI is named, not as one of the would-be assassins but as the overlord of 'Thomas', castellan of Corfe.

The tale of Edward II's escape from Berkeley Castle is improbable. How could the death of the unfortunate gatekeeper arouse no attention? The gatekeeper, although anonymous to us, was not so to his colleagues and friends. Who were the people who scooped up his body and decided instantly to pass it off as Edward II's, after first extracting the heart? It is hard to believe they were the knights who, without the knowledge of the castle guards, had come to murder him.

And again, what of the worthies of the district who saw the embalmed body? Surely, even in this state, it must have borne little resemblance, in facial features and general build, to the prisoner? Perhaps they did notice, but dared not say anything, and so began the rumours that led to the earl of Kent's conspiracy. It is remarkable that, by 1330, so many were openly supporting Kent and risking their lives if they were wrong.

There are a few inconsistencies; for example, the time between the 'escape' of Edward II and the death of the earl of Kent is two and a half years, not one and a half. It is not clear who is meant by Thomas, castellan of Corfe under the lord, 'Sir John Maltravers [VI]'. The constable at the time was Sir John Pecche, who was appointed on 16 December 1325 and was a supporter of the earl of Kent in his unsuccessful attempt to free the ex-king. As John Pecche was absent overseas in 1327 and 1328, it may be that John Maltravers was acting as constable at this time. He was certainly receiving correspondence from Berkeley Castle in September 1327, as previously mentioned. John Maltravers VI was officially constable of Corfe from 24 September 1329 until his hasty departure from the realm in November 1330. He was carrying out repairs at Corfe Castle from August 1329, which is hardly compatible with hiding Edward II there. It would also be strange if Edward II was in the castle but Maltravers did not know of his presence.

On the other hand, Fieschi mentions a pilgrimage by Edward II to Cologne, and an incident that occurred in 1338 may bear this out. In that year, a man turned up at Cologne calling himself William le Galeys (William the Welshman) and claiming to be Edward II. He was taken by his companion, an Italian, to meet Edward III, who was at Koblenz (about 70 miles away) at the time. Far from being arrested as an impostor, 'Edward, the king's father' was received politely and even went with the English royal party to Antwerp where he was kept at Edward III's expense for three weeks.[100] Was he truly who he said he was? Fieschi mentions the visit to Cologne, but not the meeting with Edward III. If the Fieschi letter was written after the meeting of Edward II and his son at Koblenz, it is surprising that the encounter is not mentioned. If the letter predates the meeting, this implies a second trip to Cologne and an awful lot of travelling for someone keeping his identity secret.

The Fieschi letter, although lacking the obvious signs of a medieval forgery, was regarded with scepticism by English historians of the early twentieth century; for example, T. F. Tout.[101] It was received more positively in Italy, where a particular abbey was identified as the place where Edward II found refuge and was eventually buried. Cuttino and Lyman found no evidence for a local tradition in Italy earlier than the publication of the Fieschi letter.[102]

The controversy was reignited by Ian Mortimer in his biography of Roger Mortimer, *The Greatest Traitor* (2003), which takes seriously the escape of Edward II. Ian Mortimer is convinced that Edward II did not die in 1327 and presents a very detailed argument for the ex-king's survival. He says that even if the Fieschi letter were shown to be a forgery, there is other evidence for the survival of Edward of Caernarfon. In his biography of Edward III, Ian Mortimer mentions the possibility that Edward II died in about 1341–42, and his remains were returned to Gloucester to be interred in the tomb where the obsequies had taken place in 1327.[103]

Ian Mortimer's work aroused a great deal of interest. As well as a biography of Edward II by Roy Martin Haines (2003), which was apparently published shortly before Mortimer's book, there have been two other biographies of Edward II in recent years: one by Seymour Phillips (2010) and one by Kathryn Warner (2014). All of them have examined the issue at length out of necessity. The fact that so many people are still discussing it shows what a strange story it is.

To sum up this tangled tale from the point of view of John Maltravers VI, John was never accused of, nor was he guilty of, the murder of Edward II. He may have been guilty of tricking the earl of Kent into believing that Edward II had escaped and hence guilty of luring Kent into committing treason. He later protested his innocence of the deception of the earl of Kent, but in 1330 he did not wait to put his case to the parliament in which he was condemned to death in his absence, but instead prudently left his home and country for exile abroad, not knowing when, if ever, it would be safe to return. If Edward II did survive, Maltravers may have had a hand in rescuing him, but the possibility was not officially admitted at the time or indeed in the lifetimes of Edward III and John Maltravers VI.

5

BARON JOHN MALTRAVERS
EXILE, SECRET MISSION, CRÉCY AND CALAIS, 1330–1347

John Maltravers VI in Flanders, 1330–1345

To return to the fortunes of John Maltravers VI in exile. After parting company with Gurney, Maltravers settled in Flanders. Far from living in total secrecy, he was involved in the politics of the area and, after a time, made contact with the English king, tentatively at first and later quite openly.

In the summer of 1332, his wife Agnes went overseas 'on pilgrimage' with the king's permission, and there is little doubt that, in fact, she went to visit her husband. The constable of Dover Castle was ordered to allow her to cross the Channel with her men, horses and equipment. In July 1332, she was awarded protection until the following Easter, and, in August, she appointed attorneys to manage her affairs in her absence.[1]

Mysteriously, John Maltravers VI sent a message to the king in 1334, saying that he 'desired to reveal to him many things concerning his honour, and the estate and well-being of the realm'.[2] William Montagu was sent to interview him and to find out what it was all about. Was it just to do with Anglo-Flemish relations or did it concern the possible survival of Edward II? We have no idea what was discussed. Maltravers's own whereabouts must have been known, but no attempt was made to arrest him. John Maltravers VI made a clandestine visit to England in 1335. The evidence for this is the pardon issued to various people for having received him in spite of his banishment from the realm. It appears that he had met William Montagu, Nicholas de la Beche, John Moleyns, Edmund de Bereford (brother of Agnes), Thomas de Berkeley, Maurice de Berkeley, William de Whitefield and Adam, abbot of Malmesbury.[3]

The long-standing conflict between England and France over Gascony became more serious in 1337. In May, the French king declared Gascony confiscate, and Edward III issued writs in October describing himself as 'King of France and England' or 'King of England and France'. With these diplomatic moves began the Hundred Years War.

In Flanders in the late 1330s, John Maltravers VI assisted in the English king's quest for allies. Most of the area comprising modern-day Belgium and Holland was ruled by counts who were subjects of the Holy Roman Emperor. The case of Flanders was particularly difficult, as the count of Flanders acknowledged the king of France, not the emperor, as his overlord. Flanders and England were linked by the wool trade: English wool was exported to Flanders and was woven into cloth there. In 1336, Edward banned the export of wool to Flanders in order to pressurise the Flemish into supporting him. This caused hardship among the weavers and cloth merchants, leading to the overthrow of the count and the establishment of a form of self-government under Jacob van Artevelde of Ghent in 1338. In the next year or two, the Flemish towns of Ghent, Bruges and Ypres formed an alliance, and the wool embargo was lifted. Flanders at first said it would be neutral in the conflict between England and France, but then entered into a military alliance with England. Later events were to show that John Maltravers had close links to van Artevelde.

So important were the negotiations with Flanders that King Edward III himself took up residence in Antwerp between 1338 and 1340. John Maltravers VI's son (John Maltravers VII) was employed in the royal service in the retinue of Henry de Ferrers, the king's chamberlain: '8 July 1338. John [VII] son of John Maltravers [VI] the younger, going beyond the seas on the king's service with Henry de Ferrers, has letters nominating… his attorneys in England until Christmas.'[4] John VII would surely have made contact with his father while in Flanders. In September 1338, the emperor crowned Edward III as vicar of the Holy Roman Empire, thus legitimising his authority over the emperor's subjects. When Edward III publicly proclaimed himself king of France in January 1340, the Flemish accepted him as their overlord.

In 1338, the French raided Portsmouth and Southampton. In about July, John VI's father, John Maltravers V, was nominated, along with others, to be a keeper of the peace for Dorset. In a petition to the king requesting that certain people should be made keepers of the peace, there are two references to defence: that the archers previously ordered to go with the king should remain in Dorset for the defence of the coast, and that the sheriff be ordered to bring armed men from Somerset into Dorset for the security of the county.[5] Defensive preparations were ordered, and on 20 October 1338 John Maltravers V was told to go to his manors nearest the sea and to be ready for an invasion.[6] His principal manor of Lytchett Matravers was about six miles from Poole Harbour, and his lands at Langton Matravers and Worth Matravers in Purbeck were also near the sea. The danger of a French invasion was averted when the English won a great naval victory at Sluys in 1340, practically destroying the French fleet and clearing the Channel for the next few years.

We do not know exactly what John Maltravers VI was up to in Flanders, but he must have been doing something useful behind the scenes, as he was given an annuity of £100 in February 1339: 'Grant for life to John [VI] son of John Maltravers [V] the elder of £100 yearly payable at Michaelmas and Easter.'[7] It is thought that this may have been for helping to bring Flanders on to England's side. Just after being awarded his annuity, he tried to capitalise on the royal approval shown to him by petitioning parliament for his sentence of banishment to be lifted 'since it had been made without him having the right to answer'[8] (ignoring the fact that he had fled the realm instead of turning up at parliament in November 1330). He asked the king to grant him safe conduct to come back to England to answer the charges. The petition was presented to parliament on his behalf by his wife Agnes, but it was not read and was therefore not proceeded with. It was too early for such a rapprochement, and his hopes of an end to his long exile were dashed.

Agnes Maltravers was now officially permitted to visit her husband. In February 1342, she was given protection for one year as she was 'going beyond the seas on the king's service', and she was given licence to stay with her husband in Flanders 'for such time as she shall please, notwithstanding that he is banished from the realm of England'.[9]

Her husband was still active on the king's behalf in Flanders. Although Edward III was anxious to remain on good terms with the people of Flanders, he could not overlook the false imprisonment of certain English merchants and the seizure of their goods, including cloth, leather, ships and wool, to the value of £6,000 in total. In October 1343, John Maltravers VI was appointed to lead a commission of three Englishmen to enquire into the matter and to secure compensation from those who had wrongfully arrested the merchants.

Politely worded letters were sent to the captains and burgomasters of Flanders, and the deacons of the weavers and fullers of Bruges, 'bringing to their knowledge' the complaint of the merchants, and 'praying them affectionately' to take inquisitions and to make restitution.[10]

In 1345, there was a crisis in Flanders that brought John Maltravers into great peril. In June, there was an armed rebellion against his friend Jacob van Artevelde. King Edward III sailed to Sluys and, on board ship, had discussions with van Artevelde. Within a fortnight, on July 17, a mob surrounded van Artevelde's house, chased him outside and killed him.

John Maltravers VI, fearing for his life in Flanders, made another attempt to lift the threat of execution as a traitor that was hanging over him. He went to the king, who was still at Sluys, and pleaded humbly to be allowed to return to England. He declared himself innocent of the misdeeds alleged against him, and willing to stand trial in parliament or in another court if anyone were to accuse him. He said his previous condemnation to death and banishment from the realm were illegal as he had not had the chance to answer the charges against him. The king, taking into consideration the good service John had rendered in Flanders and elsewhere, and the fact that he had lost all his goods thereby and was in great peril, granted Maltravers's petition with the assent of the earls, barons and others who were at Sluys at the time, and also after his return to Westminster with the assent of other great men of the king's council. Accordingly, John was promised safe passage to England with his men, servants and goods at the time of the next parliament, and the king's special protection while he remained in England during the parliamentary sitting, on the condition that he stood his trial at parliament. Sheriffs, bailiffs, ministers and others were ordered to ensure that John VI and his servants were not molested in the meantime. The judgment against him was not to be put into effect until the case was settled. The document containing these instructions, including John Maltravers's plea and the king's reply, was formally issued at Westminster on 5 August 1345. There are two slightly different versions in the Patent Rolls. In the first, the case is to be heard 'in the next Parliament';[11] in the second, the process of judgment is to be examined 'in the next Parliament or elsewhere' and is to be 'either annulled or approved in the next Parliament or before'.[12]

As it happened, the next parliament did not meet until more than a year later, in September 1346. It would have been too risky to visit England until parliament met, and John Maltravers VI seems to have stayed in Flanders. Perhaps the situation there turned out to be less dangerous than he had feared.

Lands

After his fall from grace in 1330, the lands and other possessions of John Maltravers VI were taken into the king's hands. The lands were those in his own name, not the whole of the family's estates, as his father (John Maltravers V) was still living. A commission was appointed to identify what the younger John (VI) possessed.[13] John VI was also relieved of his position as keeper of the forest south of the Trent, and Robert de Ufford was appointed as his successor on 16 December 1330.[14]

Any lands that John Maltravers VI had obtained as a result of the fall of Edmund, earl of Kent, in March 1330 were lost within the year. Following the decision in parliament in December 1330 that the earl of Kent had been deceived into committing treason, the earl of Kent's lands were restored to his son, who was also called Edmund. His widow Margaret regained her dower lands.[15] The castle of Arundel, however – which had been held by the earl of Kent since the execution of Edmund, earl of Arundel, in 1326 – was not passed to the earl of Kent's heirs but was instead awarded to Richard Fitzalan, son of Edmund, the former earl. Richard was restored to favour under the new regime of Edward III and regained the title of earl of Arundel. This was to affect the Maltravers family in a later generation.

The Dorset manors of Loders, Philipston, Up Wimborne (Wimborne St Giles) and Winterborne Houghton were granted to John de Nevill of Hornby, together with the Berkshire manor of Childrey.[16] In 1336 – after the death of John de Nevill – Loders, Philipston, Up Wimborne and Childrey were granted to Ralph Ufford and his male heirs, with reversion to the king if Ufford died without such heirs.[17]

Overstone, Northamptonshire, which John Maltravers VI had obtained on a life tenancy in April 1327, was granted to Richard Grey for seven years from November 1331.[18]

Giffard Lands

In 1331, some of the Giffard lands that John Maltravers VI had obtained in May 1330 were allocated to Roger Bavant, one of the heirs of John Giffard (d. 1322), to be held 'during pleasure'. These are listed as follows:[19]

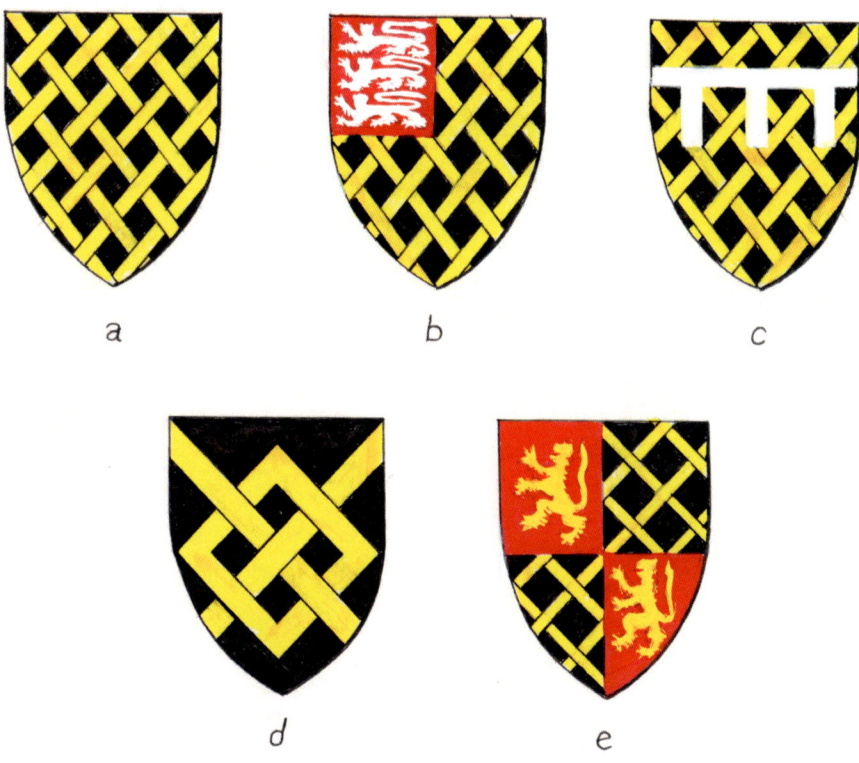

The Maltravers arms:

a. John Maltravers 'sable fretty or' c.1258.

b. William Maltravers 'sable fretty or', with the Giffard arms 'gules three lions passant guardant argent' on a canton, c.1275.

c. John Maltravers the son 'sable fretty or', with a label of three points argent, 1309.

d. Baron John Maltravers 'sable a fret or' c. 1364.

e. William Arundel, d. 1400, Arundel 'gules a lion rampant or', quartering Maltravers 'sable fretty or'.

The Norman knights landing in England 1066, based on the Bayeux Tapestry.
© iStock.com/Duncan1890

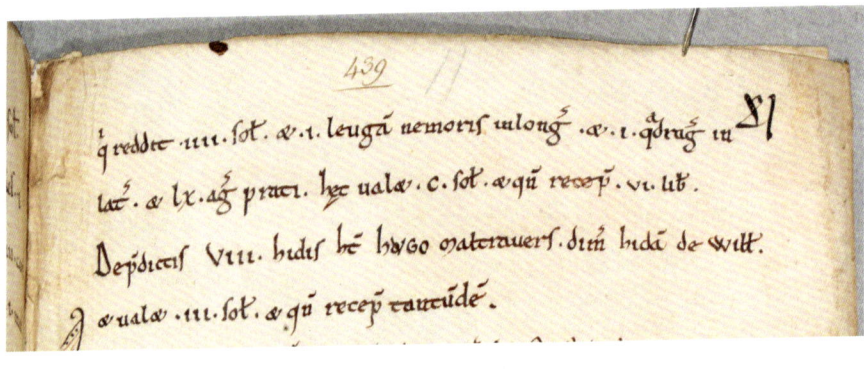

Exon Domesday: Hinton Blewett, with the names of Ralph Blewitt and Hugh Maltravers.
© The Dean and Chapter of Exeter Cathedral. MS 3500 f438v-f439r

The Church of St Nicholas at La Chaize-le-Vicomte, built by Aimery de Thouars.

Chepstow Castle, Chepstow Bridge and the River Wye. © iStock.com/susandaniels

Corfe Castle: castle and village.

The Church of St Mary the Virgin, Lytchett Matravers: the tower of c. 1200.

Castle Cornet, Guernsey.

Mont Orgueil, or Gorey, Castle, Jersey. © *iStock.com/fotofritz16*

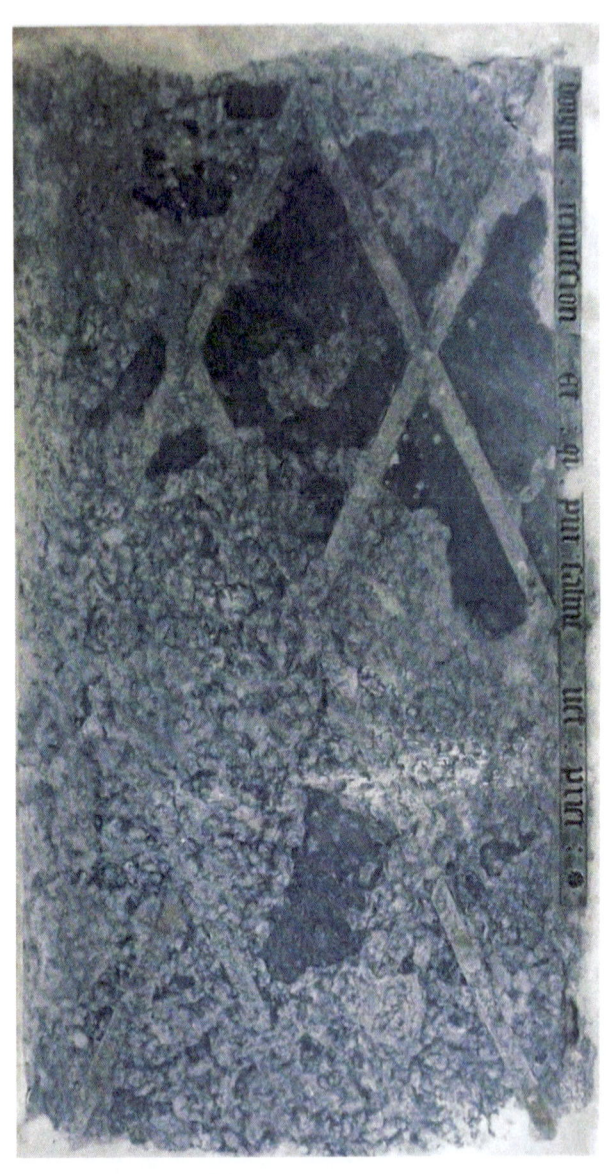

The gravestone of Baron John Maltravers, Lytchett Matravers, as it was in 2019.

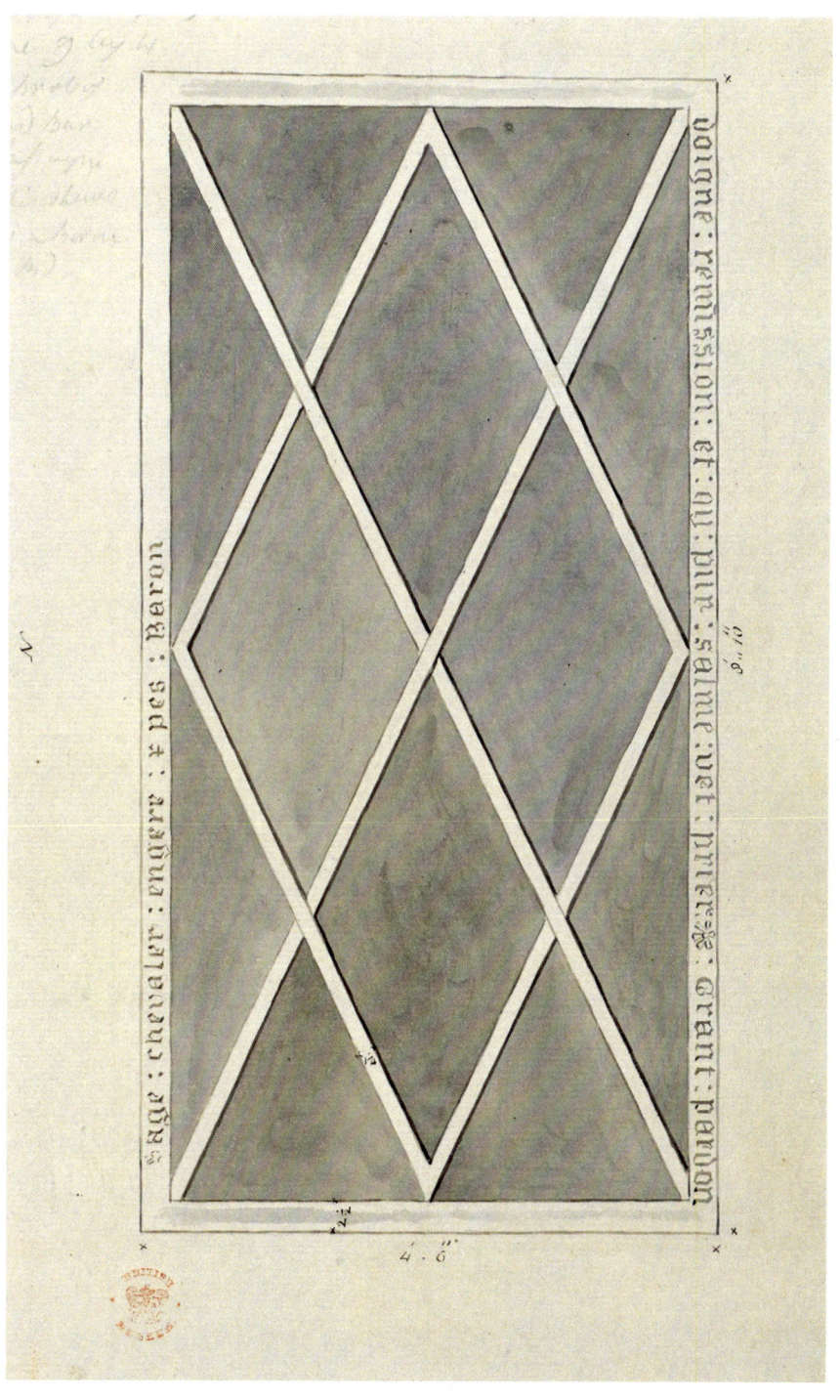

The gravestone of Baron John Maltravers, Lytchett Matravers, by David Thomas Powell c. 1810. © The British Library Board 31/01/2019 Addit. ms 17459 f115r

Arundel Castle. © *iStock.com/scottyh*

GLOUCESTERSHIRE
† Brimpsfield and Rockhampton.

WILTSHIRE
† West Codford, Sherrington and half the manor of Stapleford.

WALES
† Carreg Cennen.

Three years later, the Giffard lands as a whole – i.e. 'the castles, manors and lands in England and Wales which John Maltravers had of the inheritance of John Giffard of Brimpsfield, deceased' – were transferred to Maurice de Berkeley for life, 'for good service'.[20] This Maurice de Berkeley (1298–1347), called Maurice de Berkeley of Uley, was a younger brother of Thomas de Berkeley. They were brothers-in-law of John Maltravers VI, whose first wife was their late sister, Ela.

The manor of Ashton, Wiltshire, was to be shared between James Audley and John Lestrange under the provisions of the inquisition post mortem on John Giffard in 1327. James Audley was then a minor, but by June 1335 he was proved to be of full age and his half of the manor was ordered to be delivered to him.[21]

There was further adjustment of the Giffard inheritance in 1337. At that time, some of the lands were being held for life by Margaret, mother of John Giffard (d. 1322), and a reallocation after Margaret's death was provided for. Margaret was to die in 1338. By the 1337 arrangement, John de Wylinton acquired immediately Carreg Cennen Castle and the surrounding land of Iskennen. After the death of Margaret Giffard, he and his heirs would also be granted the Wiltshire lands of Broughton Gifford, Elston and Orcheston.[22] John de Warenne, earl of Surrey, would – after the death of Margaret Giffard – be granted the following:

WILTSHIRE
† Boyton for life.[23]

Maurice de Berkeley was to continue to hold the castle and manor of Brimpsfield, Gloucestershire, for life. He would also continue to hold the following manors, but without having to pay any farm (rent) for them:

GLOUCESTERSHIRE
† King's Stanley and Rockhampton.

WILTSHIRE
† Corton, Sherrington, Codford and Stapleford.

After the death of Margaret Giffard, Maurice de Berkeley would also get the following:[24]

GLOUCESTERSHIRE
† Stonehouse, Stoke Gifford and Walls.

WILTSHIRE
† Ashton.

At this point, in 1337, it looked as if Maurice de Berkeley had acquired an enormous windfall in the shape of the Giffard estates. But, in 1339, the year in which the king awarded John Maltravers VI his £100 annuity, the claim of the Maltravers family – if not of John VI himself – to these lands was recognised. By a convoluted legal procedure, Maurice de Berkeley of Uley was to hold the lands for life, and after his death they would pass to his nephew John Maltravers VII, whose parents were John Maltravers VI and Ela de Berkeley.[25]

Agnes Maltravers and Her Lands

The lands seized by the king on the grounds of the 'rebellion' of John Maltravers VI included the dower lands that John VI's wife Agnes de Bereford had inherited from her two previous husbands: John de Argentein and John de Nerford. In February 1331 Agnes was allowed income from these lands at the request of Queen Philippa, and in November 1331 she was granted her dower lands for life. This could hardly have been a spontaneous gesture by the queen, and it was probably Agnes who took the initiative in putting her case. She was a very bold and determined lady.[26] In 1335 she was given permission to grant leases of her dower lands which had been taken into the king's hands on account of the forfeiture of John Maltravers and afterwards 'granted to her by the king for her sustenance'.[27]

Sometimes Agnes had to deal with legal matters on behalf of her husband. For example, there was the ongoing case of Agnes Nevill who claimed she had been ousted from her manor of Barkham by John Maltravers and others before 1330. Agnes came to the king's council in 1334 to deny that she had any charters or other records concerning the case, but in the end Agnes Nevill regained her lands.[28]

In March 1336 Agnes Maltravers was pressed by Exchequer officials for the rolls and memoranda relating to her husband's position as Justice of the Forest 1329–1330. The need to return these records was probably not on John VI's mind when he fled. Agnes was given until September to deliver the documents to the treasury.[29]

John Maltravers V and the Maltravers Estates

By 1339, John Maltravers V, now aged about 73, was worried about what would happen to his lands if he died while his son was still banished and under sentence of death. The lands his son had acquired in his own name had already been forfeited. What of the core Maltravers holdings, which a traitor would not be allowed to inherit? John V therefore ensured that these lands would be inherited, not by his son but by his nephew, John Maltravers of Crowell, the son of his brother Robert. The lands were given to Henry Furneaux and Thomas de Homer, who regranted them to John Maltravers V in April 1339, with remainder to John Maltravers of Crowell. The Maltravers lands in question are listed as follows:[30]

DORSET
† Woolcombe, Langton Matravers, Lytchett Matravers and Witchampton.

WILTSHIRE
† Coate, Great Somerford and Longbridge Deverill.

SOMERSET
† Yeovil.

GLOUCESTERSHIRE
† Woodchester.

The Dorset manors of Wootton Fitzpaine, Frome Whitfield and Marshwood – forfeited by John Maltravers VI – had been granted to Robert Fitzpayn the elder and his wife Ela. In 1335, the reversion of these manors – if Fitzpayn and his wife died without any surviving children – was given to William Montagu.

Two other Maltravers manors – Worth Matravers in Dorset and La Pole in Wiltshire – were being held as dower by Maud Badlesmere, the widow of Robert Fitzpayn the younger. These manors too were to go to William Montagu if Maud, Robert Fitzpayn the elder and Ela Fitzpayn died without issue. These grants were confirmed by letters patent in 1339.[31]

Rathkeale in Ireland was demised, or leased, to John V's son Edward I, possibly as early as 1334 or 1335.[32] In January 1341, 'John Maltravers the elder' nominated two attorneys, one of whom was Edward, to look after his lands in Ireland while John V himself stayed in England.[33] By June 1341, John V had died. In that month, his widow Joan gave her lands in Cheshire to Sir Alexander de Venables, who later became her husband.[34] In September 1342, Alexander de Venables and Joan his wife, 'late the wife of John Maltravers the elder', nominated attorneys in Ireland.[35] The lease to Edward Maltravers I is mentioned again in 1351.[36]

There seems to have been no inquisition post mortem for John Maltravers V, so presumably his lands passed according to the arrangements he had made. The Maltravers manor of East Morden, Dorset, had been divided. Two-thirds of it was held from John Maltravers V by Stephen Loveras and his wife Alice, and – in January 1344, after the death of the tenants – this portion was committed to the keeping of John Maltravers the younger. The other third of East Morden was held in 1344 by James Moleyns and his wife Margaret, and it was agreed that after the death of Margaret Moleyns it, too, would pass to 'John Maltravers the younger' (presumably 'John Maltravers the younger' is John Maltravers VII, the grandson of the late John Maltravers V, but it may have been John Maltravers of Crowell, in accordance with the arrangements made by John Maltravers V in 1339).[37]

In 1344, Ralph de Ufford – the newly appointed justiciar – went to Ireland on the king's service, taking with him forty knights, a number of other men-at-arms and 200 archers. In preparation, protection was given to those accompanying him, including 'John Maltravers, chivaler' and 'John Maltravers the younger'.[38] 'John Maltravers chivaler [knight]' is probably John Maltravers of Crowell, whose career will be followed in Chapter 10. 'John Maltravers the younger' is John Maltravers VII. It is unlikely that his father, John Maltravers VI, was involved as he was still under sentence of banishment and, moreover, was occupied in Flanders.

The Crécy-Calais Campaign: Background

Edward III planned a massive invasion of France to take place in 1346. Earls and barons were to assemble with their retinues of knights, esquires, men-at-arms and archers. In addition, sheriffs were to recruit a given number of archers in their areas. The prince of Wales, later known as the Black Prince, was ordered to recruit 2,000 men in North Wales and 2,000 in South Wales, half of whom were to be spearmen and the other half archers. To encourage people to participate, those who would serve the king in the forthcoming war were offered pardons for any crimes they had committed.

The date of the muster at Portsmouth was set initially as 1 March, then postponed until May, then postponed again to the end of June due to storms. Eventually, an estimated army of 15,000 troops set sail in 700 ships, which was the largest force sent abroad in the Middle Ages. At about the same time, a small force under Sir Hugh Hastings set off for Flanders. There were already English soldiers in Gascony under the earl of Lancaster and in Brittany under Sir Thomas Dagworth. The destination of the main army was kept a secret, and the ships' captains were given sealed orders as to where to go if the vessels became separated. To everyone's surprise, it turned out that the landing place on 12 July 1346 was in none of these areas, but was at Saint-Vaast-la-Hougue in Normandy, on the eastern side of the Cotentin peninsula.

It may be that Edward III had intended to reclaim his ancestral duchy of Normandy, and hoped that the Normans would willingly accept him as their overlord. Any such plan was made impossible by the behaviour of undisciplined elements in his army, who went on an unauthorised rampage of looting and burning in Cherbourg, Barfleur, Valognes and Carentan. The people of Saint-Lô and Caen resisted as best they could, but they were overcome by Edward III's forces, with much destruction and loss of life.

The English then went on their marauding way eastward across northern France. They crossed the Seine at Poissy, which was one of several towns where a bridge had been destroyed to impede their progress. Edward III was able to deploy the carpenters he had brought with him, and, within a day, a temporary bridge had been constructed. Reluctant to force a confrontation with the French king so near Paris, Edward III changed direction and headed directly for the county of Ponthieu at the mouth of the Somme. Ponthieu had become a fief of the English Crown in 1279, but it had been confiscated by the king of France in 1337. Some of the men in Edward III's army may have known the county from the time it was under English administration. It may be that Edward III had always intended to take that route, since, while at Caen, he sent a letter to England requesting supplies and reinforcements (men-at-arms; bows, arrows and bowstrings; and money to pay the troops), which were to be conveyed to the seaport of Le Crotoy in Ponthieu.

The English army crossed the estuary of the Somme at low tide on 24 August, rested for a day in the forest of Crécy, and took up position on the hillside above the town on 26 August. They were arranged in three divisions: the right wing was commanded by the king's son, the sixteen-year-old Edward, prince of Wales; the left by the earls of Northampton and Arundel; and the centre by the king himself, who was able to view the whole battlefield from a conveniently sited windmill, and to direct the troops as necessary. The positioning of the archers has been a matter of some disagreement among historians, but it is likely that, rather than being on the extremities of the battle order, they were interspersed with the knights and spearmen for their mutual protection. The whole English army fought on foot. The French, who had been following them, marched from Abbeville to Crécy on the fateful day, but it was already afternoon by the time they arrived, and their troops were on lower ground, looking up westward towards the English. Their crossbowmen were at a disadvantage – being unable to counter the arrows from the English longbows – and retreated, blocking the advance of the mounted French knights. As night fell, chaotic hand-to-hand fighting continued. Many French nobles were killed, and their king fled the battlefield. The Battle of Crécy was a famous victory for the English against the French who had been considered the foremost military power in Europe.

The English then moved on to Calais, where they besieged the town for nearly a year. The inhabitants were starved into submission and surrendered on 4 August 1347. The English camp outside Calais grew into a small town, but it had its own problems, and many of the besiegers suffered from disease. Edward III finally returned to England in October 1347. The capture of Calais was of lasting significance as a foothold in France, and it remained an English possession for 200 years until it was lost under Mary Tudor in 1558.

The Crécy-Calais Campaign:
The Involvement of John Maltravers VI

John Maltravers VI was still under sentence of death, and could not come back to England to assemble his retinue and sail with the fleet to Normandy. He could and did, however, meet up with Sir Hugh Hastings in Flanders. Hastings sailed to Flanders soon after receiving his orders to do so on 20 June 1346.[39] John Montgomery, John Moleyns and John Maltravers VI were assigned to assist him.[40] Each of them had a personal retinue. From a later, uncertain, date in the campaign, Maltravers's retinue is given as follows: Sir John Maltravers with his retinue: one banneret (i.e. himself); two knights; nineteen esquires; twenty archers. Total: 42.[41]

Similar figures are given for two of the others: Sir Hugh Hastings with a total contingent of seventy-five and Sir John Montgomery with a total contingent of sixty-nine.[42] No figures are given for John Moleyns, but – as can be seen from adding them together – the four of them must have had over 200 men. They then recruited an army of several thousand Flemings. Estimates vary widely, but it was probably between 10,000 and 20,000.

With this sizable-but-undisciplined force, they invaded Artois in Northern France on 1 or 2 August, and besieged the town of Béthune until 24 August. The siege was then abandoned, and the Flemings returned to their homeland. Hastings and Maltravers were then about forty miles from Crécy as the crow flies, and the English king – having just crossed the Somme – was approaching Crécy from the other direction. It might have been just possible for some of Hastings's knights to ride swiftly to Crécy, if they had known in advance when and where the battle would take place, but co-ordinating troop movements in enemy territory was always difficult.[43] In any event, the link-up did not happen, and it is generally accepted that Hastings and his Englishmen were not at Crécy.

John Maltravers VI and the others joined the besiegers at Calais. By the time Calais had fallen, Hugh Hastings, John Montgomery and John Moleyns had all died due to either disease contracted at the siege or the rigours of the campaign.[44] John Maltravers VI had survived yet another hazard. Officially, he was still banished. Parliament met in September 1346, but – with the king and many lords away on campaign – the main business was raising money for the war, and Maltravers's case was not discussed.

Halfway through the siege of Calais, John Maltravers received a renewal of his permission to return to England: '26 February 1347. Renewal of the protection for John Maltravers [VI] the elder, knight, to come to England with a view to procure the reversal of the death sentence passed upon him in Parliament.'[45] The permission was repeated at the end of the year: '28 December 1347. Renewal, during pleasure, of the protection lately granted by the king to John Maltravers [VI] the elder, knight, after he had submitted himself to him in the port of Sluys in Flanders, to come to England for the purpose of endeavouring to obtain from Parliament a reversal of the judgment passed against him unheard and in his absence, in the Parliament of the fourth year of the king.'[46] Shortly before the first renewal of permission, John Maltravers appears to have risked a visit to England, since a writ addressed to the sheriff of Kent was issued on 23 January 1347, which prevented any arrest of body or distraint of goods, 'in favour of John Giffard of Bures, who had served in the retinue of Sir John de Maltravers [VI], and had gone to England with the said John de Maltravers, available to Easter'.[47]

Everyone in the army was entitled to wages at a daily rate ranging from 20 shillings for the prince of Wales to 2 pence for a Welsh foot soldier. Barons and bannerets such as John Maltravers VI would have received 4 shillings per day. On 2 June 1348, a payment is recorded to John Maltravers, banneret. The surviving Exchequer documents record the date when a payment is made, but not, unfortunately, the sum paid nor the period for which it was due.[48]

When the year-long siege of Calais was over, some of the houses in the town were taken from their French owners and given to Englishmen in order to ensure the security of the town. John Maltravers was given an inn and a house. The wording of the grant identifies the location of his property and gives a picture of how the French were being dispossessed: '10 October 1347. Grant... to John Maltravers [VI] and his heirs forever of an inn in the same town [Calais] late of Peter Rosty, contiguous to an inn late of James Doutchap towards the south, together with a low house and a wall of stone contiguous on the north to an inn late of John Gyle and now of Nicholas Shirlok, as well as the houses and void places contiguous to the same inn on the east as far as the High Street, and on the south as far as the inn late of James Pyket and on the north as far as the inn late of John Bouchecourt, "bereman".'[49] In other places, the inhabitants might be confirmed in their tenures, but now owing allegiance to the king of England, not to the king of France. One such grant was issued by John Maltravers VI, 'regarder' of the land of Louvain.[50]

At the end of the campaign, the government made good its promise to pardon felons who had served in the army. Hundreds of pardons were issued, with some specifying the crime committed, including theft of oxen, bringing false coin into England and an extraordinary number of murders. In each case, the head of the retinue vouched for the satisfactory military performance of the accused. For example, John Bidecumbe of Wodekesworth and John Broun of Knolle were pardoned for the death of John Caynel on the testimony of a John Maltravers, 2 October 1347. This must be John Maltravers VI as he was the head of a retinue.[51]

A Maltravers at Crécy

Although John Maltravers VI was not at the Battle of Crécy (but was at the siege of Calais), another member of the family was at Crécy. A soldier named John Maltravers served in the retinue of Richard Talbot, steward of the royal household. He had letters of protection on 20 May 1346 (before Crécy), and, as 'John Maltravers the younger', letters of attorney on 10 July 1347 (during the siege of Calais). Sir Richard Talbot was undoubtedly at Crécy, and there is no reason to doubt that this John Maltravers was there too.[52] The description 'the younger' is more likely to refer to the son of the elder John, rather than the cousin. Therefore, we will not deny John VII his moment of glory.

Lands

Ralph de Ufford fell ill in Ireland and died there on 9 April 1346. In his inquisition post mortem, it was found that he held land in Childrey, Berkshire. He also held Loders, Philipston and Up Wimborne by the king's grant to him and his male heirs, due to the forfeiture of John Maltravers VI. As Ufford had no male heirs, these lands reverted to the king who gave the keeping of Childrey 'during pleasure' to his clerk Walter de Worthe.[53]

6

BARON JOHN MALTRAVERS
BLACK DEATH, CHANNEL ISLANDS,
PILGRIMAGE AND RESTORATION, 1348-1354

The Black Death

In 1348, Europe was afflicted by the biggest calamity of the age: the bubonic plague, known to us as the Black Death. After arriving in Sicily at the end of 1347, in the following year it spread to Italy, then to France, and then moved inexorably northward, entering England in the summer of 1348. From 1348–49, first Dorset and then the rest of the country was affected. People died with appalling suddenness. It is estimated that between a third and a half of the population perished.

Affairs of state continued in spite of the impending catastrophe. At the parliament of January 1348, John Maltravers VI petitioned that the judgment against him – which was made in his absence in the 1330 parliament – should be reconsidered, and if it was found that the correct procedure had not been followed because he had had no chance to answer, the judgment should be quashed. He would then respond to any charges made against him. Together with 100 knights, he would swear that he was innocent of the crimes that had led to his banishment. He did not specify what these crimes might be. He stated that if his oath were not accepted, all the priests of England from the archbishops downwards should excommunicate him. He also declared that if no one would speak for him, he would defend himself personally against any accusers (other than people of 'the king's blood'). He did not attend the

January 1348 parliament in person, being 'absent in the service of the king', as indeed he had been since the judgment against him, and he referred to the 'great expense' he had incurred and how he had spurned the offers made to him by 'Philip of Valois' (being careful not to call him the king of France!).[1] There was no answer to his petition, and the matter did not come up in the next parliament, held in March 1348.

If he really was absent abroad on official business – and not just living secretly, albeit dangerously, on his English (or Irish) estates – where was he? Possibly at his house in Calais or with his friends in Flanders. As usual, the authorities knew where to find him. On 5 June 1348, John Maltravers VI and a merchant called Gilbert de Wellingborough were sent on a mission to Ghent, Bruges and Ypres on behalf of the king. They were to inform the chief men of these towns of the king's will regarding certain (unspecified) matters.[2]

Warden of the Channel Islands (1)

A few days later, on 11 June 1348, John Maltravers VI was appointed warden of the Channel Islands, which was a post that he held for several years. Although banished from England pending the review of his case, he was considered suitable for such an important job and was given responsible missions as long as they took place outside England.

The islands had been part of the Duchy of Normandy, but when the rest of Normandy was lost to France in 1204, the Channel Islands remained under the English Crown. The inhabitants continued to have cultural and family links to Normandy, and retained their own legal system. The islands were of strategic importance to England because of their position on the sea route to Gascony. The French attacked Jersey and Guernsey several times in the opening years of the Hundred Years War, and indeed took possession of Guernsey in 1338. They held it until 1345, when it was recaptured by the then warden Sir Thomas Ferrers, with a small band of Englishmen and seamen from Bayonne.[3]

Maltravers's letter of appointment refers to surveying and repairing the castles in the Channel Islands. It was important that they did not fall into French hands again:

> 11 June, 1348 Appointment for one year of John Maltravers [VI], the father, to have the keeping of the islands of Guernsey, Jersey, Sark and Alderney, and of the adjacent islands, as well as of the king's castles therein, with full power to do justice on malefactors in them as right requires and according to the laws and customs of those parts, to order and survey necessary repairs of the castles, and to see that payments [are made for these repairs and for the wages of all in the king's service] in the same islands and castles.[4]

On the same day, the sheriff of Somerset and Dorset was ordered to select a man-at-arms and 120 archers in those counties, to hold themselves in readiness to go to defend the islands of Guernsey, Jersey, Sark and Alderney when summoned by John Maltravers.[5] The documents never use a collective name for the Channel Islands, but always list the four main islands.

For the most part, John Maltravers had the authority to carry out the duties in his brief as he thought fit, but the king and his officials took a considerable interest in the Channel Islands. John received frequent instructions from Westminster on general policy matters, and even royal missives on particular cases that had come to the king's attention, which John Maltravers had to investigate and resolve.

Lands

The king's officials had not forgotten his predicament, and – as a further step towards restoring his lands – the custody of some of them was, remarkably, granted to his wife Agnes in August 1348. These were the lands formerly held by John Maltravers and now in the king's hands because of the death of Ralph de Ufford. They are listed as follows:

BERKSHIRE
† Childrey.

DORSET
† Philipston, West Moors, Up Wimborne, Loders, Eggardon, Cattescliff and Burton.

Agnes was to hold them for life. If she should predecease her husband, they were to be held by her brother Edmund de Bereford, and the clerks Philip de Weston and Nicholas Pynnok for the rest of the life of John Maltravers VI. After the death of the survivor of John and Agnes, they would revert to the king.[6]

John Maltravers VII

John Maltravers VII, son of John VI, returned home after the Crécy-Calais campaign. His uncle, Maurice de Berkeley of Uley had died on 12 February 1347 during the siege of Calais, while in possession of the Maltravers/Giffard lands. John VII was incensed to discover that an inquisition post mortem had been held – without his knowledge – on his uncle's lands, and that the heir was said to be Maurice's son Thomas, aged 13 or 14. This was contrary to the arrangement made in 1339 that these lands should pass to John Maltravers VII after his uncle's death. Accordingly, in September 1348, the younger Maltravers made a claim for the manors of King's Stanley and Rockhampton, Gloucestershire, and Sherrington, Wiltshire. A commission of inquiry was set up, but it appears that John VII's claim was not successful and the Giffard lands remained with the Berkeleys for the time being.[7]

John Maltravers VII went abroad with Richard Talbot in November 1348.[8] Sources that mention John VII do not give the purpose of this visit, and the Oxford Dictionary of National Biography entry on Richard Talbot does not mention it. However, it is likely that Richard Talbot, steward of the royal household, was accompanying the king, who went to France in that month in connection with a renewed truce with France. After the siege of Calais, a truce was arranged in September 1347, but it was failing in Flanders and northern France by July and August 1348. With the Black Death raging in France, another truce was agreed, and, unusually, Edward III decided to conduct the negotiations in person, travelling to Calais in November 1348 with the prince of Wales and other notables. The truce was extended to September 1349.[9] Richard Talbot must have asked John Maltravers VII to join his entourage on that occasion, following his good service at the Battle of Crécy.

We may imagine that John Maltravers VII returned home for Christmas 1348 hoping for further missions in the king's service. His family consisted of his wife Wentliana, his daughters Joan and Eleanor, and his infant son, called

– in a break with tradition – Henry. All around them, people were being struck down by the plague. It must have been a terrifying time.

Only a month later, on 22 January 1349, John VII died. The cause of death is not recorded, but the plague is the most likely explanation. He was probably in his thirties, and his trip abroad two months previously had been on a diplomatic mission, which was not in itself particularly hazardous.

Lands

The inquisition post mortem[10] found that John Maltravers VII held the following lands at the time of his death. Note the chilling reference to East Morden.

DORSET
† East Morden: two parts of the manor held of the king by service of rendering 8s. yearly at the Exchequer… 'The value is diminished at present because all the tenants are dead through the pestilence.'
† Lytchett Matravers: the manor held of Elizabeth de Burgh, by knight's service. Elizabeth de Burgh (or Elizabeth de Clare), 1295–1360, was one of the three sisters and co-heiresses of Gilbert de Clare, earl of Gloucester, who was killed at Bannockburn 1314.
† Martinstown: some land held of the heir of John Beauchamp of Somerset, a minor, by service of a quarter of a knight's fee.
† Witchampton: the manor lately held of Elizabeth de Burgh, but was granted to Wentliana (wife of the deceased) for her life, with remainders to the right heirs of the deceased.
† Woolcombe: the manor lately held of Elizabeth de Burgh, but was granted to Wentliana (as for Witchampton).

SOMERSET
† Yeovil: seven acres of land called the Newland, held of Elizabeth de Burgh by knight's service.
† Yeovil: the manor of Hendford, lately held of Elizabeth de Burgh, but a life interest was granted to Wentliana.

Wentliana, as the widow of a tenant-in-chief, would need the king's permission to remarry. In May 1349, the king's escheator for Somerset and Dorset was ordered to assign her, as dower, all the lands that her late husband had held at his death, provided that she took an oath not to marry without a licence.[11] In October, she was given the wardship of two parts of the manor of Rathkeale, County Limerick, to hold until John VII's heirs – her three children – came of age.[12]

Henry Maltravers

John VII's heir was his son Henry, who was 'aged one year on the feast of the Circumcision last', i.e. on 1 January 1349. If this was the actual anniversary of his birth, then he was born on 1 January 1348. Henry must have scarcely lived to his second birthday. By February 1350, he had died, possibly a victim of the plague. On 8 February 1350, the escheator of Somerset and Dorset was ordered to take Henry's lands into the king's hand and to make inquisitions post mortem.[13] There is no record of these inquisitions in the published calendars of inquisitions post mortem. Henry's sisters, Joan (aged about eight) and Eleanor (aged about five) would have been his heirs.

John Maltravers VI, Warden of the Channel Islands (2)

John Maltravers VI survived the plague. His one-year appointment as warden of the Channel Islands was due to expire in June 1349, and was renewed on 26 May 'until Michaelmas', and then was renewed on 27 September 1349 'until Easter twelvemonth', which would take him to the spring of 1351.[14]

One of John's tasks was to act as escheator, in which capacity, in 1349, he took into the king's hands the lands of Reginald and William de Carteret – father and son, respectively – who had died in early March, probably of the Black Death.[15] The heir was William's brother, Philip de Carteret, but as he had 'stayed among the king's enemies' in Normandy, Maltravers was ordered to take his oath that he would 'bear himself well and faithfully' towards the English king in future. Philip's pardon and restitution of his lands was confirmed in November 1351.[16]

The fortification of the town of St Peter Port, Guernsey, was a contentious issue between the islanders and the king. The people of the town had no safe refuge in case of attack. Castle Cornet was on an islet about a half a mile from the town, and only accessible on foot at very low tides; Jerbourg Castle, begun early in the fourteenth century, had been abandoned and was in ruins by 1350.[17]

The proposal to build a wall round St Peter Port seems to have come from the inhabitants themselves, for the king issued a licence in February 1350 for the 'good men of Port St Peter' to enclose their town 'with a good and strong wall, and to crenellate such wall', and to levy a 'custom' for the building expenses to be paid by buyers and sellers of merchandise for the period of a year from the following April.[18] The citizens liked the idea of a wall, but were unwilling to pay for it, claiming that the king had no right to impose a tax on them because they already paid a yearly tax called 'royal aid'. The king replied that the new tax was not for his own benefit, but was solely a means of raising funds for the wall, and he gave John Maltravers a commission on 4 August 1350: 'commanding him on his faith and allegiance to see that the custom is levied on all persons buying and selling merchandise in the island, for one whole year from St Bartholomew next [August 24], by some good men of the town and applied with all speed to the enclosing of the same, and that all persons found rebellious herein be committed to prison until the king give order for their punishment.'[19]

Even backed by the king's authority, Maltravers found it difficult, if not impossible, to get the islanders to carry out this task, and it may be that the wall was never built.[20] Historians differ on this point. Cox claims that it was built. Le Patourel says there is no contemporary evidence for its construction.[21] Gillian Lenfestey, in her online article on 'Medieval St Peter Port',[22] says that there would have been little point in building a wall around the town as St Peter Port is built against a steep hill and so could have come under attack from above. Five large stones, known as the Barrières de la Ville, probably mark the boundary of the medieval town. Instead of a town wall, a castle called La Tour Beauregard was built eventually at the southern end of the town. It was still under construction in 1357 (after John Maltravers VI's time as warden), and, in the 1370s, it is referred to as one of the defensive structures of the island.[23] There may also have been a Tour Gand at the northern end of St Peter Port, but very little is known about it.

The revenues that were due to the king from the Channel Islands – for example, rents, customs dues and fines – were collected by the king's receiver, who was an official appointed by the warden. In April 1350, John Maltravers was given a 'faculty' to remove the receiver and any other officials of the islands if they proved to be not suited to their duties, and to appoint others who were better suited.[24] After the payment of the wages of the castle garrisons, and other defence and administration expenses, the balance, if any, was sent to the Exchequer in London.[25] The warden was also required to audit the receiver's accounts, and to send the accounts to London.[26]

From time to time, the problem of the Church and its lands came up. The Channel Islands were in the diocese of Coutances in Normandy, and the advowsons and tithes of the parish churches were held either by Norman abbeys or by the abbey of Marmoutier near Tours. The king did not want the revenues of the Church to reach the coffers of his enemies in France. It appears that he ordered the warden to prevent priests appointed by French 'provisors' from taking up their benefices during the war. The result was that the islanders were being deprived of the rites of the Church, on which the salvation of their souls depended. The king therefore instructed John Maltravers, on 1 July 1350, to change the policy, and to allow priests to take up their duties if they agreed to reside in their parishes and to be faithful to the English king. They were to be allowed an income from their benefices sufficient for 'a reasonable maintenance', but the surplus was to be accounted for at the king's chamber.[27] Maltravers had already certified the loyalty of some of the Jersey parsons, and they were to be allowed to have possession of their benefices: Nicholas Galacien, parson of St Mary's; Nicholas Lorenir, parson of St Clement; Roger Hastein, parson of St Peter de Deserte; and Nicholas Hastein, parson of St Lawrence.[28]

Pilgrimage

John Maltravers VI soon found another project to take him far away from the islands and their troublesome inhabitants. In September 1350, he and his redoubtable wife Agnes obtained a licence to go on a pilgrimage to Rome with six grooms, several other servants and their horses. This was not just an individual decision. The pope declared 1350 to be a Jubilee year, and plenary indulgence was offered to those who made the pilgrimage to Rome. The Jubilee was a rare event, and thousands of people from all over Europe made the long and difficult journey. The English king was unhappy at the idea of barons, knights and other fighting men leaving the country when they might be needed at any moment, and required them to have licences if they wished to go on the pilgrimage. In all, over 250 pilgrims from England had licences, and – unless they were intending to walk all the way – each of them would have had horses and servants. Most of them travelled in or after September, and so John and Agnes would have had company on the journey. Of course, the fact that they had a licence does not prove that they went, but there is no reason to think they did not go. Having crossed from Dover to Calais, the journey to Rome by the ancient pilgrims' route, the Via Francigena – a round trip of about 2,400 miles – would take about six months. This route crosses the Alps at the Great St Bernard Pass, which would have been difficult in winter, so perhaps they went a different way.[29]

Warden of the Channel Islands (3)

When John returned from the pilgrimage, he involved himself again in the affairs of the Channel Islands. His appointment came up for renewal, and, on 6 April 1351, he was reappointed as warden from Easter 1351 to Easter 1352.[30]

As warden, John Maltravers VI was given 'full power to do justice on malefactors there and exercise jurisdiction in the king's name.' Usually, this was done through the bailiffs (one each for Jersey and Guernsey) and the prévôts (one each for Alderney and Sark), who presided over the courts. Judgments were given by jurats, of whom there were twelve each for Jersey and Guernsey, seven for Alderney and six for Sark.[31]

Another missive came from the king on 20 May 1351, ordering John Maltravers to compel the jurats to render justice more speedily, so that cases should not await decision for more than a year. The king had been told that some pleas before the bailiffs remained to be rendered for ten years or more as a result of favouritism and bribes, 'so that justice is denied to the people and the king is defrauded of his due'.[32] This communication from the king is referred to in a history of St Helier, Jersey, by De La Croix, published in 1845, who says that justice was so badly administered under John Maltravers VI that the king had to write him a severe letter of complaint. De La Croix correctly dates the letter to the 25th year of Edward III (25 January 1351 to 24 January 1352), but wrongly gives the calendar year as 1353.[33] This has misled later historians; for example, Langton, who says that the king's severe letter of reprimand in 1353 [sic] 'may possibly account for the appointment of William Stury as successor in the following year'.³⁴ In fact, the letter of 1351 did not lead to John VI's dismissal: he remained warden for another three years, and he would soon receive a remarkable sign of royal favour.

Meanwhile, he was continuing his duties, and going to and from the islands as required. On 28 May 1351, a safe conduct was issued for the master and mariners of a barge called *Lan*, 'which John Maltravers [VI], keeper of the islands of Jersey, Guernsey, Sark and Alderney, purposes to send to the islands for their safe-keeping, as well as for bringing back to England some anchors and cable for the king's use; and taking him and some of his men to the islands'.³⁵ This ship was to take John Maltravers to the islands, presumably from Dorset, although he had not yet cleared his name.

Restoration! (1)

A month later came a truly momentous day in John Maltravers VI's life: 20 June 1351. On that day, without waiting for a parliamentary sitting, the king's council dealt with the matter of John's outlawry and banishment. The king – with the assent of the prelates, dukes, earls, barons and others attending him in his council – ordered Maltravers's outlawry and the legal processes against him to be annulled, and his forfeited lands to be restored to him, since 'The said John both in Parliament and in councils has by his friends sued with the king with great insistence that that judgment on account of the death of the king's uncle, Edmund, earl of Kent, was not duly rendered, and that he was ready to prove himself wholly guiltless of the crime laid to his charge.'³⁶

The king granted his petition 'in consideration of the faithfulness he has always found in him' and recognising John's service 'in Flanders and elsewhere with great loss to himself and in spite of large offers from the king's adversaries to draw him from his allegiance'.

Only two days later, the clerks at the Chancery were busy sending out orders to the sheriffs and escheators in various counties to retrieve John Maltravers's forfeited lands and to restore them to him. These lands were as follows:³⁷

WILTSHIRE
† Corton, Sherrington, Codford and Stapleford: all committed to Maurice de Berkeley.

† Ashton Gifford: held for life by Margaret Giffard, with reversion to Maurice de Berkeley.
† Boyton: held for life by Margaret Giffard, with reversion to John de Warenne, late earl of Surrey.
† Broughton Gifford: held for life by Margaret Giffard, with reversion to John de Wylinton, and to his brother Ralph and to Ralph's wife Eleanor.
† Elston and Orcheston: both held for life by Margaret Giffard, with reversion to Ralph de Wylinton.

BERKSHIRE
† Childrey: granted to Ralph de Ufford.

GLOUCESTERSHIRE
† The castle and manor of Brimpsfield, and the manors of King's Stanley and Rockhampton: all granted to Maurice de Berkeley.
† Stonehouse, Stoke Gifford and Walls: all held for life by Margaret Giffard, with reversion to Maurice de Berkeley.

DORSET
† Loders, Philipston and Up Wimborne: granted to Ralph de Ufford.

The following individuals were notified that they now held certain lands from John Maltravers VI:

WILTSHIRE
John de Vere, seventh earl of Oxford, and his wife Maud de Badlesmere – who was formerly the wife of Robert Fitzpayn, the son – held the manor of La Pole as Maud's dower for her life, with reversion to William Montagu.

DORSET
Robert Fitzpayn and his wife Ela held Wootton Fitzpaine, Frome Whitfield, Marshwood and Worth Matravers, for themselves and the heirs of their bodies, with reversion to William Montagu in default of such heirs.

These instructions appear to have been sent out in a hurry, working from information readily to hand, which was out of date in some cases, as the sheriffs and escheators would no doubt discover. Three of the people named had already died: Margaret Giffard in 1338, Ralph de Ufford in 1346, and Maurice de Berkeley of Uley in 1347. Childrey, and the three Dorset manors of Loders, Philipston and Up Wimborne had been placed in the custody of Agnes Maltravers in August 1348.

On the same day, 22 June 1351, a letter was sent to Maurice Fitzthomas, earl of Desmond, concerning the manor of Rathkeale, County Limerick. It states that the manor is part of John VI's inheritance, but was held for life by Edward Maltravers I – John VI's brother – by a grant given by their father, John Maltravers V. This letter also explained that the king had learned that the earl of Desmond had entered the manor, pretending that it belonged to him by reason of John VI's forfeiture. The king stated that if it were forfeit, it would be forfeit to him and to none other. Therefore, it was to be restored to John VI in line with the pardon given to him. If the earl could show any reason why this should not be done, he was to tell the king about it without delay.[38]

There is a sequel to these transfers of lands. Ralph de Ufford, as already mentioned, died in 1346, and his lands were held by his widow Maud, who had the title countess of Ulster from her previous marriage to William de Burgh, earl of Ulster. It seems that she had to be mollified for the loss of her dower lands by the gift from the king of six tuns of wine yearly for life, to be delivered to her by the king's butler. A tun of wine was approximately 252 litres. When the butler demanded the payment of 20 shillings duty per tun, she protested. The king issued a further instruction, on 21 October 1351, that the countess was to receive the wine duty free. At the time, she was an Augustinian canoness, having entered the religious life after the death of Ralph de Ufford.[39]

Warden of the Channel Islands (4)

In Guernsey, some time before the momentous decision in the king's council, Peter de Saint Peter proposed to establish a new hospital or almshouse at Bouet ('Bowes') in St Peter Port. He intended to endow it with twenty virgates of land and eighty quarters of wheat annually. A licence in mortmain was required when founding an institution, typically a religious foundation, as the lord would no longer receive feudal dues as for an ordinary tenant; for example, on death or marriage. An inquisition *ad quod damnum* determined what damage would be done to the lord's interests or to the interests of others.

John Maltravers VI, in his capacity of warden of the Channel Islands, held the inquisition, and it was found that the king would not be disadvantaged as – by the laws and customs of the islands – he never had wardships or marriage dues there, but only received rents and services. Accordingly, a licence in mortmain was issued and recorded in the Patent Rolls on 28 June 1351.[40] This is the only detail given in some books of John Maltravers VI's time in the Channel Islands. It was probably considered significant because of the erroneous idea that Maltravers himself founded, or re-founded, the hospital. It is clear from the Patent Rolls that he merely held the inquisition *ad quod damnum*, which was a routine part of his duties.[41]

Soon after his pardon, John VI and Agnes Maltravers purchased an estate in the Channel Islands. This was Samarès Manor in Jersey, one of the three largest lay landholdings in the island. The king had confiscated it in 1340 from William de Saint Hilaire, who had sided with the French in the war, and, on 8 June 1347, granted it to Sir Geoffrey de Thoresby, a veteran of Crécy and Calais. The manor was held directly from the king, and therefore Geoffrey de Thoresby required permission to sell it to John Maltravers:

> 25 July 1351. Licence for Geoffrey de Thoresby to sell to John Maltravers [VI] and Agnes, his wife, the lands which he has of the king's gift in the island of Jersey, which escheated to the king by the forfeiture of William de Saint Hilaire, to hold in such manner as William held the same before his forfeiture, rendering to the king 24 livres [pounds] of the money current in the island yearly by the hands of his receiver there, as Geoffrey used to render…

John Maltravers thus became the seigneur of Samarès.[42]

Today, there is still a seigneur of Samarès, and the house – Samarès Manor – still stands, although it has been rebuilt over the centuries. The oldest part is the cellar or undercroft of the west wing, which dates from the eleventh or twelfth century, and has a vaulted, stone ceiling supported by two columns. It was probably used as a storeroom, perhaps for wine. Although this room is sometimes called the 'crypt', it is unlikely that the room above it was the chapel of the manor house since it is orientated north-south.[43]

Restoration (2)

Following his pardon in June, John Maltravers VI enjoyed the king's favour. In October 1351, Edward III wrote a letter to the steward of his chamber praising John Maltravers, specifically mentioning his 'goodwill and loyalty' and stating that 'he wished to do something grandiose for him'.[44]

On 18 November 1351, John received a summons to the next parliament, which was to be held from January to February 1352.[45] John VI duly attended, and personally presented a petition asking that the charter that he had received the previous June should be renewed in full parliament. His petition was read and approved by the 'lords and other great men of parliament', by the king and by the commons. The charter was therefore entered in the roll of parliament as follows:

> Edward [III] by the grace of God king of England and France and lord of Ireland to all those to whom these present letters come, greeting. Be it known that whereas John Maltravers [VI] has recently complained against a certain judgment on the occasion of the death of Edmund of good memory, late the earl of Kent, our uncle, made against the same John in our parliament held at Westminster in the fourth year of our reign of England [1330] when he was outside our said realm of England… [and] since he is prepared to stand trial in our court for every crime charged upon him in this matter… we will that the strictness of the said judgment and process that followed thereon be softened, and that he be graciously restored to the estate which he had before the return of the said judgment. And we, as a result of the fidelity and gratitude which we have always found in the said John, and for the great responsibilities which he afterwards undertook for us in various ways in parts of Flanders as well as elsewhere, in freely expending himself for us not without great loss of his goods, spurning the not insignificant offers of grace and reward made to him several times by our adversaries who would have drawn him from us to their side, …with the assent of prelates, dukes, earls, barons and other great and skilled men attending us, we have fully and completely restored the same John to the estate which he had before the return of the aforesaid judgment, in his person as well as in all his possessions and rights whatsoever, and… we wholly remit and totally annul all forfeiture, and also outlawry. And we have also granted to the same John that he shall again have all his lands and tenements which were thus said to be forfeited, being in our hands as well as in the hands of any others whatsoever by our

grant or in any other way. So that the said lands and tenements which were thus in the hands of others shall be reseized into our hands to be delivered to the same John... by us and our officials, to have and to hold to him and his heirs with knights' fees and advowsons of churches and all other things belonging to the same lands and tenements in any way, from us and our heirs and other chief lords of fees, as fully and completely as he held them before the return of the aforesaid judgment, and as he would have held them if that judgment had not been returned against him...

[If any people have acquired, between the judgment and the present date, lands belonging to John or to his heirs, their rights to these lands] shall lack all virtue of authority and shall be treated as null.

In witness of which we have made these our letters patent. Witnessed by myself at Westminster on 8 February in the twenty-sixth year of our reign of England and the thirteenth of France. [1352][46]

On the same day, 8 February 1352, letters patent were issued confirming the restitution of John Maltravers VI to his estate as it was before the judgment against him in the case of Edmund, earl of Kent, as agreed by parliament.[47]

It had taken over twenty years, but John Maltravers VI was now fully restored to his status and possessions by the king and parliament. John did not stand trial in parliament or in any other court, and there was no acquittal as such. By the king's clemency, the sentence against him was not to be enforced, his outlawry was annulled and his lands were restored to him. It may be that this painless procedure is the 'something grandiose' the king had alluded to in October. The death of Edmund, earl of Kent, is mentioned, but without specifying what John was supposed to have done in that case. Possibly, neither the king nor John Maltravers wanted to go into details of what happened in 1327–30. The death of Edward II is never an issue. John Maltravers VI resumed his life as a valued servant of the king, and the matter was never referred to again.

Warden of the Channel Islands (5)

John's appointment as warden of the Channel Islands was due to expire at Easter 1352. It was renewed well in advance – in fact, on 7 February 1352, the day before the aforementioned parliamentary proceedings. Unlike all his other letters of appointment, it had no end date, but was to be 'during pleasure'.[48]

Before long, problems arose in the Channel Islands that required his attention. On 10 March 1352, he made arrangements to spend at least a year there.[49] He had five assistants: Ralph de Horsy (described in 1353 as John Maltravers's lieutenant);[50] Alexander de Moulham; Thomas de Neuburgh, 'chivaler';[51] William de Blaunkeneye, clerk;[52] and Thomas Duraunt, king's serjeant-at-arms.[53]

A day later, the bailiffs and jurats of Guernsey were ordered to send the two best and strongest barges in the island – well fitted out, equipped and manned – to Weymouth, to bring back John Maltravers, on the king's service, before Low Sunday (April 15).[54]

Maltravers and his assistants were expecting trouble in the islands. The receiver, John Gaunt (not to be confused with John of Gaunt, son of Edward III) and John Cheny (a member of the garrison of Castle Cornet) had been assaulted by 'evildoers'. The evildoers had also prevented people from paying their rent to the receiver, thus depriving the receiver of the money needed to purchase victuals for the garrison, so that the castle was in danger of being lost. A commission of oyer and terminer was set up to deal with this crisis, with the commissioners being John de Saint Joyre, William de Feure and Robert Nicholas of Guernsey.[55] At the same time John Maltravers VI, William de Blaunkeneye and Thomas Duraunt were given a commission of oyer and terminer 'touching the accounts of bailiffs, receivers and other ministers of the king in the islands; with power to arrest any who refuse to render account before them'.[56]

Soon afterwards came news of a crime that had the makings of a diplomatic incident. The Genoese normally provided ships and crossbowmen for the French, but during this period of relative peace, on 30 July 1351, Edward gave 'protection and safe-conduct for one year' to Francis de Spinola of Genoa who was going to Guernsey to do business with merchants of Genoa on the island.[57] One of the Genoese ships was wrecked 'by the violence of the sea' at Guernsey. Sixteen named islanders and others boarded the vessel and carried off merchandise they found there, together with items washed up on the shore. Those islanders included Matthew de Sausmarez, who – as seigneur of Sausmarez – was normally entitled to the profits of wrecks occurring off the coast next to his lands. The Genoese merchants complained, and the king's council hastily added another commission of oyer and terminer, dated 18

April 1352, to John's list, for him and William de Blaunkeneye to take the necessary action. It was up to Maltravers and de Blaunkeneye to enforce the king's protection of the merchants against the islanders' customary rights.[58]

Alarmed at the general lawlessness in the Channel Islands, on 20 April 1352, the king's council authorised John Maltravers VI and William de Blaunkeneye to widen their enquiries to include 'trespasses against the king as against his ministers in the islands...'[59] and 'escheats and other profits and commodities which should pertain to the king there but have been withdrawn or concealed'.[60]

John Gaunt, who had been assaulted in early 1352, gave up his position as receiver on 15 July 1352.[61] In 1353, he complained that the government still owed him money. He said his claim had been disallowed because he 'had not the particulars thereof'. On 14 March 1353, orders were issued to John Maltravers and William de Blaunkeneye, auditors of the issues of the islands, to pay John Gaunt what he was owed, which was less than he was claiming: £8 for extents (rents, etc.); £13 18s. for his wages (he had claimed £23 18s. 6d. for wages for himself and an archer); and £17 4s. for repairing Castle Cornet.[62]

Later in 1353, John Maltravers VI left the Channel Islands, at least temporarily, for in October that year, while he was 'staying in England', he appointed an attorney to look after his interests in Ireland for one year.[63]

John Maltravers VI's wardenship of the islands came to an end on 2 April 1354. Sir William Stury was appointed warden for a three-year term to commence on that date.[64]

Summary of John Maltravers's Appointments and Periods of Office as Warden of Guernsey, Jersey, Sark and Alderney:

† On 11 June 1348: appointed for one year (until June 1349).
† On 26 May 1349: appointed until Michaelmas 1349.
† On 27 September 1349: appointed until Easter 1351.
† On 6 April 1351: appointed until Easter 1352.
† On 7 February 1352: appointed 'during pleasure', with no end date specified.
† William Stury became warden on 2 April 1354.

7

BARON JOHN MALTRAVERS
LAST YEARS, 1355–1364

When John Maltravers VI ceased to be warden of the Channel Islands he gave up his estate on Jersey. Philip de Barentin became the new seigneur of Samarès in about 1355, but there is no record of the normal permission to transfer the fief.[1]

In the last years of John's life, his adventurous days were over, and he stayed on his estates in Lytchett Matravers and elsewhere. As he was about sixty-six in 1356, the John Maltravers at the Battle of Poitiers in that year was probably his young cousin John Maltravers of Hooke and Crowell (see Chapter 10).

Lands

John VI was preoccupied with matters closer to home. Remembering the problems over his lands while he was in exile, he decided to safeguard Agnes's position by making her a joint holder with himself of the Maltravers lands. By a legal procedure, the lands were transferred to Henry de Tingewick and John Sturmy, who then regranted them to John Maltravers and Agnes his wife, to be held by John and Agnes and the 'heirs of their bodies', or in default of such heirs by the heirs of John Maltravers VI. The agreement was registered on 6 October 1356.[2]

Rathkeale in Ireland had been granted for life to John VI's brother Edward Maltravers I. After Edward's death in about 1353, John VI regained control of the manor, sending his attorneys to Ireland in 1353, 1355, 1356 and 1357.³ On the last occasion, the attorneys included John Maltravers of Crowell, to whom John VI demised (leased) the manor. When John Maltravers of Crowell died in 1360, Rathkeale reverted to the senior line of the family. Thus John VI regained this part of his inheritance and, in 1361, sent his nephew Roger to Ireland to act as his agent.⁴ (See Chapter 9 on Edward I and Roger, and Chapter 10 on the Maltraverses of Crowell.)

The Marriages of Joan and Eleanor

Baron John's granddaughters, Joan and Eleanor, needed to be found husbands. It might be supposed that Joan, the elder, would make the more prestigious match, but it was the younger sister, Eleanor, who caught the eye of the earl of Arundel as a suitable bride for his son, John Arundel. They were betrothed in 1357 when Eleanor was twelve years old and John Arundel was nine. It was arranged that the young couple would eventually inherit some of the Maltravers lands. The manors in question were Sherrington, Codford and half of Stapleford, all in Wiltshire; Kings Stanley, Gloucestershire; and East Morden, Dorset. All of these were being held by John and Agnes Maltravers for their lives. Also reserved for Eleanor was half of the manor of Elston, Wiltshire, which was held in the meantime as dower by Wentliana, Eleanor's mother, for her life.⁵ Eleanor Maltravers and John Arundel are said to have married in 1359 at the ages of about fourteen and eleven. Their first son was born in November 1364. (See Chapter 12 on Eleanor.)

There seems to have been no similar endowment of lands for Joan Maltravers, who married Sir John de Keynes in about 1362 when she was twenty and her husband was forty-one. Their first child, Wentliana, was born in 1363. (See Chapter 11 on Joan.)

Defence of the Realm

In 1360, the king asked John Maltravers VI to carry out another task that, although arduous, did not involve him personally in going anywhere to fight. Edward III was in France, initially campaigning in the north of the country, but then negotiating a peace. The outcome was the Treaty of Bretigny (1360), which brought the war to an end, but only temporarily as it turned out. England was to hold, in full sovereignty, a huge area of south-west France, including Gascony and Poitou, in addition to Calais and Ponthieu in the north. The ransom of the king of France, who had been in English custody since Poitiers, was to be three million gold crowns (worth about £500,000 in English money), which was reduced from the four million crowns previously demanded. In return, Edward III would give up his claim to the French throne.

Edward III and his council were afraid that the French might invade southern England during the king's absence. The country was put on high alert. In every county around the coast from Norfolk to Gloucestershire, and in some inland counties, men-at-arms and archers were to be arrayed ready to fight, some for local defence and others for action outside their own counties. As well as knights, there would be strong men who did not have their own armour, and these were to be suitably equipped. Men who were too weak to fight were to provide armour for the others and would contribute to the expenses. The letters appointing a commissioner for each county were sent out on 10 February 1360. Among the appointees were John Maltravers [VI] and his fellows, arrayers in the County of Dorset.'[6] John, now aged seventy, was still held in high regard.

A French force, intent on rescuing their king, did indeed invade at Winchelsea in March 1360, killing some of the inhabitants, and plundering and setting fire to the town before being repulsed by the Sussex militia.[7]

John Maltravers carried out his duties enthusiastically, but he overstepped the mark in demanding that certain priests find men-at-arms for the array. Master Richard de Netherhaven, prebendary of Slepe, and six others petitioned the king that they should be exempt from the military levy as they were already subject to the tax of a tenth for expenses of the war. This was agreed, and Maltravers was ordered to cancel the assessment on those clergymen.[8]

The Death of John Maltravers VI

After surviving many dangers in his long and eventful life, Baron John Maltravers died on 16 February 1364, aged about seventy-four, and was buried in the church of St Mary the Virgin, Lytchett Matravers, Dorset. He had been a warrior from Bannockburn to Calais; a rebel, then jailer of a king; a baron, keeper of the forest and steward of the royal household; a fugitive from the law, accused of bringing about the death of the king's uncle; an exile for twenty years who gained the wardenship of the Channel Islands and triumphant restoration; a diplomat; and a pilgrim – and, after everything, he died peacefully in his bed.

Lands

John's wife, Agnes, outlived him, and was entitled to hold most of his lands due to the agreement made in 1356. After Agnes's death, his heirs would be his two granddaughters: Joan, the wife of John de Keynes; and Eleanor, the wife of John, son of the earl of Arundel. Inquisitions post mortem showed that he held lands in three counties at the time of his death:[9]

DORSET

All his lands in Dorset were held jointly with his wife, Agnes.

- † East Morden: the manor held of the king in chief by paying 8 shillings a year.
- † Wootton Fitzpaine ('Wodeton in Marshwoodvale'): the manor and advowson of the church held of Roger de Beauchamp by knight's service.
- † Loders: the manor held of the abbot of Forde.
- † Frome Whitfield: the manor and advowson of the church held of the earl of Hereford by knight's service.
- † Lytchett Matravers: the manor and advowson of the church held of the duke of Clarence by knight's service.
- † Philipston in Wimborne St Giles: the manor held of the abbess of Wilton by knight's service.
- † Up Wimborne in Wimborne St Giles: two-thirds of the manor and half of the advowson of the church held of Robert Fitzpayn by knight's service; and other small parcels of land held of the prior of Christchurch, and of John and Joan Hamelyn.
- † Langton Matravers: the manor and advowson of the church held of the earl of Salisbury by knight's service.
- † Eggardon and Woolcombe: small parcels of land held of the abbot of Dunkeswell.
- † West Moors ('La More'): small parcels of land held of William de Beauchamp.

WILTSHIRE

The first four places listed were held jointly with Agnes.

† Sherrington: the manor held of the king in chief by knight's service.
† Codford: the manor held of the king in chief by knight's service.
† Boyton: the manor and advowson of the church held of the earl of Salisbury by knight's service.
† Corton: the manor held of Miles de Stapleton by knight's service.
† Stapleford: half of the manor held jointly by John VI and Agnes of the king by knight's service; and the other half of the manor held by John VI alone for life by gift of Henry Sturmy to whom the reversion belonged.

GLOUCESTERSHIRE

The first five places listed were held for life jointly with Agnes.

† King's Stanley: the manor held of the king in chief by knight's service, by John VI and Agnes Maltravers, and the heirs of their bodies; with remainder to John Arundel and Eleanor Maltravers, and the heirs of their bodies; and, failing such heirs, to the heirs of John Arundel.
† Woodchester: the manor and advowson of the church held of the earl of Salisbury by knight's service, with the same inheritance terms as for King's Stanley.
† Stonehouse: the manor held of the bishop of Worcester, with the same inheritance terms as for King's Stanley.
† Shurdington: the manor held of Sir James de Audley, lord of Badgeworth, by service of a pair of gilt spurs or 6 pence yearly, with the same inheritance terms as for King's Stanley.
† Minchinhampton: a small parcel of land held of the abbess of Caen, with the same inheritance terms as for King's Stanley.

The following three were held by John VI alone:

† Rockhampton: the manor and advowson of the church held by John Maltravers VI and the male heirs of his body, held of the king in chief by knight's service, with the remainder to Thomas, son of Sir Maurice de Berkeley and his heirs.
† Stoke Gifford: the manor held by John Maltravers VI and the male heirs of his body, held of the bishop of Worcester, with the remainder to Thomas, son of Maurice de Berkeley the younger, and the male heirs of his body.

† Walls: the manor held by John Maltravers VI and the male heirs of his body, held of the bishop of Worcester.

With regard to Rockhampton and Stoke Gifford, as John Maltravers VI had no surviving direct male heirs, the remainders would normally operate immediately. However, these manors, along with Walls, were assigned to his widow Agnes as dower, after she undertook not to marry without the king's licence.[10] In due course, the descendants of Thomas, son of the Maurice de Berkeley who died in 1347, took possession of Stoke Gifford, so founding the line of the Berkeleys of Stoke Gifford.[11]

There were also some manors listed as jointly held by John VI and Agnes in the 1356 agreement but that were not mentioned in the inquisitions post mortem. These were the Wiltshire manors of Coate, Winterbourne Stoke, Hill Deverill and Great Somerford (Somerford Mautravers); and the Berkshire manor of Childrey.

The Dorset manors of Witchampton and Woolcombe, and the Somerset manor of Hendford/Yeovil, were being held by Wentliana, widow of John VII, on a life tenancy.

Worth Matravers, Dorset, is not mentioned, although it was one of the manors forfeited in 1330 and restored in 1351. Later, it was a possession of Eleanor, granddaughter of John Maltravers VI, who was holding it at the time of her death in 1405.

The Gravestone of John Maltravers VI

John Maltravers VI was buried in the church of St Mary the Virgin at Lytchett Matravers. His tomb is under the floor of the north aisle, and is covered by a handsome and unusual grave slab. Instead of the normal brass effigy of a knight, it had just a brass fret (a version of the Maltravers arms) extending over the whole surface up to the inscription round the edges. The metal of the fret has long since disappeared, but the indents are still visible.

The gravestone measures approximately 2,692 x 1,371 mm (8 feet 10 inches x 4 feet 6 inches). Some older books say it is made of Purbeck marble, but the stone is now recognised as Tournai marble from the Low Countries.[12] John Maltravers must have seen monuments made of this material during the years he spent in Flanders, and would have thought – or perhaps a friend ventured to suggest – that it would make a suitable monument for himself. Whether he purchased the actual stone in his last years, or whether it was commissioned after his death, we do not know.

The black colour of the marble contrasting with the shiny brass metal made it ideal for representing 'sable a fret or' (on a black ground, a gold fret). This seems to be the first use of a single fret in the Maltravers arms instead of the previous version, 'sable fretty or'. A fret has a distinct hollow square or diamond shape, known as a 'mascle', in the centre of the design. Two long diagonal strips are woven in and out where they meet the edges of the mascle. Normally the mascle stops short of the available space, but here the diamond shape has been stretched right up to the inscription. Perhaps 'a fret' was a change in fashion, or perhaps it was considered that 'fretty' would look fussy on such a large area, as well as being more expensive to carry out. Either way, the fret certainly has a striking simplicity. (See heraldry illustrations and the drawing by Powell in this book.)

The Anglo-Norman inscription round the edge of the slab was produced in London. Two London workshops are known. The Maltravers inscription is assigned by its style of lettering to 'London B'. As is normal for the period, the lettering is in blackletter, sometimes called Gothic, with Lombardic capitals. The metal was an alloy of copper and zinc called latten, which was imported from Flanders or France.[13]

Like the fret, most of the lettering has vanished over the centuries. There is no record of the words on the two short sides. On one of them the deceased would have been identified, as in 'Here lies John Maltravers', or similar. On the two long sides were inscribed:

> *'Sage chyvaler en gere et pes Baron estoit enseigne Todiss A…*
> *… doigne remission aet qy pur salme uet prier * Grant pardon'*

This means:

> 'A wise knight in war and peace, he was ever a distinguished Baron …
> [May God] give him remission, and to whoever would pray for his soul
> * grant pardon'

The capital 'A' after '*Todiss*' is of unknown significance. The symbol '*' is a six-segment figure, possibly a rose, which perhaps symbolises the Virgin Mary.

The earliest record of the wording is in the first edition of Hutchins's *History of Dorset*, (1774), where the inscription is as previously given, but without the word 'pardon'.[14]

In 1796, Richard Gough reproduced Hutchins's illustration in his multi-volume work *Sepulchral Monuments in Great Britain*.[15] Gough visited Lytchett Matravers in person, and commented on his impressions of the church, noting that, 'There is something uncommonly plain in the windows', but did not say whether the inscription as he saw it was exactly the same as in Hutchins.

The antiquary David Thomas Powell visited Lytchett Matravers church in 1810.[16] Powell (*c*. 1772–1848) devoted most of his life to collecting materials on heraldry and genealogy, visiting churches and manor houses all over England and Wales, and making his own watercolour sketches. His drawing of the Lytchett Matravers inscription is carefully measured. He has shaded in the dark background to the fret and has drawn a little six-petal flower, which is more naturalistic than the original, after '*prier*'. He noted that some words on the first line, which he had seen in Gough's book, were now missing. At the end of the last line he added the word 'pardon', which is in no other source. He gives the surviving inscription as follows:

'*Sage chevaler en gere et pes Baron…*
doigne remission et qy pur salme uet prier * Grant pardon'

In the third edition of Hutchins in 1868,[17] which was produced after Hutchins's lifetime, it is said that the brass of the fret had gone, leaving indents in the stone where it had been. It is also wrongly said that the partial inscription recorded in the first edition had completely vanished.

When a delegation from the Dorset Natural History and Antiquarian Field Club went to examine the memorial in 1924, the members were pleasantly surprised to see that, while the fret had gone, the following words of the inscription remained, with the word 'grant' having become loose and being 'hooked out by Mr Prideaux from under the floor of the pew':[18]

'*doigne remission aet qy pur salme uet prier * Grant*'

The 1924 visitors had been told that, in the missing part of the inscription, '*Todiss*' ('always') was a mistake for '*Jadis*' ('formerly'). As a result, '*Jadis*' has been preferred in some subsequent depictions. This amendment is not justified. 'Formerly' implies something in John VI's past; as in, for example, 'he was at one time steward of the king's household'. 'Always' fits the sense of the inscription better, since the status of baron continued to the end of his life, and indeed was a title passed to his descendants. Hutchins clearly shows '*Todiss*', which is an Old French version of '*toujours*' ('always'), and as no one since his time has seen the word in question, we should rely on him to have recorded accurately what he saw.

In 1975 or 1976, the eight words: '*doigne remission aet qy pur salme uet prier *'* were still in place, and a rubbing was made by students from Hamline University, USA.[19]

The gravestone is not accessible at present and can only be seen by special arrangement with the vicar. The surface and the edges are very much degraded, due not only to the passage of time but also to the deplorable incident in the 1880s when the north aisle, including the slab, was covered by six inches of concrete on the orders of the squire of the manor. The rector of the time fought a successful campaign to have the concrete removed.[20] At some time, the west, north and east edges were repaired and partly covered in cement, and that is how it appears today. It is only possible to measure up to the edge of the cement, giving slightly lower dimensions of 2,590 x 1,346 mm (8 feet 6 inches x 4 feet 5 inches). The strip with '*doigne remission aet qy pur salme uet prier *'* is still in place and in good condition. There are, in fact, two strips butted together, with a break after '*remission*'. '*Grant*' is still missing.

According to local legend, John Maltravers was buried in full armour.

Another local story concerns a lady who was alone in the church doing the flowers, and was moved to take pity on John Maltravers. As she knelt and said a prayer for the repose of his soul, she heard a deep, long-drawn sigh close behind her and felt an icy-cold breath on her neck, at which she fled from the church and ran up the hill to her home. The incident is said to have taken place in 1924.[21]

8

AGNES DE BEREFORD, LATER ARGENTEIN, THEN NERFORD, THEN MALTRAVERS

In 1329 or 1330, Agnes de Bereford must have been happy to be marrying such an important man as John Maltravers VI, keeper of the forest south of the Trent and steward of the king's household. Her father, too, had been a royal official: he was William de Bereford, chief justice of the common pleas, who had died in 1326. Simon de Bereford, escheator south of the Trent, was probably her kinsman, although no evidence of the relationship has been found. She had already been widowed twice at that time. From her first marriage – to John de Argentein, who died in 1318 – she had one son, John, then aged eleven or twelve. Her second husband, John de Nerford, had died only lately, on 5 February 1329.

Less than two years after her third marriage, Roger Mortimer and Simon de Bereford were tried and executed, and her husband – convicted of bringing about the death of the earl of Kent – fled the country with a price on his head. Agnes was in a precarious position as the wife of a rebel, but she showed immense courage and determination in regaining control of her Argentein and Nerford dower lands, and in obtaining permission to visit John Maltravers in Flanders 'for such time as she shall please'. As a woman on her own, she would have needed an armed escort. John and Agnes must have been able to send messages to each other somehow, as she would have needed to know when it was safe to travel, and it seems that his whereabouts were not completely secret.

There must have been great relief and jubilation when he was eventually pardoned in 1351, and John and Agnes were able to resume their life together.

In February 1364, on the death of John Maltravers VI – with whom she had shared so many perils, adventures and narrow escapes – Agnes was left a widow for the third time. She was very well-off, being in possession of numerous manors spread over southern England, and one in Ireland.

Lands

Agnes still had dower lands from her previous marriages. From her first husband John Argentein, she held the Hertfordshire manors of Great Wymondley and Little Wymondley, and the Cambridgeshire manor of Melbourn. From her second husband John Nerford, she held the Suffolk manor of Wissett, and the Norfolk manors of Tharston and Shotesham.

Most of the Maltravers manors had been held jointly by John VI and Agnes, as agreed in 1356 and as recorded in John's inquisition post mortem,[1] and she was now entitled to sole possession, as conceded in the Close Rolls[2] in April 1364. There were also some manors that she was shown to hold by later events (including Agnes's own inquisition post mortem).[3]

In addition, the escheator in Gloucestershire was ordered to take Agnes's oath that she would not marry without the king's licence, and was then to assign to her, as dower, three manors that had been held by John Maltravers VI alone. These are not named in the Close Rolls, but are named in John's inquisition post mortem as Rockhampton, Stoke Gifford and Walls. After her death, the reversion would belong to Maurice (aged seven years in 1364), son of Thomas, son of Maurice de Berkeley of Uley (died 1347). There had previously been a dispute between the Berkeleys and the Maltraverses about these former Giffard manors, but the Berkeleys were going to have to be patient a bit longer.

From combining the information from these sources, Agnes's Maltravers manors were as follows:

DORSET
† The manors of East Morden, Wootton Fitzpaine, Loders, Frome Whitfield, Lytchett Matravers, Langton Matravers, Philipston, Witchampton (Agnes's inquisition post mortem); and land in Up Wimborne, Eggardon, Woolcombe and West Moors.

GLOUCESTERSHIRE
† The manors of King's Stanley, Woodchester, Stonehouse, Shurdington,

Rockhampton (dower), Stoke Gifford (dower), Walls (dower) and land in Minchinhampton.

WILTSHIRE
† The manors of Sherrington, Codford, Boyton, and Corton, and half of the manors of Elston (Agnes's inquisition post mortem) and Stapleford.

BERKSHIRE
† The manor of Childrey (later used by Agnes to endow a chantry at Lytchett Matravers).

SOMERSET
† The manor of Hendford (Agnes's inquisition post mortem) and land in Yeovil.

IRELAND
† The manor of Rathkeale (later the subject of litigation on Agnes's behalf).

Thus, she had twenty-seven manors in nine English counties, one manor in Ireland, and some other lands to her name. Even in old age, she expected to visit at least some of them in person from time to time. She must have employed a considerable number of people to help her manage her estates and would have been the lady of the manor to a huge number of tenants.

Rathkeale

Sometimes legal issues arose, at which Agnes did not hesitate to stand up for her rights. One of these concerned the manor of Rathkeale in Ireland, which had been a Maltravers possession since 1281. On an unspecified date, but probably around 1339, John Maltravers V leased it for life to his nephew John Maltravers of Crowell, in order to keep it in the family in spite of the exile of John VI. In October 1349, two-thirds of it were allocated to Wentliana, widow of John VII.

By 1351, when John Maltravers VI was pardoned, Rathkeale was being held by Edward Maltravers I on a life tenancy 'of the inheritance of John [VI]'. The earl of Desmond claimed that it should have been forfeited to him, due to the conviction and banishment of John VI, whereas the king said it was held in chief, and if it was forfeited to anyone it should be to the Crown.

After the death of John VI, the status of Rathkeale became an issue, with the king saying that – as it was held in chief – John V should not have alienated it without permission. The Maltravers family said that they held it from the countess of Desmond, thereby keeping it out of the hands of the king's escheator. There were several attempts to sort things out, but it was a complex matter that dragged on for at least nine years.

In May 1365, Exchequer officials were told to allow Agnes, widow and executrix of John Maltravers VI, more time to hand over the issues or the value of the manor of Rathkeale, while she sued in the court of Ireland.[4]

In November 1367, a date for a hearing in Chancery was set for just after the following Easter. The petitioners for the Maltravers family were John de Keynes (knight) and his wife Joan; John Arundel and his wife Eleanor; and Agnes, the widow of John Maltravers [VI].[5]

By May 1371, Agnes appeared to have won her case in Ireland ('the king has learned that it was found by due process in Ireland that the said manor is not held in chief'), but the Exchequer was still pressing her for the issues of Rathkeale. A stay until January 1372 was ordered; meanwhile, the chancellor of Ireland and others were ordered to search the rolls and memoranda there, and to report back to the Chancery in England with fuller details on the 'circumstances relating to Rathkeale'.[6]

It seems that nothing had happened by October 1372, and, in the same words as before, the officials at the Exchequer were ordered to stay their demand on Agnes for another three months, and the officials in Ireland were again ordered to search their documents and to report to the Chancery in England.[7]

The matter was still unresolved in December 1374, and by letters patent another date was fixed for a hearing 'before the king in Chancery' in June 1375. The issues were rehearsed just as in the previous commission in 1367, and no mention was made of the decision in Agnes's favour in an Irish court in 1371. The Maltravers family petitioners were now Robert Rous (knight) and his wife Joan (John de Keynes having died), John Arundel and his wife Eleanor, and Agnes, the widow of John Maltravers VI and executrix of his will.[8]

That was the end of the story as far as Agnes was concerned. It had baffled many people and remained unresolved.

Defence of the Realm

As a landowner in her own right, Agnes had responsibilities in a national emergency, and we have a glimpse of her lifestyle in 1370. The king heard that the French were assembling a great fleet to invade England, 'to wipe away the king and his realm and all the English tongue'.[9] In November of that year, the sheriffs of Dorset and all the other counties along the south coast were instructed to proclaim that all those holding land in these counties should at once go to those lands, and array their men and tenants to be ready by the following February to defend the sea coast from attacks by the king's enemies.

Agnes responded by finding men for the defence, and by sending some of her household in advance, while she herself made ready to follow them as quickly as she could, bearing in mind 'her great age, owing to which she may not suddenly depart thither without great peril of her body'. The sheriff was evidently urging her to hurry, but she protested that she was doing her best, and so a letter was sent from Westminster on 18 February 1371 to the sheriff of Dorset telling him to allow Agnes until Whitsuntide (25 May) to 'abide in Dorset'.[10]

The Maltravers Chantry at Lytchett Matravers

Later in 1371, aware of her failing health and with an eye to the hereafter, Agnes set up a chantry at Lytchett Matravers. The parson of Lytchett Matravers, John Sonnynghull, was to find three chaplains to celebrate divine service every day in the parish church for Agnes while she lived, for her soul after death, and for the souls of John Maltravers VI and the fathers, mothers, brothers, sisters and ancestors of John VI and Agnes.[11]

The chantry was endowed with the manor of Childrey and seven acres of land in Letcombe Regis. Agnes paid the king £60 to alienate the land in mortmain. The Maltravers manor in Childrey had been in the family since about 1194. In 1348, during John Maltravers VI's exile, it was entrusted to Agnes, and then, after John VI's rehabilitation, it was held by John and Agnes jointly.[12]

In May 1374, more land was added to the chantry's endowment. John Sonnynghull paid the king £10 to alienate in mortmain a 'messuage' (a dwelling house with its surrounding land), a carucate of land and 16 shillings of rent in Childrey, which was to be used for the sustenance of the three chaplains who were to celebrate divine service for Agnes and for her soul after death, and for the souls of John Maltravers VI, Edmund Danvers and their ancestors and heirs. Edmund Danvers held some land in Childrey, and presumably sold it to Agnes for the chantry.[13]

The chantry was not established immediately due to the death of John Sonnynghull around that time, but the alienation of the two portions of land is repeated in letters patent on 20 March and 28 March 1378, the Lytchett Matravers parson then being John de Claydon.[14]

A chantry could be just an institution, with a priest or priests, and an endowment to pay them. Often, the chantry took the physical form of a chapel, or at least an altar, where Mass would be celebrated for the nominated people. If Agnes's chantry had its own altar, it was probably in the north aisle, near the Maltravers tombs.

Agnes expected her chantry to continue indefinitely, but it came to an end with the dissolution of the chantries in 1547, at the beginning of the reign of Edward VI. The lands and goods of the chantries were seized by the Crown, and granted or sold to laymen. The Maltravers manor in Childrey was granted to John Fowler and John Phillpott,[15] and was never again in the hands of the Maltraverses or their descendants.

The Will of Agnes Maltravers

On 18 February 1375, Agnes made her will. A copy of it survives in the archives in Lambeth Palace.[16] In it, she commends her soul to God, and wishes her body to be buried next to that of her husband in the church at Lytchett Matravers if she dies in Dorset or Wiltshire, in the Priory of Wymondley if she dies in Hertfordshire or Cambridgeshire, or in the nearest house of friars if she dies elsewhere. She wishes her funeral to be very simple, with no pomp ('bobance'). Priests are to say Masses for her soul, and five candles are to be placed on her grave. She makes gifts to churches and to a long list of houses of friars.

Family members are remembered next in a list of bequests:

† To the earl of Arundel is given a tablet of silver and gold with an enamelled image.
† To Eleanor Arundel – Agnes's step-granddaughter, wife of John Arundel – is given a gold clasp.

† To John Argentein, Agnes's son, is given a 'dozer' (a cloth to hang at the back of a bed) in green, decorated with dolphins and swans; a set of four side pieces;[17] and her great silver goblet and various silver dishes, which are to go to the Priory of Wymondley after his death. John is enjoined not to make trouble for the executors when they take profits from the other goods.

† To Margaret, wife of Agnes's son John Argentein, is given a *'tabler de epicerie'* (a spice table) and 12 marks.

† To Maud, a daughter of John Argentein, is given Agnes's great primer, which is to be passed down through the family from one generation to the next.[18]

† To Maud's husband, Sir John Fitzwaryn, is given a gold clasp and a silver cup.

† To Elizabeth, the other daughter of John Argentein, is given a counterpane of yellow silk with four yellow carpets.

† To Elizabeth's children is given 10 marks.

† To Elizabeth's husband, Baldwin St George, is given a gold ring.

† To William Ellesfield, Agnes's nephew (son of her sister Joan), is given 100 shillings.

† To Roger Maltravers, Agnes's nephew by marriage, is given a set of bed hangings, including a coverlet with 'popinjays' (parrots), a canopy, a mattress, a pair of lintels of three leaves, a canvas and a cloth of silver; also two silver coins known as guilders. Roger is named as one of her executors.

There are bequests to friends, and executors are appointed. Servants are not forgotten, with gifts of 20 shillings each to her two damsels, to Dame Clarice Hodham, to each 'valet of menial office', to William Good and to Jack of the chamber. After paying any debts, the residue is to be used for chantry Masses for her soul.

The Death and Burial of Agnes Maltravers

Agnes died in July 1375 (the exact day is uncertain as the inquisitions post mortem in different counties give different dates), and she was buried not at Lytchett Matravers or at the Priory of Wymondley, but in the Greyfriars Church, London. Many people of high rank were buried there.

The Greyfriars friary was dissolved by Henry VIII in 1538. Many of the tombs were destroyed soon afterwards, but, fortunately, a register of burials had been compiled. From this, we learn that Lady Agnes Maltravers, '*domina* Agnes, *domina de* Matrevers', was buried in the part of the church known as 'coram altaribus' (in front of the altars).[19]

The Greyfriars church became a parish church called Christ Church. It was destroyed in the Great Fire of London in 1666. Wren's replacement church was largely destroyed by enemy bombing during the Second World War, leaving only the tower, and was not rebuilt. There is now a garden where the nave used to be.

Lands: Inquisitions Post Mortem

Agnes's lands at the time of her death are as listed under 'Lands' near the beginning of this chapter, except that she no longer held Childrey, which had been alienated for the chantry, and that her dower lands of Rockhampton, Stoke Gifford and Walls passed automatically to the Berkeley family.

Details of the succession of her other lands are in the inquisitions post mortem held in 1375.[20] The Argentein lands are to go to her son and heir, John Argentein. The Nerford lands are to go to Margery, wife of John Brewes and great-niece of John de Nerford, Agnes's second husband.

The Maltravers lands in Dorset, Somerset, Wiltshire and Gloucestershire are to go to John Arundel and Eleanor Maltravers, and then to the 'heirs of their bodies'. Contingency plans were made for there being no such heirs, but, in the event, John Arundel and Eleanor had several children and descendants, and so the lands passed to the Arundels.

No specific provision was made for Joan Maltravers, although she was a co-heiress with her younger sister Eleanor. She only had a remote chance of a look-in with regard to some, but not all, of the lands if the proposed lines of succession failed. (See Chapter 11 on Joan.)

9

ROGER MALTRAVERS I AND II, EDWARD MALTRAVERS I AND II, AND WILLIAM MALTRAVERS IV

Roger Maltravers I

Roger Maltravers I was a brother of John Maltravers V. The relationship is specifically mentioned in Roger's inquisition post mortem in 1351. Roger accompanied his brother to Ireland in 1299. In 1306, after the 'Feast of the Swans' knighting ceremony, he had letters of protection in preparation for joining the military expedition to Scotland.

Roger seems to have been based in Lytchett Matravers; he also had a connection with Gloucestershire, where he held a small amount of land. Acting as procurator for his brother John V, he presented a priest, Thomas de Bocklande, to the church of Lytchett Matravers in March 1316.[1] Roger Maltravers (probably Roger I), John Maltravers (V) and ten others were paying taxes in Lytchett Matravers in 1332.

In 1325, as a man of Gloucestershire, Roger I was summoned to Portsmouth to serve as a foot soldier in a force that was about to set out for Gascony, but he refused to go. He was by no means alone in this, and, in April, the sheriff of that county was ordered to arrest him and over 100 other reluctant soldiers,[2] and was ordered a few weeks later to arrest a further contingent of mutineers from Gloucestershire and the Forest of Dean. The king, Edward II, had the greatest difficulty in raising troops to serve with John de Warenne, earl of Surrey, who was the commander of the fleet.

Roger I died on 14 December 1348, possibly another victim of the Black Death, although he would have been quite elderly by then and so his death was not unexpected. The inquisition post mortem into Roger's lands took place, belatedly, in September 1351.[3] He was found to have a house and a small amount of land in Little Shurdington, within the manor of Badgeworth, Gloucestershire. His heir was his nephew, John Maltravers VI, identified as 'John Maltravers, son of John Maltravers brother of the deceased, aged 60 years'. This fits very well with John VI, who was born in about 1290 and therefore sixty-one in 1351. Normally, an inquisition post mortem was held within weeks of a person's death, and the long delay is unusual. Perhaps the agents of John VI were stalling in the hope that his difficulties would be overcome, as indeed they were with the annulment in June 1351 of the proceedings against him. Then he could claim his inheritance, and Shurdington duly appears in John VI's own inquisition post mortem in 1364.

Edward Maltravers I

Edward Maltravers I was a younger brother of John Maltravers VI. His date of birth is not known, though it was possibly about 1292, as John VI was born in about 1290.

Edward Maltravers enjoyed taking part in politically motivated vandalism in the reign of Edward II, but he lacked his elder brother's talent for attaching himself to a powerful patron and so raising his own status. And what a dangerous game that could be.

Edward first came to the notice of the authorities in 1320 when he was accused of breaking the park of Roger Damory at Tarrant Gunville, and a commission of oyer and terminer was set up to deal with the incident.[4]

In 1321, John Maltravers VI and his brother Edward were involved in the rebellion against the Despensers. In August, King Edward II agreed to banish the Despensers, and the rebels were pardoned. In the Patent Rolls, there is a long list of those pardoned, including Roger Mortimer; Roger Damory; John Giffard; Maurice de Berkeley and his son, another Maurice; Edward Maltravers (all on August 20); and John Maltravers VI (on September 15).[5]

Trouble between the king and the magnates soon broke out again, and, on 5 January 1322, the order was given to arrest 'John Maltravers the son [John VI]', Edward Maltravers and others.[6] This rebellion culminated in the Battle of Boroughbridge. If Edward Maltravers was still with the rebels, he seems to have slipped away and was not pursued. Apparently, he did not flee abroad, as he was still in England the following year and engaged in violence again. On 11 December 1323, a commission of oyer and terminer accused Edward and many others of entering the property of Richard de Portes: 'They broke his gates and doors at Wardesford and Winterborne Steepleton, cut down his trees and carried them and his charters, bonds and other things away, and coursed in his free warren, and carried away rabbits.'[7]

After John VI was forced to go into exile in 1330, Edward Maltravers was given a life tenancy of Rathkeale, Ireland, by his father, John Maltravers V.[8]

The name of Edward Maltravers's wife is not known. He had a son, Roger Maltravers II. Edward had died by 1354 when a settlement of the manor of Sherrington, Wiltshire, placed his son Roger – but not Edward himself – in the line of succession.[9]

Roger Maltravers II

Roger Maltravers II, son of Edward Maltravers I, married Agnes, daughter and heiress of John de Dullar, and in doing so linked the adjoining manors of Lytchett Matravers and Dullar.

Roger II's uncle, John Maltravers VI, sent him to Ireland to see to John's estates there, presumably Rathkeale: '3 April 1361, John Maltravers, "chivaler" [knight], staying in England, nominated Roger Maltravers and William Dullar as his attorneys in Ireland for one year.'[10] William de Dullar was probably a kinsman of Agnes de Dullar.

In 1375, Roger II was an executor of the will of his aunt by marriage, Agnes Maltravers. She left him some valuable items, among them bedding materials, including a canopy, a mattress and a coverlet embroidered with 'popinjays' (parrots, a fashionable motif). She also gave him a cloth of silver and two guilders of silver.[11]

Roger himself had died by about 1380. His widow, Agnes de Dullar, remarried twice: first to Robert Bont and then, by 1383, to John Levesham, who represented Salisbury in the parliaments of 1401 and 1404.[12]

Edward Maltravers II

This Edward was the son of Roger Maltravers II and Agnes de Dullar. He was left one mark in the will of John Maltravers of Hooke and Crowell who died in 1386 (see Chapter 10). Eleanor Maltravers, who died in 1405, left him a gold clasp; this may have been the same gold clasp that was left to Eleanor by Agnes Maltravers in 1375.

When Edward II's mother (Agnes de Dullar) died in 1400, the manor of Dullar came into the possession of her third and last husband (John Levesham), who then relinquished it to Edward Maltravers, his stepson. Edward leased out some of the manor, but he was still in possession of the rest of it when he died, which was at an unknown date but before John Levesham. After Edward's death, Dullar was held by John Levesham again. According to Hutchins, Edward died without issue,[13] and this is borne out by the fact that no Maltravers claimed Dullar when either Edward or John Levesham died.

John Levesham died in May 1417 or 1418. Inquisitions post mortem were held in Wiltshire and Dorset to determine who was his heir. In Dorset, the twelve jurors laid out in great detail how Dullar had been inherited by Agnes de Dullar and, after her death, had passed to John Levesham, who allowed Edward Maltravers II to hold it. The reversion (the right to the manor after John Levesham) belonged to Edward. Significantly, the jurors state that Edward died without issue, whereupon ownership of the manor descended to Thomas Hussey, a distant cousin of Agnes de Dullar, and they explain the exact relationship, going back to Agnes's grandfather John de Dullar, from whom both Agnes de Dullar and Thomas Hussey were descended.[14]

Since Edward Maltravers II died without issue, this line of the family – Edward I, followed by Roger II, followed by Edward II – comes to an end.

William Maltravers IV, Clerk

From 1314 to 1316, William Maltravers IV was the rector of the church of St Mary the Virgin, Lytchett Matravers. He was presented by Sir John Maltravers V, the lord of the manor.[15]

The relationship of William IV to the rest of the family is not known. Perhaps he was another younger brother of John VI. If so, he was probably only a teenager when he became rector, or twenty at the most. This is not impossible, especially with his father being the patron of the living. The high-flying Thomas Arundel, son of the third earl of Arundel, was made bishop of Ely at the tender age of twenty in 1373, and later became archbishop of Canterbury.

10

ROBERT MALTRAVERS AND THE MALTRAVERSES OF CROWELL AND HOOKE; BROWNING AND STRANGWAYS DESCENDANTS

Robert Maltravers and his descendants, being a junior branch of the family, were not in line to inherit Maltravers property, but within three generations – by a series of fortunate marriages to heiresses – they became considerable landowners. There was a close personal relationship with the senior branch, and Robert and his descendants could be called upon to assist in times of crisis.

Robert Maltravers, *c.* 1270–*c.* 1321

Robert Maltravers was probably born in the 1270s. He was a son of John Maltravers IV and was a younger brother of John Maltravers V.

By 1312, he was married to Lucy de Braose, a young heiress, who was born in 1297. She had inherited the manors of Crowell, Oxfordshire, and Long Wittenham, Berkshire (now in Oxfordshire), as the sole heir of her mother, Beatrice, who in turn was the daughter and sole heir of Sir John de Saint Helena. When Lucy was only a year old, her mother died, and her father, Giles de Braose, died when Lucy was seven.[1] In August 1312, an inquiry was held to prove the age of Lucy, and it was generally agreed that she had attained the age of fifteen years and was old enough to enter into her inheritance. Accordingly, in September, the escheator was ordered to give Robert and Lucy possession of Lucy's lands.[2]

Robert Maltravers took part in the Battle of Bannockburn in 1314, with other members of his family, and he was sent north again the following year to help Maurice de Berkeley defend Berwick.³

Robert and Lucy had a son, John, who was later known as John Maltravers of Crowell. Robert had died by 1321 when Lucy was described as 'late the wife' – that is, the widow – of Robert.

John Maltravers of Crowell, *c.* 1312–1360

On 18 August 1321, Lucy endowed her son John with some of the land (pasture, meadow and woodland) in Crowell and the advowson of the church there. Young John was probably about nine years old, assuming he was born in about 1312.⁴

Lucy remarried after Robert Maltravers's death. Her second husband was John Poulshot. In 1333, Lucy settled Long Wittenham on herself and John Poulshot for life, with remainder to her son John Maltravers of Crowell, and his wife.⁵ John Maltravers of Crowell's wife was Elizabeth Syfrewast of Hooke, Dorset. To begin with, she was not an heiress in her own right, but she became heir to the Syfrewast lands due to the untimely death of her brother.

John of Crowell was called upon to help safeguard the core Maltravers lands. In 1339, his uncle John Maltravers V was aged seventy-four, and his cousin John Maltravers VI could not inherit, due to being under sentence of death as a traitor and in exile abroad. There was a danger that this would still be the situation when John V died. Therefore, as mentioned in Chapter 5, it was arranged for John of Crowell to inherit these Maltravers lands: Woolcombe, Langton, Lytchett Matravers and Witchampton in Dorset; Coate, Somerford and Longbridge Deverill in Wiltshire; Yeovil in Somerset; and Woodchester in Gloucestershire.⁶ This arrangement became redundant with the restoration of John Maltravers VI in 1351.

At the Battle of Crécy in 1346 there was a 'John Maltravers the younger' in the retinue of Sir Richard Talbot. This could have been either John Maltravers VII of Lytchett Matravers (born 1313 or later) or John of Crowell (born 1312 or later). These two Johns were of similar ages and either could be described as 'John Maltravers the younger', but the warrior at the Battle of Crécy is more likely to be John VII of Lytchett Matravers, whose father was usually referred to as 'John Maltravers the elder'. (See 'A Maltravers at Crécy' in Chapter 5.)

Rathkeale in Ireland was demised (leased), by John Maltravers VI to John Maltravers of Crowell for life, with reversion to John Maltravers VI and his heirs. This demise was probably made in 1357, as John of Crowell went to Ireland as one of John VI's attorneys in that year.[7]

John Maltravers of Crowell died on 13 October 1360, and there was an inquisition post mortem on 31 October 1361 in which Rathkeale was the only place mentioned. The manor, held of the king in chief by the lease granted by John Maltravers VI, was ordered to be returned to 'John Maltravers the elder, kinsman of the deceased, aged fifty years and more'. This is John Maltravers VI, who was about seventy-one at this time.[8]

John Maltravers of Crowell and Elizabeth (née Syfrewast) had one son, born 1337, who was later known as John Maltravers of Hooke and Crowell.

John Maltravers of Hooke and Crowell

By 1354, Lucy had died. John Poulshot died on 21 March 1354, and an inquisition post mortem on his lands in Long Wittenham, held on 13 July 1354, states that he held the land for life 'of the inheritance of John (of Hooke and Crowell), aged ten years, who was the son of John Maltravers of Crowell, and a ward of Sir Edward, Prince of Wales [the Black Prince]'. The age of John Maltravers of Hooke and Crowell was underestimated. It was quite common to give the age of the heir as a round number, especially if he was clearly well over or well under twenty-one, the age of majority, so that whether he could claim his inheritance immediately was not an issue. In fact, he was sixteen, not ten years old. Young John was in wardship because he was the heir to the Syfrewast lands.[9]

Elizabeth Syfrewast's parents (Robert and Joan) and her brother John, all died between 1347 and 1354. Their inquisitions post mortem all name John, son of Elizabeth (i.e. John Maltravers of Hooke and Crowell), as the heir. The inquisitions post mortem on Robert,[10] Joan[11] and John[12] Syfrewast give differing dates of birth for him, ranging from 1338 to 1341.

However, his date of birth can be securely established from the inquiry held at Cerne Abbas on 9 May 1360 to take 'proof of age' of this John Maltravers.[13] If he could be shown to be twenty-one or more, he could take possession of his lands immediately. Various people came forward to give their recollections:

John de Haddon said that John (Maltravers of Hooke and Crowell) was born at Hooke, Dorset, on the feast of St Martin (11 November) in the eleventh year of Edward III (1337), and that he, John de Haddon, was present at the child's baptism at Powerstock, together with the child's grandfather, Robert Syfrewast. Robert Syfrewast gave him a doe from his park at Hooke and told him to remember the age of the said heir.

John Gerard, who was Robert Syfrewast's steward at the time, agreed with John de Haddon, and said he, too, was present at the baptism. The day after the birth, he held the said Robert's manorial court at Hooke, and the date would be found in the court roll.

John Wantynch (and four other named men) recalled that they were at Okeford Fitzpaine on the Tuesday after the birth, attending a great feast given by the local lord, Robert Fitzpayn. Robert Syfrewast was also at the feast and told his neighbours of the birth of his kinsman and heir.

John Giles and two others said that, on the Sunday after the birth, they took a tenancy of some land from the abbot of Milton for a term of twenty years 'which expired more than two years ago'. That is, the tenancy expired before May 1358, and therefore the tenancy started before May 1338; so, as some of the other jurors said that John's birthday was 11 November, that meant he was born on 11 November 1337.

According to the inquisitions post mortem, the Syfrewast lands, all in Dorset, were the manor of Hooke, and lands at West Shilvinghampton, Stapleford, Charlton, West Chickerell, Yard, Ernly and Frome Vauchurch.

John Maltravers at the Battle of Poitiers, 1356

A truce between England and France expired in 1355, and King Edward III planned a new campaign. Two armies were to invade France: one led by the king from the north and the other led by the prince of Wales from the south. In September 1355, the Black Prince sailed for Bordeaux, and set off in October across southern France, going all the way to Narbonne, in a *chevauchée* or destructive raid. Towns and villages were set on fire, and – in a tide of horrific violence – anyone who could not escape was killed. The next year, setting off again from English-held Gascony, the murderous army rode northward as far as the outskirts of Tours on the Loire. There the prince learned that a large French army was pursuing him, and so he turned and made towards the safety of Bordeaux. On 19 September 1356, near Poitiers, the two armies clashed in an awkward terrain of fields and hedges, bordered by a small river, which was made difficult to cross by the boggy ground. Although outnumbered, the prince won a remarkable victory, with many killed or taken prisoner. Among the captives was the king of France, John II, who was taken to Bordeaux and thence to honourable captivity in England, while efforts were made to raise his enormous ransom.

There was a John Maltravers at Poitiers, but was it John Maltravers VI, now returned from exile, aged about sixty-six; John Maltravers of Crowell, aged about forty-four; or John Maltravers of Hooke and Crowell, aged eighteen?

On grounds of age and his association with his guardian the Black Prince, John Maltravers of Hooke and Crowell is the most likely. When the expedition was announced, young John of Hooke and Crowell would have been eager to take part and earn his spurs. The Black Prince would have had no hesitation in finding a place for his ward.

The names of participants in the Black Prince's *chevauchée* and at the Battle of Poitiers were researched by H. J. Hewitt.[14] His list includes a John Maltravers. Hewitt gives one source for each person on his list, even if he found more, and for Maltravers the source is Rymer's *Foedera*[15] where 'John Maltravers' is listed among those who are given letters of protection in 1356 while they remained in Gascony with Edward, prince of Wales, on the king's business. Significantly, unlike many others, Maltravers does not have 'chivaler' after his name. It is inconceivable that Baron John Maltravers would be there without being designated as at least a knight. Therefore, it must have been either John Maltravers of Crowell, or, more likely, John Maltravers of Hooke and Crowell.

The Black Prince returned to England by sea in the spring of 1357, disembarking at Plymouth by early May. His triumphal entry into London was on 24 May. At the head of the procession came the prince with King John II of France and other important prisoners. Assuming that John Maltravers of Hooke and Crowell was present, as he had grown up in the prince's household, he was probably in the prince's entourage.

After the Battle of Poitiers and the capture of the French king, there was relative peace for a while. The Treaty of Bretigny in 1360 gave the English king full sovereignty over Aquitaine, which included Gascony and a large area of Western France, including Poitou; and also Ponthieu and Calais in the north. Brittany and Normandy remained in French hands. Edward III agreed to renounce his claim to the French throne.

John Maltravers of Hooke and Crowell: Career

John of Hooke and Crowell went on to have an active career in the king's service abroad. In 1363, he went to Bordeaux to join the Black Prince, 'Prince of Aquitaine and Wales', and stayed there until 1365.[16] The Black Prince held a luxurious court in Bordeaux, largely paid for by heavy taxes in the locality, which were much resented. In 1364, King John II of France died in London, ending all hope that the outstanding part of his ransom would ever be paid. In 1369, the war resumed: Edward III claimed again the title of king of France, and the new French king, Charles V, declared the English possessions in France confiscate.

At home, John Maltravers of Hooke and Crowell was a person of standing locally, and attended parliament as a knight of the shire for Dorset on eight occasions and for Somerset once:[17]

† For Dorset: 1368, 1381, May 1382 and October 1382.
† For Somerset: February 1383.
† For Dorset: October 1383, April 1384, November 1384 and 1385.

John Maltravers of Hooke and Crowell: Family Matters, Will and Lands

Like his father and grandfather, John Maltravers of Hooke and Crowell improved the family fortunes by marrying an heiress – in his case, Elizabeth d'Aumarle, a daughter and co-heir of Sir William d'Aumarle who died in 1361.[18] John Maltravers (of Hooke and Crowell) and Elizabeth d'Aumarle had two daughters: Matilda (Maud), who was born in 1368; and Elizabeth, who was born in 1378.

John Maltravers of Hooke and Crowell died on 15 June 1386. By his will he left his soul to God Almighty, the Blessed Mary and all saints, and his body to be buried in the abbey church of Abbotsbury, in the chapel of the Blessed Andrew. He left gifts of vestments to certain churches and silver vessels to the abbey of Abbotsbury. His two daughters, Matilda and Elizabeth, were to receive £20 each. As he had no son, he left three gilt girdles, a sword of silver gilt, a gilt dagger and all his body armour to his son-in-law Peter de la Mare, Matilda's husband. Among gifts of money to individuals was one mark to Edward Maltravers II. The monks of Abbotsbury had individual legacies of money, and the rector of Hooke was to receive 10 marks, 'to travel about the land according to the usage of religious societies for the good estate of his own soul and those of his friends and benefactors'. Sir Stephen Derby was left a grey horse; and his clerk John Savage was left forty shillings. His tenants in Hooke, Stapleford, Kingcombe and Poorton were excused paying rent for one term after his death.[19]

The inquisition post mortem[20] found that he held the following lands:

OXFORDSHIRE
† The manor and advowson of Crowell.

SOMERSET
† The manor and advowson of Middle Chinnock.
† Land at Kingsdon, Highbrook, Hardington Mandeville, Martock, Longload and Hull.

DORSET
† The manors and advowsons of Hooke, West Chickerell and 'Badecomb'.
† The manor of Woolcombe Matravers, with the advowson of the church of Melbury Bubb, held of Eleanor – the widow of John Arundel, knight – by service of a rose yearly.
† The manors of Stapleford, Higher Kingcombe, Yard, Lower Kingcombe, Frome Vauchurch, Charlton by Dorchester, 'Gorewell', South Poorton, North Poorton, Milborne Deverell (in Milborne St Andrew) and Burcombe.
† Land in 'Lescomb', Toller Porcorum, 'La Thrope' by Frampton, Martinstown, Tarrant Crawford, Spettisbury, Sturminster Marshall, Dorchester and Melcombe.

His heirs were his daughters: Matilda aged eighteen (wife of Peter de la Mare), and Elizabeth, aged eight. Matilda married twice, but had no children, and so Elizabeth became the heir to the Crowell and Hooke estates.

Several people mentioned in this chapter were remembered in a chantry set up at Abbotsbury in 1392. One of the monks was to celebrate divine service every day for Elizabeth (née d'Aumarle) while she lived and for her soul after she died, for the soul of her late husband John Maltravers (of Hooke and

Crowell), for the souls of John Maltravers (of Crowell) and his wife Elizabeth (Syfrewast), Robert Syfrewast and his wife Joan, William d'Aumarle and his wife Ellen, 'and of all the faithful departed'.[21]

Stafford, Talboys and Strangways Descendants

The male line of the Maltraverses of Hooke came to an end with John Maltravers of Hooke and Crowell in 1386. There was then a succession of three female heirs: Elizabeth Maltravers, 1378–1422, who married Sir Humphrey Stafford junior; their daughter Alice Stafford, who married Walter Talboys; and their daughter Eleanor Talboys, who married Thomas Strangways.

From them were descended many generations of Strangways of Melbury. The two manors of Melbury Sampford and Melbury Osmond were not part of the Hooke inheritance, but came to the Strangways family by purchase from a Browning descendant of John Maltravers V.

The Melbury Connection: John Maltravers V – Browning and Strangways Descendants

John Maltravers V, the father of Baron John (John VI), married Joan de Percy (née Foliot, heiress of Melbury) as his second wife, as mentioned at the end of Chapter 3. Three daughters – Alice, Joan and Elizabeth – were born of this marriage. Alice married John Browning, and their son – another John Browning (c. 1369–1416) – inherited the Melbury manors from Alice.

Two generations later, a William Browning married Katherine Wadham. After William Browning's death, Katherine married Henry Strangways, son of the aforementioned Thomas Strangways. Katherine had been left a jointure, or life interest, in Melbury Sampford and Melbury Osmond.

Henry Strangways saw an opportunity to convert this into an inheritance for his own family. In 1500, he agreed to pay the Browning heir – another William, a nephew of Katherine's late husband – the sum of 600 marks to obtain Melbury in the event that William the nephew died childless, as indeed happened. By the terms of the agreement, Melbury Sampford was then to pass to Henry Strangways immediately, while Melbury Osmond was to be held by Anne, the widow of William Browning, for her lifetime. On Anne's death in 1529, Melbury Osmond, too, passed to the Strangways family. By this time, Henry Strangways had died, and so it was his son Giles Strangways ('the elder'), who was the first of his family to hold both Melburys.

Giles Strangways the elder carried out extensive building works at Melbury House. The oldest parts of the present house date from his time. He died in 1547.[22]

11

JOAN MALTRAVERS, LATER DE KEYNES, THEN ROUS

Joan Maltravers – the eldest child of John Maltravers VII and his wife Wentliana – was overshadowed by her younger and more famous sister Eleanor, but she had an interesting and, in some ways, a tragic life. We do not have any documents by Joan herself, but we can piece together her story by dating many of the significant events in her life.

She was born in 1342, and her two siblings were Eleanor (born in 1345) and Henry (born in 1348). Soon the horrors of the Black Death raged all around, and the Maltravers family was not immune. The plague is likely to have been the cause of the deaths of Joan's father, John Maltravers VII, in January 1349 and of her little brother, Henry, by February 1350.

Joan and Eleanor would have been aware that the head of the family was their grandfather John Maltravers VI, who was mysteriously absent in their early years. Later, in 1350, grandfather John and his doughty wife Agnes went away for several months on pilgrimage to a distant place called Rome. The sisters must also have been aware of the jubilation surrounding their grandfather's pardon in 1351. Now it was safe for him to come home to Lytchett Matravers, in between his trips to Guernsey and Jersey on the king's business. Eventually, as an old man, he died and was buried in Lytchett Matravers in 1364.

Joan and Eleanor both married young, but not unusually so for that era. In about 1362, twenty-year-old Joan married Sir John de Keynes, who was aged about forty-one and was a landowner with manors in Dorset (Tarrant Keyneston and Coombe Keynes), Wiltshire (Purton), Northamptonshire

(Dodford) and Warwickshire (Oxhill).[1] No special arrangements were made to endow Joan with lands, in contrast to the settlement made for her sister Eleanor. Joan's two children were Wentliana, born in 1363 and named after Joan's mother; and John, born three years later, in January or February 1366.

A few weeks after John de Keynes junior was born, tragedy struck with the death of Joan's husband in March 1366. Thus, she was left a young widow with an infant daughter and a baby son.[2] John de Keynes senior was named as one of the litigants on the Maltravers side in the dispute about Rathkeale in November 1367. In fact, he had died more than eighteen months previously, which is perhaps an indication of the law's delays or inefficiencies.

Within a few years, Joan remarried. Her second husband was Sir Robert Rous, or Roos. Among the English combatants at Poitiers were several men surnamed Roos: Robert, John, Thomas and William.[3] No link has been found between Robert Rous and any of these men, nor has anything come to light about his parents and his early life.

Robert Rous is first mentioned in 1370, when he went to Aquitaine on the king's business.[4] From obscurity, Rous suddenly came to prominence in March 1373, when he was appointed mayor of Bordeaux.[5] Royal letters of protection were issued for him and two assistants – William de Terrington and Richard de Yeovilton – who were travelling to Aquitaine.[6] The king allocated him three knights at 3 shillings each a day, two men-at-arms at 18 pence each per day, and fifteen archers at 9 pence each per day 'for the greater security of that town and the dignity of that office',[7] and the constable of Bordeaux was ordered to pay Sir Robert Rous £222 4s. 5d. annually to cover their wages.[8] This was not nearly enough if the full complement of armed men were to be appointed. The king also granted Rous a personal annuity of 100 marks.[9]

It was not the best time to be mayor of Bordeaux. The glory days when Edward – the Black Prince, prince of Wales and prince of Aquitaine – had kept a magnificent court were over, and the prince had returned to England, a sick man, in 1371. King Edward III was aging and in failing health. While Robert Rous was mayor, there occurred the disastrous *chevauchée* led by the king's son, John of Gaunt. Normally, this type of expedition caused misery in the area attacked, but, on this occasion, the attackers also suffered. Having landed at Calais in July 1373, they left a trail of destruction across northern France; crossed the Massif Central in winter, losing half of the men and all of the horses; and arrived starving and demoralised in Bordeaux in January 1374.

Soon afterwards, Joan herself was in Bordeaux. Getting there must have been a risky undertaking. It would probably have been safest to travel by sea, and, on the voyage, Joan would have caught sight of Guernsey and Jersey where grandfather John VI had been warden, and might even have stopped off there. The reason we know that Joan was with her husband in Gascony is that letters of protection were issued for one Ellen Hatfield – executrix of the will of John Hatfield, a former citizen and pepperer of London – who was setting out for Aquitaine in the king's service, 'to stay in the city of Bordeaux, with Joan, wife of Robert Rous, mayor of Bordeaux'.[10] Sir Robert Rous remained mayor of Bordeaux until 9 April 1375, when he was succeded by Sir John de Moulton.[11]

Meanwhile, the ongoing legal tangle of Rathkeale had surfaced again in December 1374. Robert Rous was named as Joan's husband and a petitioner on behalf of the Maltravers family, together with John Arundel and his wife Eleanor, and Agnes Maltravers.[12]

The plague that devastated the population from 1348 to 1349 had not gone away completely, and there were several more outbreaks later in the fourteenth century. One of these was in 1375, and may have been the cause of further tragedy in Joan's family, when her son John, 'son and heir of John de Keynes, knight' died aged nine. The inquisitions post mortem give the date of his death as either 1 May or 9 May. It was found that he held the manors of Coombe Keynes (Dorset), Keynescourt in Purton (Wiltshire), and Oxhill (Warwickshire). There is no inquisition post mortem recorded on Tarrant Keyneston (Dorset), nor on Dodford, Northamptonshire. His heir was his sister Wentliana, then aged twelve.[13]

Scarcely four months later Wentliana, 'sister and heir of John, son of John de Keynes, knight', also died. Inquisitions post mortem were held in four counties, giving various dates between 6 August and 24 September 1375 for her death, and recording her manors as Coombe Keynes (Dorset), Oxhill (Warwickshire), Dodford (Northamptonshire) and Keynescourt in Purton (Wiltshire). Again, there is no mention of Tarrant Keyneston.[14]

As there were now no surviving children of Sir John de Keynes, his lands would go to other members of the Keynes family, not to the Maltraverses. Initially, it was said that the heir was Elizabeth de Keynes, sister of Sir John de Keynes, but further enquiries found that Elizabeth had died, either on a pilgrimage to the Holy Land or soon after her return. It was decided that the co-heirs were two sisters – Margaret de Wotton and Maud Cressy – who were distant Keynes cousins.[15]

The Keynes lands were therefore divided between Margaret and Maud. William de Brantingham purchased Margaret's share. He tried to claim Maud's share as well, saying that he had bought it from Elizabeth de Keynes before she set out on her pilgrimage. Maud's husband, Edmund de Cressy, went to law in about 1378 to recover her share, denying Brantingham's claim and saying that he did not wish to sell his wife's rights.[16] Two years later, he did exactly that, and sold half of each of the Dorset manors – Tarrant Keyneston and Coombe Keynes – to Robert Rous and his wife Joan in perpetuity, with right of inheritance to the heirs of Robert Rous. Rous paid de Cressy 100 marks of silver in each case to seal the deal.[17]

As well as losing her two children, Joan may have lost her mother at around this time. On 18 October 1375, the king presented a priest to the church of Boyton, Wiltshire, as the lands of 'Wentliana Maltravers' were in the king's hands by reason of her death.[18] Agnes Maltravers also died in 1375, but left no keepsake to Joan, her step-granddaughter. Again, Joan seems to have been deliberately ignored.

In 1376, although no longer mayor of Bordeaux, Robert Rous was intending to go to Aquitaine 'on the king's service'. Letters of protection were issued for him on 3 November 1376.[19] In Dorset, Robert Rous was now one of the leading men of the county. In 1377, there was a threat from the French, who were gathering men and ships for an invasion of England. Twice in that year, commisioners were appointed to array fighting men in many English counties. In Dorset, the commissioners were William de Montagu, earl of Salisbury; John Arundel; Robert Rous; Robert Fitzpayn; John Chideock; Edmund Fitzherbert; John Maltravers of Hooke and Crowell; Thomas Blount; and the sheriff.[20]

Edward III died on 21 June 1377. His eldest son, Edward (the Black Prince), predeceased him in 1376, and so the new king was the Black Prince's son Richard, then aged ten. Robert Rous continued his career in the royal service, and was one of Richard II's chamber knights in January 1378.[21] His annuity of 100 marks was confirmed.[22]

He was again appointed as a commissioner of array for Dorset in 1380, to call up and equip all the men of the county between the ages of sixteen and sixty, and to keep them in readiness to resist foreign invasion. The commissioners comprised those listed for 1377 (except that John Arundel, who had died, was omitted) plus some others.[23] The government had great difficulty in funding an army to repel the threatened invasion, and imposed another instalment of the notorious poll tax, which led to the Peasants' Revolt the following year.

Rous had a varied life, carrying out whatever tasks the king required of him. In 1378, he was keeper of Cherbourg for a brief time;[24] in 1380, he was a justice, standing in for the marshal of England in a military court;[25] in 1381, he was sent to York to restore peace in an unseemly dispute between the archbishop and the canons of the church of St John, Beverley;[26] and, in 1382, he was an executor of the will of Isabella de Coucy, the eldest daughter of Edward III.[27]

It is apparent that he was also well regarded by the Arundels, to whom he was related by marriage, as Joan's sister Eleanor was married to John Arundel. When John Arundel made his will in 1379, 'Sir Robert Rouse' was one of his executors.[28]

Robert Rous made his own will in May 1383. He wished to be buried in the Abbey of Tarrant, a Cistercian nunnery in the modern parish of Tarrant Crawford. He left gifts to the nuns: to every nun of Tarrant Abbey, 40 pence; to every lay sister there, 2 shillings; and, to the abbess, 'a pair of golden beades' with much other plate engraved with both his arms and those of his wife Joan. He left money for priests to pray for the souls of his father and mother for one year after his death, in various churches, including Tarrant Keyneston and Witchampton. Other churches to which he left money were Salisbury Cathedral (£5), Poole (50 shillings) and Lincoln Cathedral (50 shillings). To the earl of Kent, he left a gilded salt cellar with a lion decoration. Rous's executors were his wife, Sir Bartholomew Pigot and others.[29] Robert Rous died on 2 December 1383. An inquisition post mortem was held at Blandford in August 1384, but the jurors found that 'He held no lands in Dorset. Heir not known'. No inquisitions post mortem for other counties are recorded.[30]

Joan had died by 1389. On 18 February in that year, a chantry for Robert and Joan was set up on a permanent basis. The bishop of London paid the king £100 to alienate in mortmain the manor of Tarrant Keyneston to the abbess and convent of Tarrant, who would find two chaplains to celebrate divine service daily in the abbey church for the souls of Robert Rous (knight); his wife Joan; and the father, mother and friends of Robert and others; and for doing other acts of piety in the abbey every year for their souls, and for the souls of the father and mother of the said Joan.[31]

There is no firm evidence for the date of Joan's death. As she apparently did not hold any lands (having been effectively cut out of the Maltravers succession by arrangement with the Arundels), there was no inquisition post mortem. After Joan's death, Eleanor was indisputably the Maltravers heiress. As Joan had no surviving children, and Robert Rous had no descendants, the half share in the manor of Coombe Keynes reverted to the Cressy family.[32]

12

ELEANOR MALTRAVERS, LATER ARUNDEL, THEN COBHAM

Eleanor, younger sister to Joan Maltravers, was born in about 1345. Their brother, Henry, died in infancy in 1350, making the sisters co-heirs to their grandfather, John Maltravers VI. When Eleanor was twelve, she was betrothed to John Arundel, a younger son of Richard, earl of Arundel. She may have been dismayed to learn that her fiancé was only nine years old. At the request of the earl, some of the Maltravers lands were earmarked for the young couple after the lifetime of the current holders.

Richard, third earl of Arundel, had himself been betrothed at a young age, when he was seven and his bride-to-be, Isabella Despenser, was eight. That had not worked out well. Although he had a son (Edmund) and two daughters with Isabella, he later claimed that he had been forced to marry her. He obtained a papal annulment in 1344 and married Eleanor of Lancaster in the following year. Wanting to ensure that his lands – including his castle of Arundel – would go to his heirs by his second marriage, in 1347, he entailed the lands on himself and Eleanor for their joint lives, and subsequently on his 'male heirs begotten on the body of the aforesaid Eleanor'.[1] This legal arrangement was to have unexpected consequences for Maltravers descendants in a later generation. Edmund Arundel was understandably aggrieved to find himself, at the age of twenty, declared illegitimate and disinherited. For the rest of his life, he attempted to claim his rights. At one point, he was imprisoned in the Tower of London, when his guards included Robert Rous.[2]

Richard, earl of Arundel, went on to have three sons and four daughters with Eleanor of Lancaster. The sons were Richard, born in 1346; John Arundel, born in about 1348, who married Eleanor Maltravers; and Thomas Arundel, born in 1353, who became archbishop of Canterbury. The daughters included Joan, who married the earl of Hereford; and Alice, who married the earl of Kent. The other daughters died young.

Sir John Arundel, *c.* 1348–1379, the First Husband of Eleanor Maltravers

The marriage between John Arundel and Eleanor Maltravers is said to have taken place on 17 February 1359, when they were eleven and fourteen years old, respectively. Their first son was born in 1364, and altogether they had five sons and two daughters.

In his early adult life, John Arundel assisted his father in the management of the family estates. It was quite unusual for lords to take a personal interest in details of administration. The Arundel lands became even more extensive when augmented by the Warenne inheritance. John de Warenne, earl of Surrey, died without legitimate children in 1347, and his estates and the title passed via his sister Alice to Richard Earl of Arundel.

Richard, third earl of Arundel, died in 1376, having made his will the previous year, and left bequests to many members of his family. To his son John Arundel, he left 5,000 marks, all the stock on his lands, and a house in London, called Bermondsey Inn, near Fish Wharf.[3] John Arundel was knighted with his elder brother Richard, who became the fourth earl. John was individually summoned to parliament at the beginning of Richard II's reign, as 'John de Arundel', but apparently this did not make him a baron, and he was summoned by the right of his wife Eleanor (Baroness) Maltravers.[4]

John Arundel pursued a military career and was appointed marshal of England in 1377. He was granted £100 a year for life, which was later doubled to £200. He successfully defended Southampton when it was attacked by the French. In 1377–78, he went to Brittany, the duke of Brittany being an ally of the English, and managed to relieve the siege of Brest. In 1378–79, he went to defend Cherbourg.[5]

By now a seasoned commander, he prepared to go on another expedition to Brittany in support of the duke. The troops assembled near Southampton. While waiting for favourable winds, they evidently caused a lot of trouble in the neighbourhood, for the king's council sent an instruction to 'John de Arundel, marshal of England', to the admirals Thomas de Percy and Hugh de Calvyle, and to others, ordering them to enquire into complaints from local people that the soldiers had taken – without payment – horses, oxen, cows, cocks, hens, geese, victuals and other goods.[6]

John Arundel and his soldiers then committed the atrocities for which he is remembered. They sought lodgings in a convent and, in spite of the mother superior's protests that the men might be tempted to commit an unforgiveable sin and that they should therefore seek lodgings elsewhere, they forced their way in and assaulted and raped the nuns and other women who were staying in the convent. As previously mentioned, they seized from the neighbourhood whatever supplies they needed for the voyage, without paying. Finally, at the end of Mass they stole a chalice from the altar and ran to the ships, with the priest pursuing them to the shore, where he excommunicated the thieves on the spot.

Once at sea, a dreadful storm raged for several days and blew the ships off course. To lighten the load, they threw overboard first any unimportant objects, then their plunder and, finally, sixty women whom they had abducted from the convent. Eventually, they found themselves off the coast of Ireland. There was then a furious argument between Sir John Arundel and his sailors as to whether it was better to wait in deep water for the winds to die down or to risk everything by making straight for the shore. The sailors were for waiting, but Sir John was impatient and, it is said, cruelly murdered some of them. The shipmaster succeeded in driving Sir John's ship on to the beach of an island, and the men jumped down and made for firm ground. Sir John stood on the beach for too long and became stuck in the quicksands. Some of his men attempted to rescue him, but were themselves drowned by a huge wave, along with their leader. Some survived, but the bodies of Sir John and others were recovered three days later. Sir John was buried in an abbey in Ireland. He died on 15 December 1379. This account is from Thomas Walsingham's chronicle.[7] The gist of the story, that John Arundel was shipwrecked and died, is true. From the commission sent to Arundel before the voyage, it can be said that his troops were not behaving well. The appalling tale of the nuns, however, may be an invention by the chronicler. Although Walsingham says he was buried in Ireland, his body was taken to Lewes, where his widow Eleanor later requested burial for herself.

Just before setting off on this expedition, while waiting for favourable winds, John Arundel made his will, which was dated 26 November 1379.

He wished to be buried in Lewes Priory. He left legacies to Eleanor his wife; to each of his children; to his brother Richard, earl of Arundel; and to his sister Joan, the wife of the earl of Hereford. His daughter Joan was left 1,000 marks. His executors were Sir Robert Rous and a 'Sir... Maltravers', who was probably Sir John Maltravers of Hooke and Crowell.[8] The inquisitions post mortem on Sir John Arundel list many manors in Northamptonshire, Kent, Northumberland, Somerset, Warwickshire, Sussex and Surrey. He was also holding, jointly with Eleanor, almost all the Maltravers lands (all manors unless stated)[9]:

SOMERSET
† Hendford and Yeovil (rent).

DORSET
† Martinstown (a toft and land), East Morden, Worth Matravers, Frome Whitfield, Woolcombe, Lytchett Matravers, Up Wimborne (Wimborne St Giles), Philipston, Langton Matravers, Loders, Wootton Fitzpaine, Eggardon (land) and West Moors.

GLOUCESTERSHIRE
† Minchinhampton (land).

WILTSHIRE
† Sherrington, Codford, Elston (half the manor), Stapleford (half the manor), Boyton, Corton, Winterbourne Stoke, Coate, Hill Deverill and Somerford Mautravers (Great Somerford).

Missing from the list are the Gloucestershire manors of King's Stanley, Woodchester, Stonehouse and Shurdington, which later continued to be held by Arundel descendants. King's Stanley and Woodchester passed to John Arundel's son of the same name, and Stonehouse and Shurdington appear in Eleanor's own inquisition post mortem in 1405. Three other Gloucestershire manors – Rockhampton, Stoke Gifford and Walls – would have reverted to the Berkeley family after the death of Agnes Maltravers. The inquisitions post mortem were held in the first half of 1380, and found that John Arundel's heir was his son, John de Arundel, knight, aged fifteen.

The Children of John Arundel and Eleanor Maltravers

1) Sir John Arundel, 1364–1390

Born on 30 November 1364,[10] he was brought up in the royal household alongside Prince Richard (born in 1367), who was to become King Richard II.[11] John was with the army in Scotland in 1383 and with the English fleet in 1388. He was certainly a knight, being referred to as 'John de Arundel, knight' in his son's proof of age in 1406 and in his own inquisition post mortem in 1390. He married Elizabeth Despenser, and they had a son, another John Arundel (1385–1421).[12] John died on 14 August 1390 and was buried in Missenden Abbey. At his death, he held the manors of King's Stanley and Woodchester jointly with his wife, and several manors in Surrey. His heir was his son John, then aged five, being born on 1 August 1385.[13]

2) Joan

Her grandfather – Richard, third earl of Arundel – made his will in 1375 and awarded a very generous 1,000 marks to 'the eldest [unnamed] daughter of my son John'.[14] This is assumed to be Joan. She is mentioned before the legacies to her brothers, so perhaps she was the eldest (or the favourite?) grandchild. She was left a further 1,000 marks in the will of her father, John Arundel, who died in 1379.[15] Joan married firstly Sir William de Bryan and secondly Sir William Etchingham. She died on 1 September 1404. Joan, Sir William Etchingham and their son Thomas are depicted in a famous brass in Etchingham church.

3) Henry and 4) Edward

Henry and Edward were left 500 marks each in the earl of Arundel's will of 1375, where they are named and called 'the younger sons of my son John'.[16]

5) Sir William Arundel KG

The earl of Arundel also left 500 marks to William, 'another son of my son John'.[17] King Richard II appointed him to be a knight in his service: '21 September 1392. Grant for life to William de Arundel, because retained to stay for life with the king, of 100 marks a year.'[18] William was made a Knight of the Garter in about 1395, for service in Ireland with the king.[19] William's garter stall plate – dating, it is said, from 1421 – is in St George's Chapel, Windsor. It quarters the Arundel lion with 'sable fretty or' for Maltravers. In this case, it is definitely fretty, not a fret. His arms are also seen in a modern interpretation on the ceiling of St George's Hall, which was restored after the Windsor Castle fire of 1992; here, they have used a fret, not fretty, for the Maltravers quarters.[20]

William was governor of Rochester Castle and city, and, in his will of 1 August 1400 he desires to be buried in the Priory of Rochester. He died later in the same month. His wife was a lady called Agnes, her surname unknown. They had no children. In her will of 1401, she wishes to be buried in Rochester Priory with her husband. She left gifts for her sisters-in-law Joan de Bryan (no. 2 in this list), Margaret de Ros (no. 6 in this list), and Margaret Cobham (a child of Eleanor Maltravers's second marriage, detailed later in this chapter).[21]

6) Margaret

She was the younger daughter, and was living in 1375. Her existence is implied in the earl of Arundel's will, where he mentions 'the eldest daughter of my son John', who is presumed to be Joan, so there must have been at least one other daughter. The earl makes no provision for Margaret. She married William de Ros, the sixth Baron de Ros. Her husband died in 1414, and she died in 1438.[22]

7) Richard

He is not mentioned in the earl of Arundel's will. Perhaps he was the youngest and not yet born in 1375. He succeeded his brother William as governor of Rochester Castle from 1401 to 1413.[23] William Arundel, in his will, calls Richard his 'carnal brother' (an unusual phrase that just seems to mean his full brother in the ordinary sense), and leaves him all his lands and his vessels of silver. Richard is also mentioned in the will of William's wife Agnes.[24]

Under Henry V, Richard was one of the king's knights and was awarded 100 marks a year in 1415 'for good service to the king's father and to the king'.[25] For the campaign in France, he undertook to serve with nine men-at-arms and thirty archers.[26] He was probably at the Battle of Agincourt on 25 October 1415, but details of his part in it are not recorded. He was at the siege of Rouen in 1418, where his arms were the Arundel arms of 'gules a lion rampant or' quartered with 'sable a fret or' for Maltravers.[27]

He was lord of the manor of Witchampton, Dorset. In an inquisition (writ of mandamus) in 1421, it was said that he held Witchampton 'long before his death', but that, in 1415, he granted it by a charter to Joan de Bohun, countess of Hereford and others.[28] Richard made his will in 1417 and asked to be buried in Rochester Abbey. He desired his executors to find someone to go to Rome, to the Holy Land and to 'The Holy Blood' in Germany for the good of his soul.[29] He asked for his goods to be divided equally among his three daughters – Philippa, Joan and Eleanor – from his marriage to Alice, widow of Roger Burley.[30] He died on 3 June 1419, leaving his daughters as his heirs.[31]

Sir Reynold (or Reginald) Cobham, 1348–1403, the Second Husband of Eleanor Maltravers

At the end of 1379, Eleanor Arundel, née Maltravers, was a widow aged 34 with seven children. Within the year, she had married Reynold Cobham, the second Baron Cobham of Sterborough.[32] Before long, they had three children: John[33] and Elizabeth, who both died young, and Reynold junior, who became the Cobham heir. In 1384, the parents discovered that they should not have married, as they were related within the third degree of consanguinity. Their common ancestor was their great-grandfather Maurice, Lord Berkeley, who fought at Bannockburn, was warden of Berwick and died in 1326.[34]

There are two versions of how Eleanor and Reynold overcame the problem. One is that they were given absolution for having contracted an illegal marriage, and the children were legitimated by a 'bull' from the pope. The other is that the marriage was annulled, and then they separated for a few days before remarrying with a dispensation. They went on to have two more children: Thomas, who died young; and Margaret, who grew up to marry Reynold Curteys.

Reynold Cobham senior died on 6 July 1403. His heir was his son, Reynold junior, who was said to have been twenty-one on 11 November of the previous year.[35] There seems to have been no problem at that time about his right to inherit his father's lands, but twelve years later the controversy about his parents' marriage suddenly surfaced again. It was said that Reynold was a child of his parents' unlawful first marriage, and he had not been legitimated by their second marriage. The heir should therefore have been Margaret Curteys, born during the second marriage. An inquiry was held in January 1416, in which it was alleged that Reynold senior and Eleanor had both been aware of their family connection, but had gone ahead and married anyway. In 1417 Reynold junior asserted at the Exchequer, apparently successfully, his right to inherit.[36]

Eleanor was widowed for the second time by the death of Reynold Cobham. She had many manors in her possession, but it was at Lytchett

Matravers that she made her will on 26 September 1404. In it, she calls herself 'Alianor Arundell [sic]' and asks to be buried at Lewes Priory with her first husband, '*mon tres honorable seigneur* [my very honourable lord] John Arundel'. This indicates that John's body had been returned to Lewes from Ireland, as Eleanor would surely have known where he lay. A copy of Eleanor's will is in the Register of Archbishop Arundel, held in the archives at Lambeth Palace, folio 221v–222v.[37] There are many legacies to individuals, including her sisters-in-law Joan, countess of Hereford; and Alice, countess of Kent. From her first marriage, she mentions her daughters (Margaret) de Ros and Joan (Etchingham, formerly Joan de Bryan), and her son Richard Arundel. Evidently, she did not know that Joan Etchingham had just died, on 1 September. She leaves gifts for the children of her second marriage: 'my son Reynold' and 'my daughter Margaret Curteys'. Also mentioned is Edward Maltravers II, great-nephew of John Maltravers VI.

Eleanor died on 10 January 1405. Inquisitions post mortem were held in several counties.[38] Since her son, John Arundel (1364–1390) had already died, the heir for her Maltravers lands – except Witchampton – was her grandson, another John Arundel, who was born in 1385.

She held the following Maltravers lands:

DORSET

† Witchampton: the manor. (This manor alone was to go to her son, Richard Arundel, who was aged twenty-six years or more at Eleanor's death.)
† Loders: rent from the manor, and from land in Eggardon, Litton Cheney, Woolcombe and West Moors, which have been let on a life tenancy with reversion to Eleanor's heirs.
† Frome Whitfield: rent from the manor, which is let on a life tenancy as per Loders.
† Lytchett Matravers: the manor; some of the land is let on a life tenancy per Loders.
† Philipston: the manor
† Worth Matravers: the manor.
† Langton Matravers in Purbeck: the manor.
† East Morden: the manor.
† Wootton Fitzpaine: the manor.
† Wimborne St Giles: the manor called 'French's'.

† Martinstown: half a toft and some land.

GLOUCESTERSHIRE
† Stonehouse: the manor.
† Minchinhampton: land.
† Shurdington: land.

SOMERSET
† Hendford: the manor.
† Yeovil: rent from lands.

WILTSHIRE
† Sherrington and Codford: the manor.
† Elston: half the manor;
† Boyton: the manor.
† Corton: the manor.
† Winterbourne Stoke: the manor.
† Coate: the manor.
† Hill Deverill: the manor.
† Great Somerford: the manor, let to John Chelreye for life.

She held the following lands jointly with her first husband, John Arundel, and they were to go to his heirs after her death. As these have not been mentioned before, they are possibly her dower lands from the Arundel estates:

SOMERSET
† The manors of Cucklington, Stoke Trister and Bayford, and the bailiwick of the forester at Selwood.

She held the following manor, which John Arundel acquired by purchase in about 1370. It is to go to the heirs of herself and John Arundel:

KENT
† Postling.

She also had dower lands in Wiltshire and Kent from her marriage to Reynold Cobham. These manors probably went to the Cobham heirs:

WILTSHIRE
† Langley Burrell.

KENT
† Aldington near Maidstone, Hulberry, East Shelve and Boardfield, a tenement at Westwell, Orkesden, and Bowzell.

John Arundel, 1385–1421, the Sixth Earl of Arundel, the Grandson of Eleanor Maltravers

Since Eleanor's eldest son, John Arundel, had died in 1390, her heir was her grandson, another John. The grandson was born on 1 August 1385 and baptised at St Mary's church, Datchet, Buckinghamshire. When he was later required to prove his date of birth, various jurors came forward, and some recalled their part in the ceremony:[39] 'William Spelyng said that on that day [he] went to the house of John Benet, vicar of Datchet, to ask him to be godfather.' Others recalled personal events: 'Walter Clerk of Horton said that in that week his wife Isabel was delivered of his eldest son John'; and 'John Sperman on that day was sent to London by Margery Lady Moleyns to discover where John the father could be found.'

John was knighted in 1399, when he was only fourteen. On the death of Eleanor Maltravers in 1405, he became the third Baron Maltravers, counting Eleanor as the second baroness in her own right. In 1406, having proved that he had attained the age of twenty-one, he took possession of the Maltravers estates. He married Eleanor de Berkeley and they had a son, John, who was born in 1408. John, the third Baron Maltravers, fought in France in 1415. He was probably at Agincourt.[40]

In the same year, 1415, he found himself able to claim the earldom of Arundel as a result of the death of Thomas, the fifth earl, without any legitimate children (although he had an illegitimate son, John). Earl Thomas had three sisters who considered that, as co-heirs, they were entitled to the estates. They were Elizabeth, wife of Thomas Mowbray, duke of Norfolk; Joan, wife of William Beauchamp, Baron Abergavenny; and Margaret, wife of Sir Roland Lenthall. They acquired some of the Arundel lands.[41]

There was a difficulty for the sisters, however. As we have seen at the beginning of this chapter, in 1347, Richard (third earl of Arundel) settled his estates – including the castle, town and manor of Arundel – on himself and his second wife, Eleanor of Lancaster, for their joint lives, with remainder to the male heirs of his body by the said Eleanor. John Arundel – grandson of the John Arundel who died in 1379 and great-grandson of Richard, the third earl – was clearly the 'male heir', and it was further argued that the earldom of Arundel automatically went with the castle. This claim was disputed by the Mowbray family, and the question was never resolved in John's lifetime.

There is evidence that John Arundel was summoned to parliament as earl of Arundel in 1416. The summons was partially erased from the rolls of parliament in 1658–88, suggesting that someone still had a grudge against his family all those years later.[42]

John died on 21 April 1421, in possession of the Maltravers estates as held by Eleanor Maltravers in 1405, as well as many Arundel holdings (for example, Clun and Oswestry in Shropshire; Castle Acre in Norfolk; and, not least, two-thirds of the castle, township and manor of Arundel, Sussex). It was not unusual for someone to inherit part of a manor, but two-thirds of a castle is harder to imagine. In his inquisition post mortem, he is called 'John de Arundel, Lord Arundel and Maltravers'.[43]

John's widow – Eleanor de Berkeley, who later remarried twice – lived on until 1455. She had no doubt of her status as the widow of an earl, and in her will she describes herself as 'Countess of Arundel and Lady Maltravers'. She asks for her body to be buried with 'my late husband, John Earl of Arundel'.[44] Her wish was carried out, and there is a joint tomb for the sixth earl and his wife in the Fitzalan Chapel at Arundel.

John Arundel, 1408–1435, the Seventh Earl of Arundel, the Great-grandson of Eleanor Maltravers

In the next generation, Eleanor Maltravers's great-grandson – another John Arundel – was born at Lytchett Matravers, Dorset, on 14 February 1408. He was thirteen when his father died in 1421, and eighteen when, as Lord Maltravers, he was knighted in 1426.

There was an inquiry in 1429 to prove that he was twenty-one years of age and entitled to the possession of his lands. He is there referred to as 'John Arundel, knight, son of John Arundel, knight'.[45] In the same year he was summoned to parliament as Lord Maltravers.[46]

In 1430, he went to France on military service, a career he followed with distinction for the rest of his short life. He was made a Knight of the Garter in 1432. He had been calling himself the earl of Arundel since going to France in 1430, although his title was not yet officially recognised.

The parliament of 1433 adjudicated on the dispute between John Arundel and the duke of Norfolk about which of them had the right to the castle of Arundel and the other lands, and hence the earldom of Arundel. Detailed arguments were put by each side. The duke (John de Mowbray, who had succeeded his father in 1399) said his ancestors had held the castle both before and after the Norman Conquest, and had been earls of Arundel automatically. John Arundel, however, held a trump card in the form of the entail by Richard, the third earl, by which the castle, honour and lordship of Arundel were to pass to male heirs only. The terms of the entail and its legal authority were set forth, and the descent of the lordship to John Arundel, the petitioner, was recited thus:

† from Richard, the third earl of Arundel;
† to his son Richard, the fourth earl;
† to his son Thomas, the fifth earl (died without legitimate male issue);
† to John, the sixth earl (died in 1421), who was the grandson of John Arundel (died in 1379), the latter being a brother of Richard, the fourth earl;
† to John, the seventh earl of Arundel, the current claimant.

After due discussion and deliberation, the king accepted the claim of John Arundel to the castle, honour and lordship of Arundel by special hereditary right, and he decreed that John Arundel should sit in parliaments and royal councils as earl of Arundel as his ancestors had done. In reaching this judgment, the king weighed in the balance the 'strenuousness in arms and maturity in counsel' that John had displayed. John Arundel had won his case, and not only he, but also his late father, could be considered earls of Arundel.[47]

John (the seventh earl of Arundel) was injured while on campaign in France, and his leg was amputated, but, nevertheless, on 22 June 1435 he died. He was buried, it was believed, in the Greyfriars church at Beauvais in France. In the Fitzalan Chapel at Arundel, a monument was erected, which was for a long time thought to be a cenotaph, or empty tomb. In the mid-nineteenth century, a document came to light that told another story. This was the will, dated 1454, of a man who claimed to have brought the body back to Arundel. Intrigued by this evidence, Canon M.A. Tierney obtained permission to excavate around the tomb, and he discovered underneath it a grave containing the bones of a man over six feet tall, who was missing a leg.[48]

Although John de Mowbray, duke of Norfolk, was unsuccessful in his claim to the earldom of Arundel in 1433, the Arundel and Norfolk titles were combined in later generations as a result of the marriage in 1555 of an Arundel heiress, Mary Fitzalan, to Thomas Howard, duke of Norfolk.

The Maltravers family had come a long way from the humble knight Hugh Maltravers, who was employed by William d'Eu and rewarded with a host of manors in South West England. Over the centuries, his descendants served nobles and kings, and many people knew the name Maltravers for good or ill. With the death of John Maltravers VII without a male heir, and the subsequent marriage of his daughter Eleanor, the barony of Maltravers was subsumed in the house of Arundel, and became a subsidiary title of the earls of Arundel.

At the present day, the duke of Norfolk – the premier duke in the peerage of England – has among his subsidiary titles 'Earl of Arundel' and 'Baron Maltravers'. He is descended from the Arundels and Maltraverses in this history.

In Dorset, the names Lytchett Matravers, Langton Matravers and Worth Matravers are a reminder of lives lived there in times gone by.

Maltravers Family Tree 1: 1066–c.1300

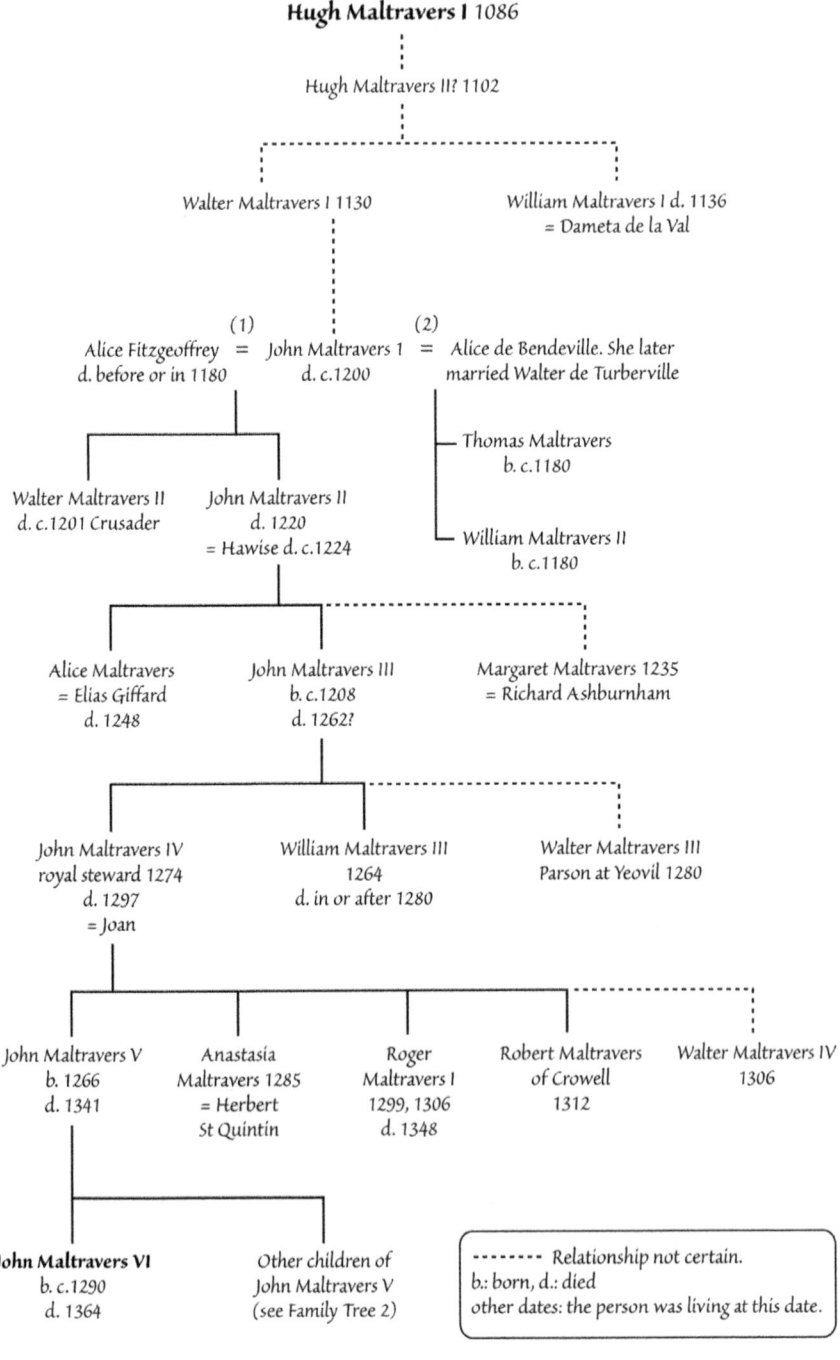

FAMILY TREES ♦ 155

Maltravers Family Tree 2: John Maltravers VI, c.1290–1364, first Baron Maltravers

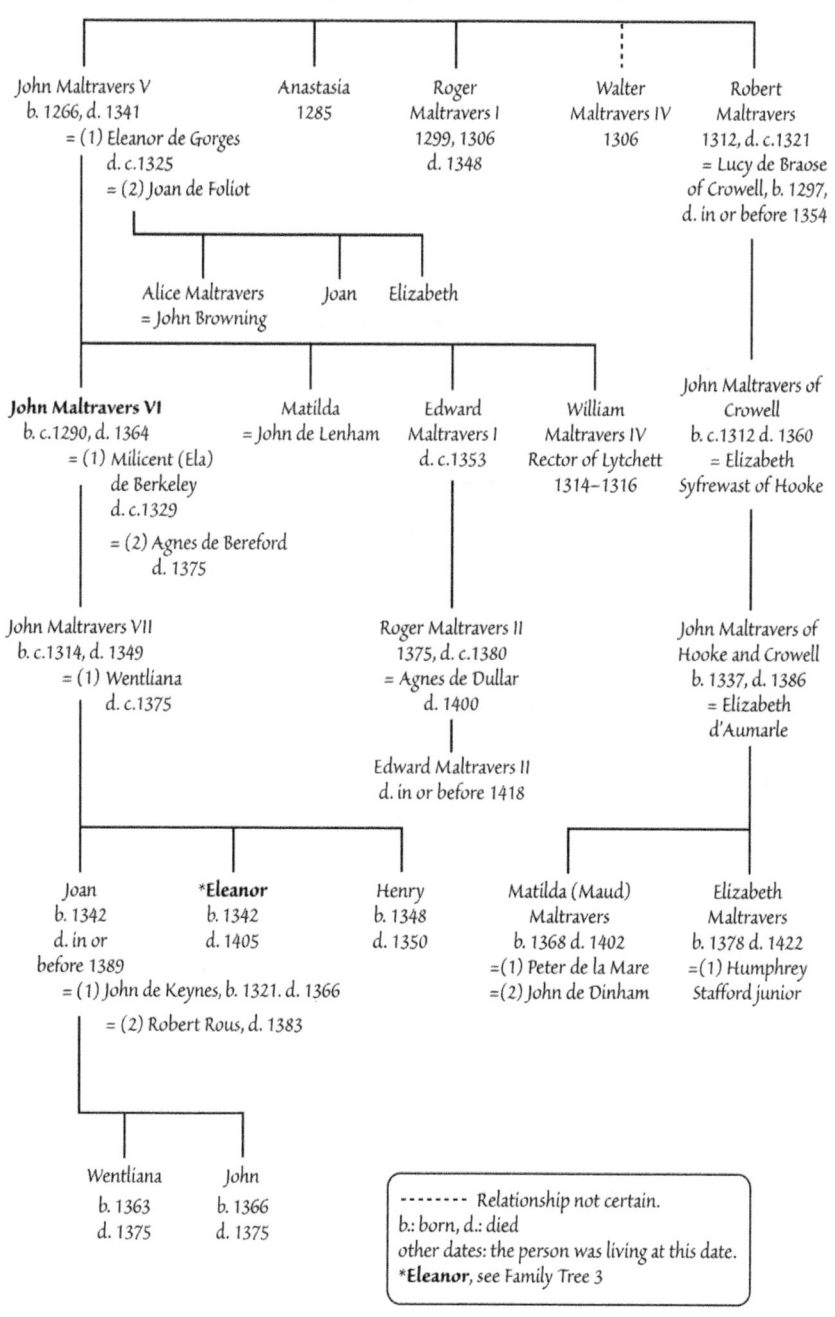

156 ♦ FAMILY TREES

Maltravers Family Tree 3:
Eleanor Maltravers/Arundel/Cobham 1345–1405

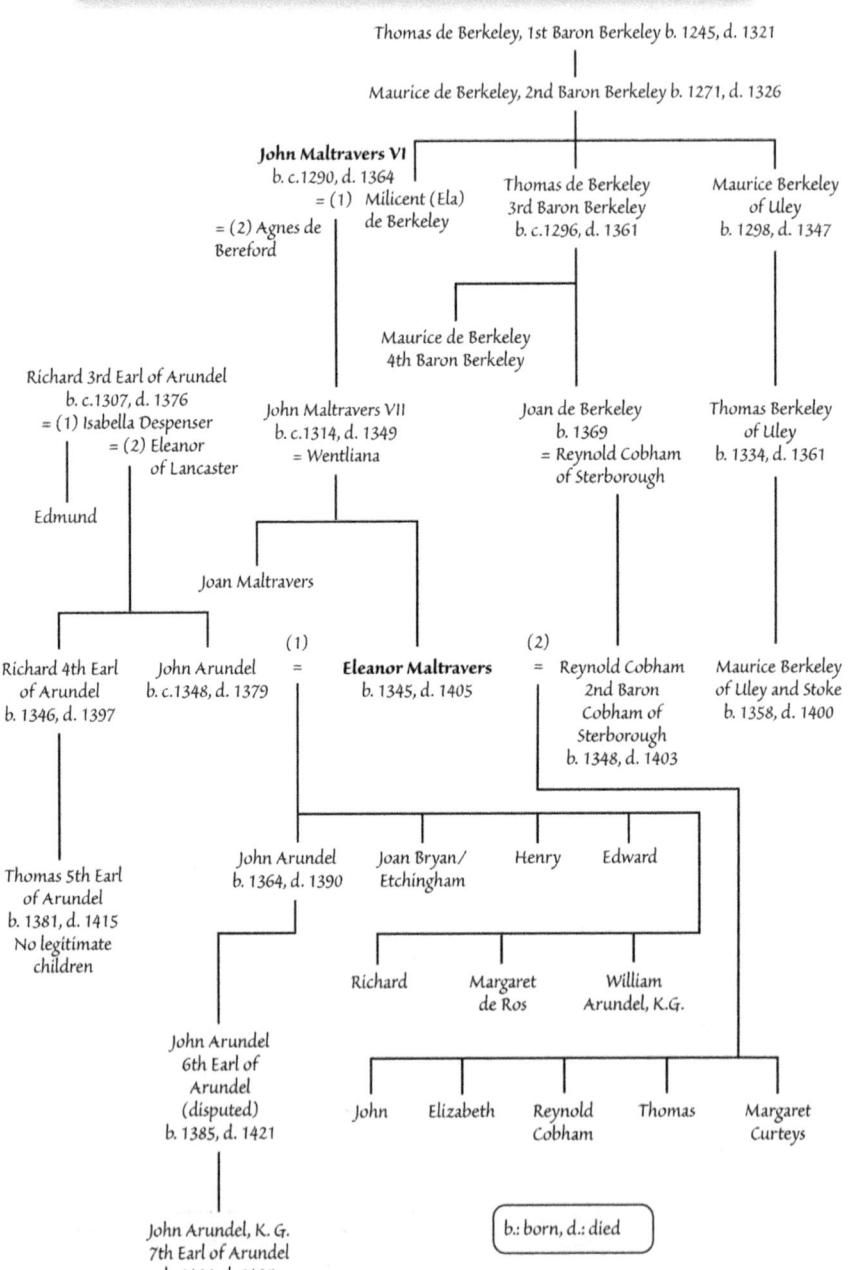

b.: born, d.: died

ABBREVIATIONS FOR NOTES AND REFERENCES

CChR	*Calendar of the Charter Rolls 1257–1341*, 3 vols (HMSO, 1906–1912).
CCR	*Calendar of the Close Rolls 1313–1374*, 16 vols (HMSO, 1893–1911).
CDS	*Calendar of Documents Relating to Scotland*, vols I–IV (HMSO, 1881–1888); supplementary vol V (Scottish Record Office, 1986).
CFR	*Calendar of the Fine Rolls 1269–1356*, 6 vols (HMSO, 1911–1921).
CGR	*Calendar of Gascon Rolls 1373–1377* (Gascon Rolls Project, Universities of Oxford, Liverpool and Kings College London, 2014).
CIPM	*Calendar of Inquisitions Post Mortem 1291–1418*, 18 vols (HMSO, 1912–1995); *1418–1432*, 3 vols (Boydell, 2002–2004).
CLR	*Calendar of the Liberate Rolls 1240–1251*, 2 vols (HMSO, 1930–37).
CPR	*Calendar of the Patent Rolls 1247–1416*, 49 vols (HMSO, 1908–1910).
G.E.C., *Complete Peerage*, I	G. E. C. [G. E. Cokayne], *Complete Peerage*, 2nd edn, 14 vols (St Catherine Press, 1910–1959), I: *Ab-Adam to Basing*, ed. by Vicary Gibbs, 1910). [Includes Argentine and Arundel]
G.E.C., *Complete Peerage*, III	G. E. C. [G. E. Cokayne], *Complete Peerage*, 2nd edn, III: Canonteign to Cutts, ed. by Vicary Gibbs and H.

	Arthur Doubleday (1913). [Includes Cobham]
G.E.C., *Complete Peerage*, VIII	G. E. C. [G. E. Cokayne], *Complete Peerage*, 2nd edn, VIII: Lindley to Moate, ed. by H. A. Doubleday and Lord Howard of Walden (1932). [Includes Mautravers (Maltravers)]
Hutchins, *Dorset*	John Hutchins, *The History and Antiquities of the County of Dorset*, 3rd edn, rev. by W. Shipp and J. W. Hodson, 4 vols (1868; repr. E. P. Publishing, 1973). [References are to this edition except where noted]
ODNB	*Oxford Dictionary of National Biography* (Oxford University Press, 2004). [Online access is available by subscription or via public library membership]
PROME	*The Parliament Rolls of Medieval England 1275–1504*, general editor Chris Given-Wilson, 16 vols (Boydell, 2005).
PROME-ONLINE	*Parliament Rolls of Medieval England*, ed. by Chris Given-Wilson and others (Boydell, 2005), online edition (subscription required), in British History Online <http://www.british-history.ac.uk/no-series/parliament-rolls-medieval>
TNA	The National Archives
VCH	*Victoria History of the Counties of England* (Institute of Historical Research, 1901–).

NOTES

Chapter 1. Hugh Maltravers

1   P. H. Reaney, *A Dictionary of English Surnames*, 3rd edn (Routledge, 1991). Eilert Ekwall, *The Concise Oxford Dictionary of English Place-Names*, 4th edn (Oxford University Press, 1960). Surname database: Moultrie, <www.surnamedb.com/surname/Moultrie> [accessed 14 September 2016]
2   Frank McLynn, *1066: The Year of Three Battles* (Pimlico, 1999), pp. 185–186. Pierre Bouet, *Hastings 14 octobre 1066* (Tallandier, 2014), pp. 59–61.
3   Jules Gabilly, *Montravers autrefois et aujourd'hui* (Société Française d'Imprimerie et de Librairie, 1910; repr. Hérault Éditions, 1989), p. 10.
4   McLynn, p. 186; Jane Martindale, 'Aimery de Thouars and the Poitevin Connection', *Anglo-Norman Studies*, 7 (1984), 224–245.
5   Martindale, 225–226, rejects the figure of 4,000 for the men from Poitou, as found in the writings of nineteenth-century writers such as Vaudoré and Imbert: De la Fontenelle de Vaudoré, 'La Cooperation des Poitevins à la conqête de l'Angleterre', *Revue Française*, 1 (1833), 36–51; Hugues Imbert, *Histoire de Thouars* (Clouzot, 1871), p. 46.
6   Estimate 14,000: McLynn, p. 185.
7   Estimate 15,000: Bouet, p. 27.
8   *Le Roman de Rou* is a narrative poem written c. 1160–1170 by Wace (sometimes referred to as Robert Wace), and dedicated to Henry II, king of England, and his wife, Eleanor of Aquitaine. Wace made use of oral tradition and written sources, all of which would have been familiar to his audience at the court of Henry II. Wace wrongly names the Breton leader as Alan Fergent instead of Alain le Roux. With 'Aimery the warrior', Alan commanded the Poitevins, the Bretons and the barons from Maine. *The History of the Norman People: Wace's Roman de Rou*, translated by Glyn S. Burgess (Boydell, 2004), p. 177.
9   William of Poitiers was a Norman who had studied at Poitiers, hence his name. He wrote his account of the Battle of Hastings soon after the event. He was not present at the battle himself, but he was personally acquainted with Duke

William and his court. In his account of the battle, he refers to 'the Breton knights and other auxiliaries on the left wing'. William of Poitiers, *Gesta Guillelmi of William of Poitiers,* ed. by R. H. C. Davis and M. Chibnall (Oxford University Press, 1998), p. 129.
10 William of Poitiers, p. 149.
11 *Histoire de La Chaize-le-Vicomte* (Commune de La Chaize-le-Vicomte) <www.lachaizelevicomte.fr/fr/information/86894/1-histoire> [accessed 14 September 2016]
12 George Beech, 'The Participation of Aquitanians in the Conquest of England 1066–1100', *Anglo-Norman Studies, 9* (1986), 1–24; Imbert, pp. 45–49.
13 Orderic Vitalis, *The Ecclesiastical History of England and Normandy*, trans. by Thomas Forester, 4 vols (Bohn, 1853–56), I, 480–491.
14 The names in the versions of the *Battle Abbey Roll* by Brompton, Leland, Holinshed and Duchesne are in the following two books:
Anthony J. Camp, *My Ancestors Came with the Conqueror* (Society of Genealogists, 1988; corrected reprint 1990). Includes an alphabetical index of names; and
M. Jackson Crispin and Leonce Macary, *The Falaise Roll* (Butler and Tanner, 1938; with additions and corrections by G. Andrews Moriarty, 1939; repr. Genealogical Publishing, 1969), pp. 199–220. Includes lists of names arranged by source.
The names from Leland, Holinshed, Duchesne and the Dives Roll are in the following:
Duchess of Cleveland, *The Battle Abbey Roll with Some Account of the Norman Lineages,* 3 vols. (Murray, 1889), I, pp. xix-xxxvi. <www.battle-abbey.co.uk/battleabbeyrollw01battuoft_tjw> [accessed 1 May 2018]
The version of the list by Guillaume le Tailleur, *Chronicles of Normandy,* which gives the name 'Mautrauers', is included in the following:
John Stow, *Annales: A General Chronicle of England* (1615), pp. 103–106 (p. 106).
15 L. Delisle, *Liste des Compagnons de Guillaume-le-Conquérant à la Conqête de l'Angleterre en 1066.* (Bibliothèque Nationale, Paris, 1872). Pièces Justificatives, L.K.2, 2 pages.
16 Crispin and Macary, *Falaise Roll*. As above
17 *Domesday Book: A Complete Translation*, ed. by G. Martin (Penguin, 2002).
18 *Domesday Book*, general editor J. Morris (Phillimore, 1975–1992). Volumes for individual counties, with Latin text, English translation and notes.
19 <www.opendomesday.org> [accessed 10 August 2017]
20 *Domesday Book: Somerset* (Phillimore, 1980), section 26.5;
Victoria County History: Somerset, I, ed. by William Page (Victoria County History, 1906), p. 508;
Exeter Cathedral Library Archives reference MS 3500, f438v–f439r, see

illustration reprinted in this book by permission of the Dean and Chapter of Exeter Cathedral.
21 *Victoria County History: Somerset*, I, 514;
Exeter Cathedral Library Archives reference MS 3500, f78r. This entry is less clear than the aforementioned, being obscured by a stain on the page.
22 *Domesday Book: Dorset* (Phillimore, 1983), section 34.4.
23 *Domesday Book: Dorset* (Phillimore, 1983), section 34.5.
24 *Domesday Book: Dorset* (Phillimore, 1983), section 34.7.
25 *Domesday Book: Dorset* (Phillimore, 1983), section 34.14.
In 1304, an inquest on Ingelram de Waleys showed that he had held land at Stoke Gaylard from John Maltravers (V), as follows:
Calendar of Inquisitions Post Mortem 1300-1307, no. 222.
26 *Domesday Book: Dorset* (Phillimore, 1983), section 34.15.
27 *Domesday Book: Somerset* (Phillimore, 1980), section 26.6.
28 *Domesday Book: Somerset* (Phillimore, 1980), section 26.5.
29 *Domesday Book: Wiltshire* (Phillimore, 1979), section 32.5. In 1256, John Maltravers held the manor and sued his tenant in his manorial court at Lytchett Matravers: *Victoria County History: Berkshire*, ed. by P. H. Ditchfield and William Page, IV (Victoria County History, 1924) <http://www.british history.ac.uk/vchberks/vol4/pp183-200> [accessed 2 May 2018]
30 *Domesday Book: Wiltshire* (Phillimore, 1979), section 32.6.
31 *Domesday Book: Wiltshire* (Phillimore, 1979), section 32.15.
32 *Domesday Book: Gloucestershire* (Phillimore, 1982), section 31.9.
33 Orderic Vitalis, *Ecclesiastical History*, III, 21–22.
34 *Two Cartularies of the Augustinian Priory of Bruton and the Cluniac Priory of Montacute* (Somerset Record Society, 1894).
Hugh's gift is mentioned in charter 9, pp. 123–124, dated c. 1155; and the text is in charter 32, p. 134.
35 Montacute Priory, a house of the Cluniac order of Benedictine monks, is not mentioned in the *Domesday Book*. In its earliest charter, William, count of Mortain, gave to the monastery the church of St Peter near his castle of Montacute; the borough and its market, with the toll, the castle and chapel; his orchards and vineyards; the manor of Bishopstone; and numerous other lands in Somerset, Dorset, Devon and Cornwall. 'Bishopstone' was the place where William's father, Robert count of Mortain, had built his castle by 1086; later, the town itself became known as 'Montacute'. Count William's charter can be dated as between 1095 (when he succeeded his father as count of Mortain) and 1104 (when he was banished by King Henry I).
Two Cartularies of the Augustinian Priory of Bruton and the Cluniac Priory of Montacute (Somerset Record Society, 1894), charter 1, pp. 119–120.

Chapter 2. Maltravers Knights

1. G.E.C., [G. E. Cokayne], *Complete Peerage*, 2nd edn, 13 vols (St Catherine Press, 1910–1959), VIII, 577–578.
2. W. E. Wightman, *The Lacy Family in England and Normandy 1066–1194* (Oxford University Press, 1966), p. 70.
   Magnum Rotulum Scaccarii vel Magnum Rotulum Pipae de anno Tricesimo-primo Regni Henrici I [The Great Roll of the Pipe 1130–31] (Record Commission, 1833), p. 34.
   This pipe roll is an isolated survival; no pipe rolls have survived from the next two decades. A continuous record of the pipe rolls begins in 1155.
3. *The Oxford Illustrated History of Medieval England*, ed. by Nigel Saul (Oxford University Press, 1997), pp. 81–82.
4. Richard of Hexham, 'The Acts of King Stephen, and the Battle of the Standard', in *The Church Historians of England*, trans. by J. Stevenson, 5 vols (1856), vol. IV, part 1, pp. 33–58 (p. 35).
5. Richard of Hexham, as above.
6. John Hutchins, *The History and Antiquities of the County of Dorset*, 3rd edn, rev. by W. Shipp and J. W. Hodson, 4 vols (1868; repr. E. P. Publishing, 1973), III, 314;
   G.E.C., *Complete Peerage*, VIII, 577–578;
   Magnum Rotulum Scaccarii [1130–31], pp. 15, 87, 124.
7. John Maltravers paid into the treasury 1 mark in 1157–58: *The Great Rolls of the Pipe for the Second, Third and Fourth Years of the Reign of King Henry the Second* [1155–58] (Record Commission, 1844), p. 119.
   And a further 1 mark in 1158–59: *The Great Roll of the Pipe for the Fifth Year of the Reign of King Henry the Second* [1158–59] (Pipe Roll Society, vol. I, 1884), p. 39.
8. John Maltravers paid 50 marks into the treasury in 1164–65: *The Great Roll of the Pipe for the Eleventh Year of the Reign of King Henry the Second* [1164–65] (Pipe Roll Society, vol. VIII, 1887), p. 65;
   And another 50 marks in 1165–66: *The Great Roll of the Pipe for the Twelfth Year of the Reign of King Henry the Second* [1165–66] (Pipe Roll Society, vol. IX, 1888), p. 98.
9. *The Great Roll of the Pipe for the Eighteenth Year of the Reign of King Henry the Second* [1171–72] (Pipe Roll Society, vol. XVIII, 1894), p. 77.
   The *Complete Peerage* mentions the possibility, but not the certainty, of a different John in 1172: 'John, whom we suppose to be son and heir of John abovenamed': G.E.C. *Complete Peerage*, VIII, 578.
10. In 1184–85, he paid 25 marks, leaving 75 marks owing: *The Great Roll of the Pipe for the Thirty-first Year of the Reign of King Henry the Second* [1184–85] (Pipe Roll Society, vol. XXXIV, 1913), p. 182.

For the next year, the debt is given in pounds, so the 75 marks he owed is given as £50, of which he paid £24, leaving £26 to pay: *The Great Roll of the Pipe for the Thirty-second Year of the Reign of King Henry the Second* [1185–86] (The Pipe Roll Society, vol. xxxvi, 1914), p. 139.

The debt was gradually paid off over the following two or three years.

11 George Thomas Clark, 'The Earls, Earldom and Castle of Pembroke, 3', *Archaeologia Cambrensis*, 3rd ser., vol. 5, issue 19 (July 1859), 188–202 (p. 191).
12 G.E.C., *Complete Peerage*, viii, unnumbered page, Maltravers pedigree.
13 G.E.C., *Complete Peerage*, viii, 578.
14 Torquato Tasso, *Jerusalem Delivered*, trans. by J.H. Wiffen, 3rd edn (1830), p. lxxvi. 'Walter de Maltrevers' is in the list of crusaders in the reign of Richard I.
15 *An Inventory of the Historical Monuments in Dorset*, 5 vols (Royal Commission on Historical Monuments of England, 1952–1975), ii: *South East* (1970), pp. 154–157.
16 Great Somerford: *Victoria County History: Wiltshire*, xiv (1991) <http://www.british-history.ac.uk/vch/wilts/vol14/pp194-204> [accessed 18 June 2018]
Filands: *VCH Wiltshire*, xiv <http://www.british-history.ac.uk/vch/wilts/vol14/pp229-240> [accessed 18 June 2018]
Coate: *VCH: Wiltshire*, vii (1953) <http://www.british-history.ac.uk/vch/wilts/vol7/pp187-197> [accessed 18 June 2018]
17 G.E.C., *Complete Peerage*, viii, unnumbered page, Maltravers pedigree.
18 *Curia Regis Rolls Richard I and John*, prepared by C.T. Flower, 7 vols (HMSO, 1922–72), i, pp. 219, 224, 271, 273, 332, 356, 380–381, 393, 441;
Paul R. Hyams, *Rancor and Reconciliation in Medieval England* (Cornell University Press, 2003), pp. 294–296.
19 Henry de Bracton, *Bracton's Note Book: A collection of cases decided in the King's courts during the reign of Henry the Third, annotated by a lawyer of that time, seemingly by Henry of Bratton*, ed. by F. W. Maitland, 3 vols (1887), ii, case 77, pp. 69–70.
20 Letters Patent, cited in Hutchins, *Dorset*, iii, 316.
21 G.E.C., *Complete Peerage*, viii, 578.
22 Son underage in Trinity term, May/June 1220: Bracton *Note Book*, iii, case 1437, pp. 389–390.
Property escheated in 1221: Hutchins, *Dorset*, iii, 316; *CFR 1220–21*, no. 132 <http://www.finerollshenry3.org.uk> [accessed 20 June 2018]
23 Hawise 1222: De Bracton *Note Book*, ii, case 191, p. 156.
24 Inquisition post mortem on John Giffard, d. 1322: refers to the grant of Ashton by John Maltravers III to his sister Alice, grandmother of the John Giffard who died in 1322. *CIPM 1327–36*, no. 78.
25 *CLR 1240–45*, p. 26.
26 G.E.C., *Complete Peerage*, viii, 578–579.
27 *CLR 1245–51*, p. 98.

28 *CPR 1247–58*, p. 523.
29 *Two Cartularies of the Augustinian Priory of Bruton and the Cluniac Priory of Montacute* (Somerset Record Society, 1894), charter no. 33, p. 134. In the printed version, Maltravers is recorded as 'John Maltravers of Gunle', which is probably a mis-transcription for Gyvele (Yeovil).
30 Lewes and Evesham:
F. M. Powicke, *King Henry III and the Lord Edward*, 2 vols (Oxford University Press, 1947), II, 493–502.
David Crouch, 'Giffard, John, first Lord Giffard (1232-1299), baron' in *ODNB*, online edn, Jan. 2008 <http://www.oxforddnb.com/view/article/10651> [accessed 23 March 2011]
D. A. Carpenter, *The Battles of Lewes and Evesham 1264/5* (Mercia, 1987).
Lewes:
William Maltravers was at Lewes with John Giffard; they captured two royalist knights: Reginald FitzPiers and Alan de la Zouch: W. H. Blaauw, *The Barons' War, including the Battles of Lewes and Evesham*, 2nd edn (1871), p. 201.
Evesham:
O. de Laborderie, J. R. Maddicott and D. A. Carpenter, 'The Last Hours of Simon de Montfort: A New Account', *English Historical Review*, 115, issue 461 (2000), 378–412.
Robert of Gloucester, *Chronicle* [in English verse]. Text in *The Metrical Chronicle of Robert of Gloucester*, ed. by W. A. Wright (1887), part 2. Translated into modern English in *The Church Historians of England*, trans. by J. Stevenson (1858), vol. 5, part 1. The actions of William Maltravers III in cutting off de Montfort's feet and hands; and the description of Evesham as 'The murder of Evesham for battle was it none'.
Arnald FitzThedmar, *Chronicle* <www.nationalarchives.gov.uk/battle.of.evesham> [accessed 26 June 2018] Translation of an extract on the killing of Simon de Montfort, including hanging de Montfort's testicles on either side of his nose.
31 *Abbreviatio Placitorum* (1811), pp. 160, 165.
32 W. H. Blaauw, *The Barons' War*, p. 375. Gives a list of participants, including, among the royalist gentry, 'John de Maltravers, Dorset; William de Maltravers, Dorset'. Blaauw's source cited as *Abbreviatio Placitorum*.
33 *CIPM 1291–1300*, no. 149.
34 *CChR 1257–1300*, pp. 227–28.
35 *CIPM 1327–36*, no. 78.
John Giffard died in 1322, his inquisition post mortem was in 1327 and further inquiry was conducted in July 1327.
When John Lestrange died in 1361, an inquiry duly found that he held half of the manor of Ashton from Sir John Maltravers: *CIPM 1361–1365*, no. 202.
36 *The Royal Charter Witness List of Edward I 1272–1307*, transcribed and ed. by Richard Huscroft, List and Index Society, 279 (List and Index Society, 2000).

Handbook of British Chronology, 3rd edn (Royal Historical Society, 1986).
37 Roger Dodsworth, *Monasticon Anglicanum* (1655), p. 992.
38 Henry Gough, *Itinerary of King Edward the First Throughout his Reign A.D. 1272–1307*, 2 vols (Gardner, 1900), I: *1272–1285*, p. 41.
39 Thomas Blount, *Fragmenta Antiquitatis or Antient* [sic] *Tenures of Land and Jocular Customs of Some Manors* (first published 1679; new edition with notes by Beckwith, 1784), p. 334.
40 G. J. Turner, 'The justices of the forest south of the Trent', *English Historical Review*, 18, issue 49 (1903), 112–116.
41 *CPR 1258–66*, p. 435.
42 *CFR 1269–70*, no. 1134 <http://www.finerollshenry3.org.uk> [accessed 27 June 2018]
43 *CFR 1272–1307*, p. 28.
44 *CPR 1272–81*, p. 443.
45 *CPR 1281–92*, p. 84.
46 *CFR 1272–1307*, p. 382.
47 *CFR 1307–19*, p. 1.
48 'Neville, Geoffrey de (d. 1285), baron' in *Oxford Dictionary of National Biography* (Oxford University Press, 2004) <https://doi.org/10.1093/ref:odnb/19933> [accessed 19 June 2019]
49 'Vescy, William de, Lord Vescy (1245–1298)', in *ODNB* <https://doi.org/10.1093/ref:odnb/28255> [accessed 19 June 2019] Includes William de Vescy's two periods of office, 1285–1290 and 1295–1297, and John de Vescy's period of office 1290–1295.
50 'Clifford, Robert, first Lord Clifford (1274–1314)' in *ODNB* <https://doi.org/10.1093/ref:odnb/5658> [accessed 19 June 2019]
51 'Royal Forests', in *Victoria County History: Wiltshire*, (VCH, 1959), IV, 391–433 <http://www.british-history.ac.uk/vch/wilts/vol4/pp391–433> [accessed 27 June 2018];
Earl of Cardigan, *The Wardens of Savernake Forest* (Routledge & Kegan Paul, 1949).
52 *Full Abstracts of the Feet of Fines Relating to the County of Dorset from Their Commencement in the Reign of Richard I*, ed. by E. A. Fry and G. S. Fry, Dorset Records, 5 (1896), p. 199. This volume covers the years 1195–1327.
53 *Feet of Fines Dorset from Richard I*, Dorset Records 5, pp. 244–45.
54 *CPR 1272–81*, pp. 390, 443, 444, 459.
55 G.E.C., *Complete Peerage*, VIII, 579; *CPR 1281–92*, p. 154.
56 *CPR 1281–92*, p. 316.
57 *Feet of Fines, Dorset from Richard I*, Dorset Records 5, p. 204; *CIPM 1300–1307*, no. 153.
58 Henry Gough, *Itinerary of King Edward the First*, I, 173;
C. Cochrane, *Poole Bay and Purbeck 3000 BC–AD 1660* (Friary Press, 1970), p. 60.

59 F. M. Powicke, *The Thirteenth Century 1216–1307* (Oxford University Press, 1953), p. 440–443;
    Marc Morris, *A Great and Terrible King: Edward I and the Forging of Britain* (Hutchinson, 2008), pp. 275–279;
    Parliamentary Writs and Writs of Military Summons 1273–1327, ed. by F. Palgrave (1827);
    'Giffard, John, first Lord Giffard 1232–1299' in *ODNB* <https://doi.org/10.1093/ref:odnb/10651> [accessed 2 September 2018]
60 Joan, born 1272, was a daughter of Edward I, and by 1297 had become the young widow of her much older husband, Gilbert de Clare, Earl of Gloucester and Hertford, who was born in 1243 and died in 1295.
61 *CIPM, 1291–1300*, no. 404.
62 Samantha Letters, *Online Gazetteer of Markets and Fairs in England and Wales to 1516: Somerset*, updated 2013 <www.history.ac.uk/cmh/gaz/gazweb2> [accessed 27 June 2018]

Chapter 3. War and Rebellion

1 Hutchins, *Dorset*, III, 316.
2 Chronicle of Walter of Guisborough, previously known as Walter of Hemingborough: *Walter of Hemingborough, Chronicon*, ed. by H. C. Hamilton, 2 vols (English Historical Society, 1849), II, 121.
3 Marc Morris, *A Great and Terrible King: Edward I and the Forging of Britain* (Hutchinson, 2008), pp. 297–300.
4 *Calendar of Patent Rolls 1292–1301*, p. 417.
5 Anthony Mitchell, *Kingston Lacy, Dorset* (National Trust, 1994), p. 6.
6 Henry Gough, Itinerary of King Edward the First Throughout his Reign, 2 vols (Gardner, 1900), II: 1286–1307, p. 258.
7 The payment to Melior at Plympton on 23 April 1297 is recorded in the following, with the source given as the royal household accounts of Edward I, Edward II, and Edward III, Addit. MS No. 7965.: The Graphic and Historical Illustrator, ed. by E. W. Brayley, I (1834), p. 89. These documents are now in the British Library with the same reference number: British Library, Add. MS 7965 Wardrobe Accounts 25 Edward I: 20 November 1296–20 November 1297. Confirmation that the king was at Plympton for about a month in April 1297 is in Gough, *Itinerary*.
8 *Calendar of Charter Rolls 1300–26*, p. 66.
9 *Calendar of Documents relating to Scotland*, v, supplementary (1986): John, Walter and Roger Maltravers, protection 12 June 1306, p. 441, no. 2610; John Maltravers, letters of attorney 22 July 1306, p. 354, no. 1607.
10 Roger Mortimer, protection 26 May 1306, *CDS*, v, 436–437, no. 2600.

11 *CPR 1307–13*, December 1307, p. 30, and March 1308, p. 53.
12 *CPR 1307–13*, May 1308, p. 87; May 1309, p. 172; March 1310, p. 255. Luke: *Calendar of Fine Rolls 1307–19*, p. 93.
13 *CPR 1307–13*, October 1307, p. 10. [attorneys Robert Lovel and William le Clerk];
    CPR 1307–13, April 1308, p. 66. [attorney William Denebaud];
    CPR 1307–13, September 1310, p. 281. [attorneys John de Middleton and Henry de Glanville].
14 The original roll has disappeared, but a copy is in a document in the British Library: MS Cotton Caligula A, xviii, fols. 3–21.
    It has been printed several times, including N. H. Nicolas, *A Roll of Arms of the Reign of Edward the Second* (1829), in which John Maltravers is on page 12.
15 John Buckledee, 'Tournaments', in *Medieval Dunstable* <www.medievaldunstable.org.uk> Includes list of participants; place and date Dunstable 1309. [accessed 1 October 2016]
    C. E. Long, 'Tournament at Stepney, 2 Edw. II', in *Collectanea Topographica et Genealogica*, iv (1837), 61–72. This includes a list of participants; John Maltravers is no. 191. This is from an eighteenth-century manuscript. The location 'Stepney' is wrong, it should be Dunstable; and the date should be 1309, not 1308.
    A. Tomkinson, 'Retinues at Dunstable 1309', *English Historical Review*, 74 (1959), 70–89. This corrects the place and date to Dunstable, 1309.
16 *CPR 1307–13*, 13 May 1313, 'Protection for John Maltravers going with Robert son of Payn', p. 581.
17 *CPR 1307–13*, 31 May 1313, p. 590.
18 *Calendar of Close Rolls 1313–18*, p. 77.
    Bridget R. Harvey, 'The Berkeleys of Berkeley, 1281–1417: A Study in the Lesser Peerage of Late Medieval England' (PhD Thesis, University of St Andrews, 1989), pp. 43–44.
19 *Full Abstracts of the Feet of Fines Relating to the County of Dorset from Their Commencement in the Reign of Richard I*, ed. by E. A. Fry and G. S. Fry, Dorset Records, 5 (1896), p. 323.
20 *CChR 1300–26*, p. 269.
21 John Maltravers with Maurice de Berkeley, letters of attorney, 3 May 1314: *CDS*, v, p. 364, no. 1729;
    John Maltravers and Robert Maltravers with him, protection, 6 May 1314: *CDS*, v, p. 464, no. 2971.
22 Thomas de Berkeley: *CPR 1313–17*, p. 107; Maurice de Berkeley: *CPR 1313–17*, p. 123.
23 John Barbour, *The Bruce* [poem written c. 1371–75], trans. by Michael Macmillan, *The Bruce of Bannockburn Being a Translation of the Greater Part of Barbour's Bruce* (E. MacKay, 1914).

24 Nicholas Trivet, *Annalium Continuatio* (Theatro Sheldoniano, Oxford, 1722; repr. Kessinger, 2009).
   This includes the list of captives. The chronicler Nicholas Trivet died c. 1334.
25 *The Chronicle of Lanercost 1272–1346*, trans. by Sir Herbert Maxwell (Maclehose, 1913).
26 Trivet, *Annalium*, p. 15.
   T. F. Tout, *Chapters in the Administrative History of Mediaeval England*, 6 vols (Manchester University Press, 1920–33), II (1920), 294–295.
27 *Vita Edwardi Secundi*, ed. by and revised translation by Wendy Childs (Oxford University Press, 2005), p. 97.
   For the Battle of Bannockburn in general:
   David Cornwell, *Bannockburn: The Triumph of Robert the Bruce* (Yale University Press, 2009);
   Peter Reese, *Bannockburn* (Canongate Books, 2003).
28 Date of appointment: John Scott, *Berwick-upon-Tweed: The History of the Town and Guild* (1888), pp. 40–41.
29 *Calendar of Documents Relating to Scotland*, ed. by Joseph Bain, 4 vols. (Public Record Office, 1881–88), III, 1307–57 (1887), p. 85, no. 452.
30 *CDS*, III, 89–90, no. 470.
31 *CDS*, III, 91, no. 477.
32 *CCR 1313–18*, pp. 352–353.
33 *Collectanea Topographica et Genealogica*, VI (1840), 340; Hutchins, *Dorset*, III, 316.
34 *Close Rolls Cl. 10 Edw. II m. 26d.*, cited in *Parliamentary Writs and Writs of Military Summons 1273–1326*, ed. by F. Palgrave, vol. 2, division 1 (1830), p. 185.
35 *Coll. Top. & Gen.*, VI (1840), 340; and Hutchins, *Dorset*, III, 316 [both these sources give the wrong year, 1317, it should be 1316].
36 *CPR 1313–17*, 17 June 1316, p. 480; 12 July 1316, p. 508.
37 *Calendar of Chancery Warrants*, I: 1244–1326, p. 455.
38 *Parliamentary Writs and Writs of Military Summons*, ed. by F. Palgrave, vol. 2, division 1 (1830), p. 191.
39 *CPR 1317–21*, p. 64.
40 *Feet of Fines Dorset from Richard I*, Dorset Records 5, p. 289, no 114A.
41 *CPR 1317–21*, pp. 451–452, pp 364–365;
   J. R. S. Phillips, *Aymer de Valence* (Oxford University Press, 1972);
   R.M. Haines, 'Sir Thomas Gurney of Englishcombe in the County of Somerset, Regicide?', *Somerset Archaeological and Natural History Society Proceedings*, 147 (2004), 45–65.
42 *CChR 1300–26*, p. 391, no. 76.
43 *Parliamentary Writs and Writs of Military Summons*, vol. 2, division 1 (1830), p. xxxv.

44 *Parliamentary Writs and Writs of Military Summons*, cited in *Coll. Top. & Gen.*, VI (1840), p. 340. The letters of protection issued on 8 August 1319 for 'John Maltravers' do not specify John Maltravers the younger, so it is probably for John Maltravers V;
CDS, v (1986), p. 487, no. 3250.
45 *CPR 1317–21*, p. 477.
46 Appointment: *Gascon Rolls C 61/33*, m. 12, nos. 104–105;
Repayment ordered on 6 March 1320: *CCR 1318–23*, p. 183;
Protection for Maurice de Berkeley and companions of 7 March 1320: *CPR 1317–21*, p. 432;
Successor: *Gascon Rolls C 61/33*, m. 7, nos. 230 and 232.
47 *Feet of Fines Dorset from Richard I*, Dorset Records 5, p. 303, no. 155.
48 *CCR 1318–23*, pp. 541–543.
49 *CPR 1321–24*, pp. 15–16.
50 *CPR 1321–24*, p. 40.
51 *CPR 1321–24*, p. 46; *CFR 1319–27*, p. 87.
52 *Parliamentary Writs and Writs of Military Summons*, vol. 2, division 1 (1830), p. 272.
53 *CCR 1318–23*, p. 519.
54 *CCR 1318–23*, p. 427.
55 Ian Mortimer, *The Greatest Traitor: The Life of Roger Mortimer, Ruler of England 1327–1330* (Jonathan Cape, 2003), pp. 124–125;
May McKisack, *The Fourteenth Century 1307–1399* (Oxford University Press, 1959), p. 73;
Kathryn Warner, *Edward II: The Unconventional King* (Amberley, 2014), pp. 158–160.
56 James Greenstreet, 'The Boroughbridge Roll of Arms', *The Genealogist*, new series, 1 (1884), 51–54, 117–121 (p. 119);
Vicary Gibbs, 'The Battle of Boroughbridge and the Boroughbridge Roll', *The Genealogist*, 21 (1905), 222–226;
Bridget Wells-Furby, 'The "Boroughbridge" Roll Reconsidered', *Historical Research*, 86 (2013), 196–206.
57 'The French Chronicle of London 1259–1343' in *Chronicles of the Mayors and Sheriffs of London 1188–1274* (1863).
58 *CCR 1318–23*, p. 586.
59 *CPR 1324–27*, p. 223.
60 *CCR 1318–23*, p. 474.
61 *Coll. Top. & Gen.*, VI, p. 340; Hutchins, *Dorset*, III, 316
[both these sources give the correct year for the summons (1322), but the wrong year for the muster (1323), it should be 1322].
62 Mortimer, *The Greatest Traitor*, p. 135.
63 John Maltravers V: *Coll. Top. & Gen.*, VI, 341; Hutchins, Dorset, III, 317

[both these sources give the wrong year (1326); it should be 1325].
64 Roger Maltravers I: Coll. Top. & Gen., VI, 341; Hutchins, *Dorset*, III, 317;
   [both these sources give the wrong year (1326); it should be 1325].
   Calendar of Gascon Rolls, TNA C 61/36:290.
65 Additional list of deserters: CGR, TNA C 61/36:472.
66 *CGR*, TNA C 61/38:37.
67 *CPR 1327–30*, p.59.
68 G.E.C., *Complete Peerage*, VIII, 580.
69 *CPR 1324–27*, p. 232.
70 Hutchins, *Dorset*, III, 317; G.E.C., *Complete Peerage*, VIII, 580.

Chapter 4. The Death of a King?

1 *CPR 1324–27*, pp. 325–328.
2 Maltravers oath: *Calendar of the Plea and Memoranda Rolls of the City of London*, I: 1323–1364, ed. by A. H. Thomas (HMSO, 1926), p. 12;
   Roy Martin Haines, *King Edward II: Edward of Caernarfon, his Life, his Reign and its Aftermath, 1284–1330* (McGill-Queen's University Press, 2003), pp. 193–194.
   Maltravers was not a knight of the shire for Dorset: *Parliamentary Writs and Writs of Military Summons*, vol. 2, division 1, compiled and ed. by F. Palgrave (1830), p. xxxvi.
3 Close Rolls 1 Edw. III, p. 1, m. 22., cited in Hutchins, Dorset, III, 318.
4 *CPR 1327–30*, p. 59.
5 *CPR 1327–30*, p. 59.
6 *CPR 1327–30*, p. 101.
7 *CPR 1327–30*, p. 346.
8 *CPR 1327–30*, p. 130.
9 *CPR 1327–30*, p. 209.
10 *CPR 1327–30*, p. 182.
11 Roy Martin Haines, 'Sir Thomas Gurney of Englishcombe in the County of Somerset, Regicide?', *Somerset Archaeological and Natural History Society Proceedings*, 147 (2004), 45–65.
12 *CPR 1321–24*, p. 17.
13 John Smyth, *The Lives of the Berkeleys*, ed. by Sir John Maclean, 3 vols (1883–85), I (1883), pp. 291–292.
14 Adam Murimuth, *Continuatio Chronicarum*, ed. by Edward Maunde Thompson (1889; repr. Cambridge University Press, 2012), p. 52.
15 Geoffrey le Baker, *The Chronicle of Geoffrey le Baker of Swinbrook*, trans. by David Preest, (Boydell Press, 2012; repr. 2018), pp. 29–30.
16 *CCR 1327–30*, p. 77; Geoffrey le Baker, p. 31; Murimuth, p. 52.

17 Close Rolls 1 Edw. III, p. 1, m. 2 d., cited in Hutchins, *Dorset*, III, pp. 317–318.
18 *CPR 1327–30*, p. 95.
19 *CPR 1327–30*, p. 130.
20 *CPR 1327–30*, p. 154.
21 Seymour Phillips, *Edward II* (Yale University Press, 2010), p. 544, note 133.
22 *CPR 1327–30*, pp. 156–157.
23 T. F. Tout, 'The Captivity and Death of Edward of Carnarvon', *Bulletin of the John Rylands Library*, 6, no. 1 (1920; repr. Longmans, 1920).
    Ian Mortimer, *The Greatest Traitor: The Life of Sir Roger Mortimer, Ruler of England 1327–1330* (Jonathan Cape, 2003), pp. 186–187.
    Phillips, *Edward II*, pp. 547–548.
24 Murimuth, pp. 53–54.
25 Payment to Berkeley and Maltravers: *CCR 1327–30*, p. 284.
26 Ian Mortimer, *Greatest Traitor*, pp. 197–198; Phillips, p. 553.
    Heritage: Cathedral History < www.gloucestercathedral.org.uk > [accessed 26 July 2018]
27 Ian Mortimer, *Greatest Traitor*, pp. 198–199, 292–293 note 11. This quotes an account by Hugh de Glanville, the royal clerk who escorted the woman to Worcester.
28 Ian Mortimer, *Greatest Traitor*, pp. 212, 295 note 33.
    The chronicle that mentions Lancaster's murder accusation is *The Brut*, ed. by F.W.D. Brie, 2 vols (1906–08), I (1906), 259.
29 Natalie Fryde, *The Tyranny and Fall of Edward II 1321–1326* (Cambridge University Press, 1979; repr. 2003), p. 220.
30 *CPR 1327–30*, p. 423.
31 *CPR 1327–30*, pp. 212, 221–223, 434, 476, 565.
32 *CFR 1327–37*, pp. 107, 155.
33 Maltravers steward, 1328: *Handbook of British Chronology*, 3rd edn (Royal Historical Society, 1986), p.76;
    Ian Mortimer, *Greatest Traitor*, p. 203.
34 Maltravers steward, 1329: *Handbook of British Chronology*, p. 76;
    Witnessing charters in 1329: Ian Mortimer, *The Perfect King: the Life of Edward III, Father of the English Nation* (Jonathan Cape, 2006), p. 422.
35 Ian Mortimer, *Perfect King*, pp. 72–74;
    Rymer, *Foedera*, cited in Hutchins, *Dorset*, III, 318;
    On 30 May 1329 Maltravers nominated attorneys until 1 August to cover for his absence: *CPR 1327–30*, p. 390.
36 *CFR 1327–37*, p. 128.
37 *CFR 1327–37*, p. 206.
38 *CCR 1327–30*, p. 568; *CPR 1327–30*, p. 421.
39 *CCR 1327–1330*, p. 576; *CPR 1327–1330*, p. 449.
    This eyre may not have taken place, as no plea rolls have been found in the

Exchequer records:
Jane Winters, 'The Forest Eyre 1154–1368' (Unpublished doctoral thesis, University of London, King's College, 1999).
40 15 January: CCR 1327–30, p. 588.
Revised date 26 February: *CPR 1327–30*, p. 466.
41 *CCR 1330–1333*, p. 31; *CPR 1327–30*, pp. 521–522.
42 *CCR 1327–30*, p. 568.
43 *CCR 1327–30*, p. 575.
44 Earl of Cardigan, *The Wardens of Savernake Forest* (Routledge & Kegan Paul, 1949), p. 64–68;
H. C. Brentnall, 'The metes and bounds of Savernake Forest', *Wiltshire Archaeological and Natural History Magazine*, 49 (1941), 391–434.
45 *CCR 1327–30*, p. 458.
46 Charles R. Young, *The Royal Forests of Medieval England* (University of Pennsylvania Press, 1979), p. 154.
47 *CCR 1327–30*, p. 450.
48 *CCR 1330–33*, p. 18.
49 *CFR 1327–37*, p. 179.
50 Murimuth, pp. 253–257.
51 Kathryn Warner, *Edward II: The Unconventional King*, (Amberley, 2014), p. 248.
Melton's letter was first partly published in 1911: J. Harvey Bloom, 'Simon de Swanland and King Edward II', *Notes and Queries*, 11th ser., 4 (Jul.–Dec. 1911), p. 1.
The letter is summarised, including Melton's request for secrecy, but its significance was not immediately realised, as the letter was not dated by year. In recent times, it is discussed in this article:
Roy Martin Haines, 'Sumptuous apparel for a royal prisoner: Archbishop Melton's letter, 14 January 1330', *English Historical Review*, 124 (2009), 885–894.
And it is also referred to in recent biographies.
52 Appointment of John Pecche: *CPR 1324–27*, p. 202.
Appointment of John Maltravers: *CFR 1327–37*, p. 149.
Repairs: *CCR 1327–30*, p. 487.
53 *CPR 1327–30*, p. 477.
54 Summons to parliament (RDP): *Reports from the Lords Committees touching the Dignity of a Peer of the Realm*, 5 vols (1829), IV, p. 393.
55 Geoffrey Le Baker, pp. 39–40. The original is in Latin.
56 *The Brut, or, the Chronicles of England*, ed. by F. W. D. Brie, 2 vols (Early English Text Society, 1906; repr. 1960), I, 263–265.
57 *CPR 1327–30*, p. 556.
58 *CPR 1327–30*, p. 571.
59 *CPR 1327–30*, pp. 563–564.

60 Hugh Turplington, steward: *Handbook of British Chronology*, p. 76.
61 Argentine: G.E.C., *Complete Peerage*, I, 196–197.
62 *CPR 1324–27*, p. 346.
63 *CIPM 1327–36*, no. 78.
64 *CIPM 1327–36*, no. 78.
65 *CIPM 1327–36*, no. 78.
66 *CIPM 1327–36*, no. 79.
67 *CIPM 1327–36*, no. 78.
68 *CFR 1327–37*, p. 113.
69 *CChR 1327–41*, pp. 116–117.
70 *CPR 1327–30*, p. 527; *CCR 1330–33*, p. 140.
71 *CPR 1327–30*, p. 429.
72 *CPR 1327–30*, p. 10.
73 *CPR 1327–30*, p. 404.
74 *CFR 1327–37*, p. 174.
75 *CPR 1334–38*, p. 445.
76 'Beal fitz, beal fitz, eiez pitie de gentil Mortymer.':
   Chronicon Galfridi le Baker de Swynebroke, ed. by Edward Maunde Thompson (Clarendon Press, 1889), p. 46;
   Geoffrey Le Baker, *Chronicle*, trans. by D. Preest, p. 41.
77 *CCR 1330–33*, p. 158–159.
78 Summons to parliament (RDP): *Reports from the Lords Committees touching the Dignity of a Peer of the Realm*, IV (1829), p. 398.
79 *The Parliament Rolls of Medieval England* [PROME], IV: *Edward III, 1327–1348*, ed. by Seymour Phillips and Mark Ormrod
   'Edward III: November 1330, C65/2 mm 7-5', [PROME-ONLINE], <http://www.british-history.ac/no-series/parliament-rolls-medieval/november-1330> [accessed 3 July 2018]
80 *PROME-ONLINE*, November 1330.
81 *PROME-ONLINE*, November 1330.; Hutchins, *Dorset*, III, 318.
82 *PROME-ONLINE*, November 1330.
83 *PROME-ONLINE*, November 1330.
84 *PROME-ONLINE*, November 1330.
85 *CCR 1330–33*, p. 165.
86 *CPR 1330–34*, p. 144.
87 Haines, 'Sir Thomas Gurney of Englishcombe in the County of Somerset, Regicide', pp. 58–59.
88 Phillips, p. 576.
89 *CPR 1330–34*, p. 201.
90 *CFR 1327–37*, pp. 207, 217–218, 226.
91 *PROME-ONLINE*, November 1330.
92 The order to restore the title of earl and the lands: *CCR 1330–1333*, p. 292.

93 Ian Mortimer, *Greatest Traitor*, p. 189–190.
94 Polychronicon Ranulphi Higden, ed. by J. R. Lumby, 8 vols. (Longman, 1882) VIII, 324: cited by Ian Mortimer, The Greatest Traitor, p. 191.
95 Geoffrey Le Baker, *Chronicle*, trans. by D. Preest, p. 32.
96 Ian Mortimer, 'The Death of Edward II in Berkeley Castle', *English Historical Review*, 120 (2005), 1175–1214 (p. 1190).
97 Roy Martin Haines, *King Edward II*, pp. 226, 467 (footnote 36).
98 The full text of the Fieschi letter is in the following:
G. P. Cuttino and Thomas W. Lyman, 'Where is Edward II?', *Speculum*, 53 (1978), 522–543, English translation pp. 526–527;
Ian Mortimer, *Greatest Traitor*, English translation pp. 251–252;
The Auramala project: facsimile, Latin text and English translation <https://theauramalaproject.wordpress.com/2016/11/10/the-fieschi-letteria/lettera-fieschi/> [accessed 10 June 2019]
99 Cuttino and Lyman, 'Where is Edward II?', 522–543.
100 Ian Mortimer, *Perfect King*, p. 152–154.
101 Tout, *Captivity*, p. 39.
102 Cuttino and Lyman, pp. 522–543.
103 Ian Mortimer, *Greatest Traitor*, pp. 251–252.
Ian Mortimer, 'The Death of Edward II in Berkeley Castle', *English Historical Review*, 120 (2005), 1175–1214.
Ian Mortimer, *Perfect King*, p. 201.

Chapter 5. Exile, Crécy and Calais

1 Dover: *CCR 1330–33*, p. 584;
Protection and attorneys: *CPR 1330–34*, p. 324.
2 *CPR 1330–34*, p. 535.
3 Pardons issued in March 1335 to Montagu, Beche and Moleyns: *CPR 1334–38*, p. 88;
Pardons issued in April 1335 to Bereford: *CPR 1334–38*, p. 89;
Pardons issued in June 1335 to Thomas and Maurice Berkeley, William de Whitefield and Adam the Abbot of Malmesbury: *CPR 1334–38*, p. 111.
4 *CPR 1338–40*, p. 112.
5 *TNA Special Collections: Ancient Petitions*, SC 8/107/5327.
6 Rot. Alemann., 12 Edw. III, p. 2, m. 7d., cited in *Coll. Top. & Gen.*, VI (1840), 341.
7 *CPR 1338–40*, p. 378.
8 *TNA Special Collections: Ancient Petitions*, SC 8/272/13564. Dated to the parliament of Feb. 1339.
9 *CPR 1340–43*, pp. 370, 378.

10 *CPR 1343–45*, p. 173.
11 *CPR 1343–45*, p. 535.
12 *CPR 1343–45*, pp. 541–542.
13 *CCR 1330–33*, p. 207.
14 *CFR 1327–37*, p. 206.
15 *CPR 1330–34*, pp. 72–73.
16 *CPR 1330–34*, p. 116, May 1331.
17 *CChR 1327–41*, p. 352, charter no. 62.
18 *CFR 1327–37*, p. 287.
19 *CFR, 1327–37*, p. 274.
20 *CFR 1327–37*, p. 423, Nov. 1334.
21 *CIPM 1327–36*, no. 78; *CCR 1333–37*, p. 402.
22 *CPR 1334–38*, pp. 560–561.
23 *CPR 1334–38*, p. 562.
24 *CPR 1334–38*, pp. 563–564.
25 *CPR 1338–40*, p. 239.
26 *CPR 1330–34*, pp. 84, 215.
27 *CPR 1334–38*, p. 134.
28 *CCR 1333–37*, p. 233.
29 *CCR 1333–37*, p. 558.
30 *CPR 1338–40*, p. 239.
31 *CChR 1327–41*, pp. 348–349; *CPR 1338–40*, p. 393.
32 Edward Maltravers held Rathkeale in 1334–35: Pipe Rolls Ireland, 44, p. 55, cited in Brian Hodkinson, Who Was Who in Medieval Limerick, Manuscript Sources (updated 2014): <https://www.limerick.ie/sites/default/files/atoms/files/who_was…> [accessed 16 July 2018]
33 *CPR 1340–43*, p. 124.
34 Chester Inquisitions Post Mortem, cited in G.E.C., *Complete Peerage*, VIII, 580–581.
35 *CPR 1340–43*, p. 511.
36 *CCR 1349–54*, pp. 313–314, 323.
37 *CPR 1343–45*, p. 210; *CFR 1337–1347*, p. 353.
38 *CPR 1343–45*, pp. 244, 245.
39 French Roll 20 Ed. III m.1, cited in George Wrottesley, *Crécy and Calais from the Original Records in the Public Record Office* (Harrison, 1898; repr. Kessinger Legacy Reprints, [n.d.]), p. 88.
40 The English captains assigned to the Flanders expedition were Lord Hugh Hastings, Lord John Moleyns and Lord John Maltravers: Henry Knighton, *Chronicon*, ed. by Joseph Rawson Lumby, 2 vols (1895), II, 34–35.
John Montgomery, John Moleyns and 'a devious adventurer', John Maltravers, were assigned as Hastings's assistants: Jonathan Sumption, *The Hundred Years War*, (1990–), I: *Trial by Battle* (Faber,1990; repr. 1999), p. 498..

41 Wrottesley, *Crécy and Calais*, p. 197.
42 Wrottesley, pp. 196–197.
43 The movements of the Flemish troops and their failure to link up to king's forces before Crécy: Yuval Noah Harari, 'Inter-frontal cooperation in the fourteenth century and Edward III's 1346 campaign', *War in History*, 6 (1999), 379–395.
44 Wrottesley, pp. 280–281.
45 *CPR 1345–48*, p. 532.
46 *CPR 1345–48*, p. 448.
47 Wrottesley, p. 108.
48 Wrottesley, p. 212.
49 *CPR 1345–48*, p. 565.
50 *CPR 1345–48*, p. 566.
51 *CPR 1345–48*, p. 555.
52 Wrottesley, pp. 98, 130.
53 *CIPM 1336–47*, no. 629.
   CFR 1337–47, p. 474.

Chapter 6. Channel Islands

1 *Parliament Rolls of Medieval England* [PROME], IV: Edward III, 1327–1348, ed. by Seymour Phillips and Mark Ormrod.
   'Edward III: January 1348, C65/13, item 65, Petition of John Maltravers', [PROME-ONLINE], <http://www.british-history.ac.uk/no-series/parliament-rolls-medieval/january-1348> [accessed 30 July 2018]
2 *CCR 1346–49*, p. 523.
3 Sumption, *The Hundred Years War*, I: *Trial by Battle*, pp. 459, 471.
4 *CPR 1348–50*, p. 115.
5 *CPR 1348–50*, p. 165.
6 *CPR 1348–50*, p. 134.
7 *CIPM 1347–52*, no. 46; *CPR 1348–50*, pp. 239–240.
8 Treaty Roll, 22 Edw. III, m. 3, cited in G.E.C., *Complete Peerage*, VIII, 585. Talbot was steward from May 1345 to September 1349: *Handbook of British Chronology*, p.76.
9 Ian Mortimer, *The Perfect King*, p. 262;
   Jonathan Sumption, *The Hundred Years War*, II: *Trial by Fire* (Faber, 1999), pp. 16–17.
10 *CIPM 1347–52*, no. 190.
11 *CCR 1349–54*, p. 33.
12 *CFR 1347–56*, p. 169.
13 *CFR 1347–56*, p. 209.
14 *CPR 1348–50*, pp. 299, 441.

15 William de Carteret died in the first week of March; i.e. 1–8 March 1349: *CIPM 1347–52*, no. 406.
    Reginald de Carteret died in the second week of Lent; i.e. 4–10 March 1349: *CIPM 1347–52*, no. 407.
    The Black Death: Peter Bisson, 'The Fief and Seigneurs of Samarès in the Middle Ages', *Société Jersiaise Annual Bulletin*, 24 (1987), 339–353 (p. 343).
    Online reprint: *Samares in the Middle Ages*, <https://www.theislandwiki.org/index.php/Samares_in_the_Middle_Ages> [accessed 24 August 2018]
16 Order to take the Carteret lands into the king's hands, June 1349: *CFR 1347–56*, p. 121.
    Order to receive the oath of Philip de Carteret, August 1349: *CCR 1349–54*, p. 103.
    Conditional pardon of Philip de Carteret and restitution of his lands, 1351: *CPR 1350–54*, p. 174.
17 J. H. Le Patourel, *The Medieval Administration of the Channel Islands 1199–1399* (Oxford University Press, 1937), pp. 68–69.
18 *CPR 1348–50*, p. 478.
19 *CPR 1348–50*, p. 559.
20 C. Cox, 'St. Peter Port in Bygone Times', *Transactions of la Société Guernesiaise*, 5 (1907), 333–348.
21 Le Patourel, pp.70–71.
22 Gillian Lenfestey, 'Medieval St Peter Port' (n.d.), <museums.gov.gg/CHttpHandler.ashx?id=76720&p=0> [accessed 5 August 2018].
23 Le Patourel, pp. 70–71; Lenfestey, *Medieval St Peter Port*.
24 *CPR 1348–50*, p. 492.
25 Warden's responsibility for revenues: Le Patourel, pp. 86–87.
    The details of individual receivers during John Maltravers VI's wardenship are in Le Parourel, pp. 9–10 as follows [modern TNA reference numbers have been added]:
    John Carteret, Receiver from Michaelmas 1348 to Michaelmas 1349: TNA E 101/89/20 (Jersey), TNA E 101/90/3 (Guernsey).
    John Carteret, Receiver from Michaelmas 1349 to 8 August 1350, in *Société Jersiaise Annual Bulletin*, 7 (1912), 180–184 (Jersey only).
    Nicholas Hastein, Receiver from 8 August 1350 to 8 August 1351: TNA E 101/89/21 (Jersey only).
26 Order to audit the accounts of John Carteret 6 April 1350: CPR 1348–50, p. 528.
27 *CCR 1349–54*, p. 193.
28 *CCR 1349–54*, p. 191.
29 Thomas Rymer, *Foedera*, 4 vols in 7 (London, no publisher, 1825), vol. III, part 1, p. 204;
    Diana Webb, *Pilgrims and Pilgrimage in the Medieval West* (Tauris, 2001), pp. 165–166;

Confraternity of Pilgrims to Rome <http://pilgrimstorome.org.uk/via.francigena> [accessed 6 August 2018]
30 *CPR 1350–54*, p. 59.
31 Le Patourel, pp. 88–92.
32 *CCR 1349–54*, pp. 317–318.
33 Jean De La Croix, *Les Etats: Episode Historique d'une Histoire Inedite de Jersey*, in *La Ville de St Helier* (1845), p. 51.
34 C. Langton, 'Seigneurs of Samarès', *Société Jersiaise Annual Bulletin*, 11 (1931), 376–427 (pp. 383–384);
Online reprint: *Seigneurs of Samares* <www.theislandwiki.org/index.php/Seigneurs_of_Samares> [accessed 25 August 2018]
35 *CPR 1350–54*, p. 76.
36 *CPR 1350–54*, p. 110.
37 *CCR 1349–54*, pp. 312–313.
38 *CCR 1349–54*, pp. 313–314; *CCR 1349–54*, pp. 323.
39 *CPR 1350–54*, p. 153.
40 Inquisition ad quod damnum held in the regnal year 24 Edward III, 25 January 1350 to 24 January 1351: TNA C 143/298/20; Licence in mortmain issued 28 June 1351: *CPR 1350–54*, pp. 116–117.
41 The error in the part played by John Maltravers VI was pointed out in Cox, (1907) p. 340. Cox wrongly dates the licence to 28 June 1362, which, as he says, would have been after Maltravers's time as warden. The site of the hospital is identified as 'the Bosq'.
42 *CPR 1350–54*, p. 123.
43 Peter Bisson, 'Philippe de Barentin and the Payns of Samarès', *Société Jersiaise Annual Bulletin*, 26 (1996), 537–552 (550–552);
Online reprint: <www.theislandwiki.org/index.php/Philippe_de_Barentin_and_the_Payns_of_Samares> [accessed 27 August 2018];
Bisson, 'Samarès in the Middle Ages';
Langton, 'Seigneurs of Samarès'.
Samarès Manor is a listed building, grade 1. There is an architectural description on the States of Jersey website: (Samarès Manor reference CL0085): <https://www.gov.je/citizen/Planning/Pages/HistoricEnvironments.aspx> [accessed 9 August 2018]
44 TNA E 101/391/8, m.2, cited in Ian Mortimer, *The Perfect King*, p. 294, note 7.
45 Hutchins, *Dorset*, III, 319.
46 *The Parliament Rolls of Medieval England* [PROME], v: Edward III, 1351–1377, ed. by Mark Ormrod.
Online edition: 'Edward III: January 1352', items 54-56, [PROME-ONLINE], <http://www.british-history.ac.uk/no-series/parliament-rolls-medieval/january-1352> [accessed 5 March 2019]
The quotation from the Parliament Rolls on the restoration of John Maltravers

VI is printed in this book with the consent of the publishers and by the kind permission of the editors of PROME.
47 *CPR 1350–54*, p. 224.
48 *CFR 1347–56*, p. 320.
49 Protection given and attorneys appointed: *CPR 1350–54*, p. 240.
50 February 15, 1353. Protection for one year for Ralph de Horsy, lieutenant of John Maltravers, keeper of the islands of Guernsey, Jersey, Sark and Alderney, in the said islands.': *CPR 1350–54*, p 407.
51 *CPR 1350–54*, p. 248.
52 *CPR 1350–54*, p. 253.
53 *CPR 1350–54*, p. 254.
54 Treaty Roll, 26 Edw. III, m. 13, cited in G.E.C., *Complete Peerage*, VIII, 584.
55 *CPR 1350–54*, p. 279.
56 *CPR 1350–54*, p. 280.
57 *CPR 1350–54*, p. 122.
58 *CPR 1350–54*, p. 283.
    Rights of wreck:Le Patourel, p. 80.
59 *CPR 1350-54*, p. 283.
60 *CPR 1350–54*, p. 284.
61 Le Patourel, p. 10: [modern TNA reference numbers have been added] *John Gaunt*, Receiver of Guernsey, Sark and Alderney, from Michaelmas 1351 to 15 July 1352: Account TNA E 101/89/23.
62 *CCR 1349–54*, pp. 533–534.
63 *CPR 1350–54*, p. 490.
64 Appointment of William Stury: *CCR 1354–60*, p. 61;
    General account of John Maltravers, from 11 June 1348 to 2 April 1354: Pipe Roll, 31 Edw. III, m. 40, cited in Le Patourel, p. 10.

Chapter 7. Baron John Maltravers: Last Years

1 C. Langton, 'Seigneurs of Samarès', *Société Jersiaise Annual Bulletin*, 11 (1931), 376–427.
2 Feet of Fines Divers Counties CP 25/1/287/45, no. 524, <www.medievalgenealogy.org.uk/fines/dorset> then search under the reference number. [accessed 12 September 2018]
3 *CPR 1350–54*, p. 490; *CPR 1354–58*, pp. 248, 417, 621.
4 *CPR 1358–61*, p. 578.
5 *CPR 1354–58*, p. 595.
6 *CPR 1358–61*, pp. 405–408.
7 Jonathan Sumption, *The Hundred Years War, II: Trial by Fire* (Faber, 1999), pp. 436–437.
8 *CCR 1360–64*, p. 26.

9 *CIPM 1361–64*, no. 592.
10 Inquisiton on John Maltravers VI includes assignment of dower: CIPM 1361–64, no. 592.
11 The first of the Berkeley family to take possession of Rockhampton, Walls and Stoke Gifford was Sir Maurice Berkeley (1358–1400), who was the son of Thomas (c. 1334–1361) and the grandson of Maurice Berkeley of Uley (1298–1347):
The History of Parliament: the House of Commons 1386–1421 (Boydell & Brewer, 1993) <www.historyofparliament.org/volume/1386-1421/member/berkeley-sir-maurice-1358-1400> [accessed 12 September 2018]
12 P. I. McQueen, 'The Maltravers fret', *Monumental Brass Society Transactions*, 10.4 (1966), 244–248.
13 Sally Badham, 'Monumental brasses and the Black Death: a reappraisal', *Antiquaries Journal*, 80.1 (September 2000), 207–247.
14 John Hutchins, *The History and Antiquities of the County of Dorset*, 1st edn, 2 vols (1774), II, 117.
15 Richard Gough, *Sepulchral Monuments in Great Britain*, 2 vols (1786–1796), vol. 1, part 2, (1796), pp. 117–118.
He says his illustration is from Hutchins vol. 2, p. 117 [the first edition of Hutchins, Dorset, II, as in the previous note).
16 Drawing of the Maltravers brass by David Thomas Powell, c. 1810:
British Library, *Western Manuscripts*, vol. IV: Devonshire and Dorset, Add MS 17459, fol. 115r.
17 John Hutchins, *The History and Antiquities of the County of Dorset*, 3rd edn, 4 vols (1861–73; repr with additions 1973), III (1868) 332.
18 Vere L. Oliver, 'The Maltravers brass at Lytchett Matravers', *Proceedings of the Dorset Natural History and Antiquarian Field Club*, 46 (1925), 65–70.
19 www.hamline.edu/offices/archives/brass-rubbings [follow the link to 'Matravers' or 'Maltravers'] [accessed 17 June 2019].
This is an archive of over 1,000 brass rubbings made by students from Hamline University, St Paul, Minnesota, USA in 1975–76. It includes the surviving part of the Matravers inscription.
20 Shirley Percival, *A Dorset Village: Lytchett Matravers* (1982), pp. 61–62.
Other publications on the Lytchett Matravers fret:
William Lack, H. Martin Stuchfield and Philip Whittemore, *The Monumental Brasses of Dorsetshire* (Monumental Brass Society, 2001), pp. 112–113.
Doris Sibun, *Dorset Brasses and the Persons They Commemorate* (Sherborne: Abbey Press, 1974), pp. 38–40, plate 19.
A. G. Sadler, *The Indents of Lost Monumental Brasses in Dorset and Hampshire* (1975), pp. 16–17.
21 Florence Carré, *Folklore of Lytchett Matravers, Dorset* (Toucan Press, 1975), p. 7.

Chapter 8. Agnes de Bereford

1 *CIPM 1361–64*, no. 592.
2 *CCR 1364–68*, pp. 8–9.
3 *CIPM 1374–77*, no. 180.
4 *CCR 1364–69*, pp. 180–181.
5 *CPR 1367–70*, pp. 59–60.
6 *CCR 1369–74*, p. 231.
7 *CCR 1369–74*, p. 411.
8 *CPR 1374–77*, pp. 59–60.
9 *CCR 1369–74*, pp. 202–203.
10 *CCR 1369–74*, p. 215.
11 *CPR 1370–74*, p. 116.
12 Childrey in *Victoria County History: Berkshire,* IV (1924), pp. 272–279 (274–275) <http://www.british-history.ac.uk/vch/berks/vol4/pp272-279> [accessed 15 September 2018]
13 *CPR 1370–74*, p. 448.
14 *CPR 1377–81*, pp. 160, 162.
15 *Victoria County History: Berkshire.*
16 Lambeth Palace Library Archives, Register of Archbishop Sudbury, fols 78r–79r: The text of the will is in French. It is dated 1374, but, by modern reckoning and starting the year in January, the year is 1375.
The will is translated in the following:
J.S. Bothwell, 'Agnes Maltravers (d. 1375) and her husband, John (d. 1364): rebel wives, separate lives and conjugal visits in later medieval England', in *Fourteenth Century England,* 4, ed. by J.S. Hamilton (ISBN 9781843832201, Boydell Press, 2006), pp. 80–92 (pp. 91–92).
Material from the translation by J.S. Bothwell is reprinted here by kind permission of Boydell & Brewer Ltd., 23 October 2018. Lambeth Palace Library has kindly agreed to the use of the original French text, 15 October 2018.
There is also a partial translation in the following: *Testamenta Vetusta*, ed. by Nicholas Harris Nicolas, 2 vols (1826), I, 91–92, 'Lady Anne Maltravers'.
17 Beds and bedding: Bedding materials were prized possessions in those days. There might be a framework, either freestanding or attached to the ceiling beams, from which curtains could be suspended. At the back was a hanging called a dosser; for example, the 'dozer' left to John Argentein. On the bed itself was a mattress filled with straw or wool, with a canvas sheet on top. There might be a bolster to serve as a pillow. Richer people would have linen sheets. Then came blankets and a coverlet, embroidered with attractive designs or even with the owner's device. All these hangings and items of bedding could be transported with the lord or lady when they travelled to another of their manors.
18 A primer, or book of hours, is a prayer book for the laity, which includes the

Little Office of the Blessed Virgin, Vespers, Matins and Lauds, and some psalms. It was usually in Latin. Agnes's copy is a precious item, to be treated as an heirloom, and may have been illustrated.

19 Register of burials: C. L. Kingsford, *The Greyfriars of London* (Aberdeen University Press, 1915), pp. 70–133, footnote 298 <http://www.british-history.ac.uk/brit-franciscan-soc/vol6/pp70-133> [accessed 15 September 2018]
20 *CIPM 1374–77*, no. 180.

Chapter 9. Roger and Edward Maltravers

1 Hutchins, *Dorset*, III, 317, 334.
2 *Calendar of Gascon Rolls*, TNA C 61/36:290. See also The Threat from Gascony, in Chapter 3.
3 *CIPM 1347–52*, no. 648.
4 *CPR 1317–21*, p. 477. See also Land Transactions and Property Disputes 1318–1320, in Chapter 3.
5 *CPR 1321–24*, pp. 15–16. See also The Despenser Wars 1321–1322, in Chapter 3.
6 *CPR 1321–24*, p. 46. See also The Despenser Wars 1321–1322, in Chapter 3.
7 *CPR 1321–24*, pp. 444–445.
8 In 1334–35, 'Edward Fitzjohn Maltravers held Rathkeale': *Pipe Rolls*, cited in Brian Hodkinson, *Who was Who in Medieval Limerick from Manuscript Sources*, updated 2014 <www.limerick.ie/sites/default/files/atoms/files/who_was_who_in_medieval_limerick_-_from_manuscript_sources> [accessed 16 September 2018];
When John VI's lands were restored to him in 1351, it is stated that Rathkeale had been held by John V, who had demised it to Edward, brother of John Maltravers VI, for life: *CCR 1349–54*, pp. 313–314, 323.
Rathkeale later came into the hands of John Maltravers of Crowell, who was holding it when he died in 1360.
9 In 1354, Sherrington in Wiltshire was settled on John Maltravers VI and his wife Agnes, and then in tail male successively to the following: 1) Baldwin, son of Edmund de Bereford; (2) Joan, the granddaughter of John Maltravers VI; (3) John, the grandson of Robert Maltravers; and (4) Roger, son of Edward Maltravers:
Chancery Inq. ad quod damnum, in *Abstracts of Wiltshire Inquisitiones Post Mortem, 1327–77* (British Record Society, 1914), p. 230.
In the event, Sherrington was the subject of a different arrangement in 1357, in connection with the marriage of Eleanor Maltravers to John Arundel.
10 *CPR 1358–61*, p. 578.
11 For other bequests of Agnes Maltravers, see Chapter 8.

12 'Levesham, John (d. 1418), of Salisbury, Wilts', in *The History of Parliament: the House of Commons 1386–1421* (Boydell & Brewer, 1993) <www.historyofparliamentonline.org/volume/1386-1421/member/levesham-john> [accessed 18 January 2013]
13 Hutchins, *Dorset*, III, 320.
14 *CIPM 1418–22*, nos. 17, 489.
The Wiltshire inquisition post mortem no. 17, gives his date of death as 12 May 1418. The Dorset inquisition post mortem, no. 489, which includes the detailed proof of the descent of the manor of Dullar, gives his date of death as 10 May 1417. Revised versions of these inquisitions post mortem are as follows:
King's College London, Mapping the Medieval Countryside (2014) <http://www.inquisitionspostmortem.ac.uk/view/inquisition/21-017/> [accessed 20 October 2018]
King's College London, Mapping the Medieval Countryside (2014) <http://www.inquisitionspostmortem.ac.uk/view/inquisition/21-489/> [accessed 20 October 2018]
15 Hutchins, *Dorset*, III, 334.

Chapter 10. Maltraverses of Crowell and Hooke

1 Giles de Braose: *CIPM 1300–1307*, no. 317;
Crowell: *Victoria County History: Oxfordshire*, VIII (1964) <http://www.british-history.ac.uk/vch/oxon/vol8/pp80–91> [accessed 19 September 2018]
Long Wittenham: Victoria *County History: Berkshire*, IV (1924) <http://www.british-history.ac.uk/vch/berks/vol4/pp384–390> [accessed 18 September 2018]
2 Proof of age: *CIPM 1307–16*, no. 417;
Possession of lands: *CCR 1307–13*, p. 479.
3 Calendar of Documents Relating to Scotland, vol. V, supplementary (1986):
6 May 1314 Protection for John Maltravers [V] and Robert Maltravers with him: p. 464, no. 2971;
1 May 1314 Protection for John Maltravers [V]... Robert Maltravers... with Maurice de Berkeley: p. 467, no. 3011.
4 *CPR 1321–24*, p. 22.
5 *Victoria County History: Berkshire*, IV.
6 *CPR 1338–40*, p. 239.
7 *CPR 1354–58*, p. 621.
8 *CIPM 1361–64*, no. 137; *CFR 1356–68*, p. 255.
9 *CIPM 1352–60*, no. 149.
10 Robert Syfrewast died on 20 May 1347 and his inquisition post mortem was in 1360: *CIPM 1352–1360*, no. 563.
11 John Syfrewast died on 30 October 1350 and his inquisition post mortem was

in 1360: *CIPM 1352–1360*, no. 583.
12 Joan Syfrewast died on 6 January 1354 and her inquisition post mortem was in 1354: *CIPM 1352–1360*, no. 191.
13 *CIPM 1352–60*, no. 646.
14 H. J. Hewitt, *The Black Prince's Expedition of 1355–1357* (Manchester University Press, 1958), p. 207.
15 Thomas Rymer, *Foedera*, vol. III, part 1, pp. 325–326.
16 Letters of attorney and letters of protection for one year, commencing April 1363: *Calendar of Gascon Rolls 1363–1364*, TNA C 61/76/14; C 61/76/15.2. Letters of protection renewed for one year commencing May 1364: *CGR*, TNA C 61/77/34.
17 S. W. Bates Harbin, *Members of Parliament for the County of Somerset* (Somerset Archaeological and Natural History Society, 1939), pp. 65–66.
18 Sir William d'Aumarle: *CIPM 1361–64*, nos. 272, 273.
19 Hutchins, *Dorset*, III, 321.
20 *CIPM 1384–92*, nos. 262 (Oxford), 263 (Somerset), 264 (Dorset).
The calendar gives the place names in their original spelling. As many as possible are given their modern spelling here with the aid of A. Fagersten *The Place Names of Dorset* (1938) and other sources.
21 *Somerset and Dorset Notes and Queries*, 8 (1903), pp. 191–192; CPR 1391–96, pp. 116–117.
22 Melbury House:
Sidney Heath and W. de C. Prideaux, *Some Dorset Manor Houses with Their Literary and Historical Associations* (Bemrose, 1907), pp. 133–153.
The indenture of 1500: Heath and Prideaux, p. 151.

Chapter 11. Joan Maltravers

1 *CIPM 1336–47*, no. 504.
2 The inquisitions post mortem in four counties on Sir John de Keynes do not agree on the exact date of his death, nor on the age of his son and heir, but the consensus is that Sir John died between 1 March and 9 March 1366, and that young John was born between 19 January and 23 February 1366: *CIPM 1365–70*, no. 66.
3 H. J. Hewitt, *The Black Prince's expedition of 1355–57* (Manchester University Press, 1958), p. 210.
4 *Calendar of Gascon Rolls 1370–71*, TNA C 61/83, item 86 (Gascon Rolls Project, Universities of Cambridge, Liverpool and Kings College London, 2014) <www.gasconrolls.org/en/edition/calendars>
Search under 'view the rolls'. [Accessed 23 September 2018]
5 *CGR 1373–74*, TNA C 61/86, item 18.

6 *CGR 1373–74*, TNA C61/86, item 7;
   CGR 1373–74, TNA C61/86, item 25;
   CGR 1373–74, TNA C61/86, item 55.
7 *CGR 1373–74*, TNA C61/86, item 9.
8 *CGR 1373–74*, TNA C61/86, item 42.
9 *CPR 1370–74*, p. 288.
10 *CGR 1374–75*, TNA C61/87, item 2.
11 *CGR 1375–76,* TNA C61/88, item 44.
12 *CPR 1374–77*, p. 60.
13 *CIPM 1374–77*, no. 233.
14 *CIPM 1374–77*, no. 234.
15 *CIPM 1374–77*, no. 234; *CPR 1385–89*, pp. 105–107.
16 *TNA Special Collections: Ancient Petitions*, TNA SC 8/101/5026 and TNA SC 8/103/511.
17 *Full Abstracts of the Feet of Fines Relating to the County of Dorset from the Commencement of the Reign of Edward III to the End of the Reign of Richard III, 1327–1485,* ed. by E. A. Fry and G. S. Fry, Dorset Records, 10 (1910), pp. 189–190.
18 *CPR 1374–77*, p. 180.
19 *CGR 1376–77*, TNA C 61/89, item 39.
20 *CPR 1374–77*, pp. 496–500; *CPR 1377–81*, pp. 38–40.
21 *CCR 1377–81*, p. 49.
22 *CCR 1377–81*, p. 49; *CPR 1377–81*, p. 105.
23 *CPR 1377–81*, pp. 471–474.
24 Walsingham says 1379, but the date is corrected by the editor of the following edition to 1378:
   The *Chronica Maiora of Thomas Walsingham, 1376–1422*, ed. by James G. Clark, trans. by David Preest (Boydell, 2005).
25 *CPR 1377–81*, p. 485.
26 *CPR 1377–81*, p. 633.
27 *CPR 1381–85*, p. 205.
28 *Testamenta Vetusta*, ed. by N. H. Nicolas, 2 vols (1826), I, 105.
   See also Chapter 12.
29 Hutchins, *Dorset*, III, 315;
   Collectanea Topographica et Genealogica, 8 vols (1834–43), III (1836), 99–100.
   The original is in The National Archives, reference TNA PROB 11/1/2.
30 *CIPM 1384–92*, no. 190.
31 *CPR 1388–92*, p. 17.
32 Half of Coombe Keynes was held in 1407 by John Cressy, deceased, whose heir was his son Thomas. *CIPM 1405–1413*, no 370.

Chapter 12. Eleanor Maltravers

1 *Feet of Fines Divers Counties 1347–1350*, CP 25/1/287/43, no. 401 <http://www.medievalgenealogy.org.uk/fines/abstracts/CP_25_1_287_43> [accessed 27 September 2018]
2 Michael Burtscher, *The Fitzalans: Earls of Arundel and Surrey, Lords of the Welsh Marches 1267–1415* (Logaston, 2008), pp. 47–48.
3 *Testamenta Vetusta*, ed. by N. H. Nicolas (1826), I, 94–96.
4 G.E.C., *Complete Peerage*, I, p. 259.
5 'Sir John Arundel' in ODNB (2004) <https://doi.org/10.1093/ref:odnb/718> [accessed 28 September 2018];
   G.E.C., *Complete Peerage*, I, 259–60.
6 *CPR 1377–81*, pp. 420–421.
7 The *Chronica Maiora of Thomas Walsingham, 1376-1422*, trans. by David Preest, introduction and notes by James G. Clark (Boydell & Brewer, 2005).
   Another edition, with text and translation:
   The St Albans Chronicle: the Chronica Maiora of Thomas Walsingham, ed. by John Taylor and others, 2 vols (Oxford University Press, 2003–11), I: 1376–394.
8 *Testamenta Vetusta*, I, 105.
9 *CIPM 1377–84*, nos. 179–189.
10 Inquisitions on his father, John Arundel, died 1379: *CIPM 1377–84*, nos. 179–189.
11 Nigel Saul, *Richard II* (Yale University Press, 1999), p. 18.
12 G.E.C., *Complete Peerage*, I, p. 260.
13 *CIPM 1384–92*, nos. 951–952;
    Proof of age: *CIPM 1399–1406*, no. 1123.
14 *Testamenta Vetusta*, I, 94–96.
15 *Testamenta Vetusta*, I, 105.
16 *Testamenta Vetusta*, I, 94–96.
17 *Testamenta Vetusta*, I, 94–96.
18 *CPR 1391–96*, p. 178.
19 Information obtained from St George's Chapel, Windsor.
20 Seen on a visit to Windsor on 8 February 2014.
21 Hutchins, *Dorset*, III, 322; *Testamenta Vetusta*, I, 150 (William), 156 (Agnes).
22 Hutchins, *Dorset*, III, 322.
23 *CPR 1399–1401*, p. 389.
24 *Testamenta Vetusta*, I, 150 (William), 156 (Agnes).
25 *CPR 1413–16*, p. 284.
26 Dan Spencer, *18-24 May 1415: Royal Patronage* <www.agincourt600.com/2015/04/02/18-24-may-1415-royal-patronage> [accessed 25 April 2017]
27 A. C. Fox-Davies, *A Complete Guide to Heraldry*, revised edn, revised and annotated by J. P. Brooke-Little (Bloomsbury, 1985), p. 115.

28 *CIPM 1418–22*, no. 713a.
29 The church that became known as Holy Blood Church is in Wilsnack, Germany, and it was the site of a miracle that was supposed to have taken place in 1383. In that year, the church was destroyed in a fire, but three consecrated hosts were found on the altar, intact but stained with blood. The site became a popular place of pilgrimage.
30 *Testamenta Vetusta*, I, 196.
31 Hutchins, *Dorset*, III, p. 322.
32 There were several branches of the Cobham family, so 'of Sterborough' must be included in the title. For the Cobhams in general:
'Cobham family' in ODNB (2004) <http://www.oxforddnb.com/view/printable/52781> [accessed 26 Apr 2017];
G.E.C., *Complete Peerage*, III, pp. 353–354.
33 *CPR 1413–16*, p. 389.
In January 1416, Reynold junior is referred to as the brother and heir of John, son of Reynold Cobham (senior).
34 Cobham descent:
Maurice de Berkeley's son, Thomas (d. 1361), had a daughter Joan who married Reynold de Cobham, first Baron Cobham of Sterborough. Joan and Reynold were the parents of Reynold de Cobham, second Baron Cobham of Sterborough, 1348–1403, and husband of Eleanor Maltravers.
Maltravers descent:
Maurice de Berkeley's daughter Ela married John Maltravers VI, Eleanor's grandfather.
35 *CIPM 1399–1405*, nos. 760–770.
36 *Calendar of Inquisitions Miscellaneous*, vol. 7, 1399–1422, pp. 284–285, case no. 507;
'Cobham Family' in *ODNB*.
37 Lambeth Palace Library Archives, *Register of Archbishop Arundel*, fols 221v–222v. Details of the will are published in this book by kind permission of Lambeth Palace Library Archives, 15 October 2018.
38 *CIPM 1399–1405*, nos. 1115–1122.
39 *CIPM 1399–1405*, no. 1123.
40 G.E.C., *Complete Peerage*, I (1910), p. 247.
41 Burtscher, *The Fitzalans*, pp. 110 and 128.
42 M. A. Tierney, *The History and Antiquities of the Castle and Town of Arundel* (1834), pp. 101–102.
43 *CIPM 1418–22*, nos. 811–823.
44 *Testamenta Vetusta*, I, 277, 279.
45 *CIPM 1427–32*, no. 312;
Percival, *A Dorset Village: Lytchett Matravers*, p. 16.
46 'John Fitzalan (VI), 7th earl of Arundel' in *ODNB* <http://www.oxforddnb.

com/wiew/printable/9532> [accessed 27 April 2014]

G.E.C., *Complete Peerage*, I, pp. 247–248.

47 *The Parliament Rolls of Medieval England* [PROME] XI: Henry VI, 1432–1445, ed. by Anne Curry.

'Henry VI: July 1433, items 32–35', [PROME-ONLINE] <http://www.british-history.ac.uk/no-series/parliament-rolls-medieval/july-1433> [accessed 30 September 2018]

For the entail, see the following:

Feet of Fines Divers Counties 1347–1350, CP 25/1/287/43, no. 401.

48 M. A. Tierney, 'Discovery of the Remains of John, 17th Earl of Arundel, obit. 1435', *Sussex Archaeological Collections*, 12 (1860), pp. 232–239.

Note, there are different ways of numbering the earls of Arundel.

INDEX OF MALTRAVERS LANDS

Ashton Gifford (Wilts), 61, 79, 80, 97
Boyton (Wilts), 62, 79, 97, 109, 116, 138, 144, 149
Brimpsfield (Gloucs), 15, 61–62, 79, 98
Broughton Gifford (Wilts), 62, 79, 98
Burcombe (Dorset), 132
Burton (Dorset), 90
Carreg Cennen Castle (Wales), 62, 79
Cattescliff (Dorset), 90
Charlton (Berks), 6–7
Charlton by Dorchester (Dorset) 129, 132
Chepstow Castle, 11–12
Childrey (Oxon), 24, 39, 78, 87, 90, 98, 110, 116, 118–119
Chilfrome (Dorset), 39
Coate (Wilts), 12, 39, 81, 110, 144, 149
Codford (Wilts), 62, 79, 80, 97, 106, 109, 116, 144, 149
Coombe Keynes (Dorset), 135, 137, 138, 140
Corfe Castle (Dorset) 49–50
Corton (Wilts), 80, 97, 109, 116, 144, 149
Crowell (Oxon), 126, 127, 132
Dullar (Dorset), 124, 125
East Morden, (Dorset), 82, 92, 106, 108, 115, 144, 148
Easton (Wilts), 15
Eggardon (Dorset), 90, 108, 115, 144, 148
Elston (Wilts), 62, 79, 98, 106, 116, 144, 149

Ernly, (Dorset), 129
Filands (Wilts), 12
Frome Vauchurch (Dorset), 129, 132
Frome Whitfield (Dorset), 82, 98, 108, 115, 144, 148
Gorewell (Dorset), 132
Grafton (Wilts), 6–7
Great Somerford (Wilts), 12, 39, 81, 110, 144, 149
Hendford, Yeovil (Somerset), 6, 11–12, 24, 92, 110, 116, 144, 149
Higher Kingcombe (Dorset), 132
Hill Deverill (Wilts), 39, 110, 144, 149
Hinton Blewett (Somerset), 6–7
Hooke (Dorset), 127, 128–129, 132
Iskennen (Wales), 62
King's Stanley (Gloucs), 61, 62, 80, 91, 98, 106, 109, 116, 145
La Pole (Wilts), 82, 98
Langton Matravers (Dorset), 23, 25, 76, 81, 108, 115, 144, 148
Little Shurdington (Gloucs), 123
Litton Cheney (Dorset), 148
Loders (Dorset), 39, 49, 78, 87, 90, 98, 108, 115, 144, 148
Loders Bingham (Dorset), 33
Long Wittenham (Oxon), 126, 127, 128
Longbridge Deverill (Wilts), 81
Lower Kingcombe (Dorset), 132
Lytchett Matravers (Dorset), 6–7, 23, 25, 29, 39, 76, 81, 92, 108, 115, 118–119, 125, 144, 148

Mappowder (Dorset), 6–7
Marshwood (Dorset), 49, 82, 98
Martinstown (Dorset), 92, 144, 149
Melbury Bubb (Dorset), 132
Melbury Osmond (Dorset), 63, 133–134
Melbury Sampford (Dorset), 63, 133–134
Middle Chinnock (Somerset), 132
Milborne Deverell (Dorset), 132
Minchinhampton (Gloucs), 109, 116, 144, 149
North Poorton (Dorset), 132
Orcheston (Wilts), 62, 79, 98
Overstone (Northants), 48, 78
Philipston (Dorset), 38, 39, 49, 78, 87, 90, 98, 108, 115, 144, 148
Rathkeale (Ireland), 23, 27, 37–38, 62, 82, 92–93, 99, 105–106, 116–117, 128, 136, 137
Rockhampton (Gloucs), 62, 79, 80, 91, 98, 109, 110, 115, 116, 121
Samarès (Jersey), 100, 105
Sherrington (Wilts), 39, 62, 79, 80, 91, 97, 106, 109, 116, 124, 144, 149
Shipton Dovel (Gloucs), 6–7
Shurdington (Gloucs), 109, 116, 123, 149
Sopworth (Wilts), 6–7, 39
South Poorton (Dorset), 132
Stapleford (Dorset), 129, 132
Stapleford (Wilts), 48, 62, 79, 80, 97, 106, 109, 116, 144
Stock Gaylard, (Dorset), 6–7
Stoke Giffard (Gloucs), 62, 80, 109, 110, 115, 116, 121
Stonehouse (Gloucs), 62, 80, 109, 116, 149
Stourton Caundle (Dorset), 6–7
Sutton Mandeville (Wilts), 48
Syde (Gloucs), 62
Tarrant Crawford (Dorset), 139
Tarrant Keyneston (Dorset), 135, 138, 139
Up Wimborne (Dorset), 40, 78, 87, 90, 98, 108, 115, 144
Walls (Gloucs), 62, 80, 110, 115, 116, 121
West Chickerell (Dorset), 129, 132
West Moors (Dorset), 90, 108, 115, 144, 148
West Shilvinghampton (Dorset), 129
Wimborne St Giles, (Dorset), 149
Winterborne Houghton (Dorset), 48, 78
Winterbourne Stoke (Wilts), 110, 144, 149
Witchampton (Dorset), 23, 25, 39, 81, 92, 110, 115, 139, 146, 148
Woodchester (Gloucs), 15, 24, 39, 43, 81, 109, 116, 145
Woolcombe (Dorset), 6–7, 13–14, 23, 39, 81, 92, 108, 110, 115, 132, 144, 148
Wootton Fitzpaine (Dorset), 82, 98, 108, 115, 144, 149
Worth Matravers (Dorset), 76, 82, 98, 110, 144, 148
Yard (Dorset), 129, 132
Yeovil (Somerset), 6–7, 39, 81, 116, 144, 149